A CRITICAL INTRODUCTION TO THE PHILOSOPHY OF GOTTLOB FREGE

A Critical Introduction to the Philosophy of Gottlob Frege

GUILLERMO E. ROSADO HADDOCK
University of Puerto Rico at Rio Piedras, Puerto Rico

ASHGATE

Published by
Ashgate Publishing Limited
Gower House
Croft Road
Aldershot
Hampshire GU11 3HR
England

Ashgate Publishing Company
Suite 420
101 Cherry Street
Burlington, VT 05401-4405
USA

Ashgate website: http://www.ashgate.com

British Library Cataloguing in Publication Data
Rosado Haddock, Guillermo E., 1945-
 A critical introduction to the philosophy of Gottlob Frege
 1.Frege, Gottlob, 1848-1925 2.Frege, Gottlob, 1848-1925.
 Begriffsschrift
 I.Title
 193

Library of Congress Cataloging-in-Publication Data
Rosado Haddock, Guillermo E., 1945-
 A critical introduction to the philosophy of Gottlob Frege / Guillermo E. Rosado Haddock.
    p. cm.
 Includes bibliographical references and index.
 ISBN 0-7546-5471-0 (hardback : alk. paper)
 1. Frege, Gottlob, 1848-1925. I. Title.

B3245.F24R67 2006
193—dc22

                                                                        2005031884

ISBN-13: 978-0-7546-5471-1
ISBN-10: 0-7546-5471-0

Printed and bound in Great Britain by Antony Rowe Ltd, Chippenham, Wiltshire.

Contents

Preface

The publication of a new book in English on Frege could seem at first sight to be completely unnecessary. As Ivor Grattan-Guinness has put it on p. 177 of his recent book *The Search for Mathematical Roots: 1870-1940*, there is a massive Frege industry in English, though of a refurnished Frege, which Grattan-Guinness calls 'Frege' in order to distinguish him from the real Frege. In fact, a series of writings, mostly in English, have flourished in the last two decades, presenting Frege as a sort of epistemologist in the Kantian or, at least, neo-Kantian tradition. A similar massive bulk of writings, also mostly in English, has followed a programme of trying to derive as much arithmetic as possible from a weakening of Frege's logical system. The last group of authors seems to conceive Frege primarily as a philosopher of mathematics – and they are right in doing so – but have adhered to a programme that not only has attained only modest goals, but that even if successful, would probably still be unsatisfactory – as argued at the very end of this book. A third trend in Fregean scholarship, and probably the oldest, is the view made famous by Michael Dummett's first book on Frege, the very influential *Frege: Philosophy of Language* of 1973. According to that book, Frege was primarily a philosopher of language – though he published only one paper, namely 'Über Sinn und Bedeutung', that can be considered a writing on the philosophy of language. Moreover, in that book Dummett presents Frege as a sort of 'philosophical Adam', with almost no roots in the philosophical tradition. Dummett's contention – which seems to have been already abandoned by its distinguished proponent – has been rightly criticized by many Fregean scholars and is nowadays upheld by almost nobody. However, it has produced an exaggerated reaction in those who try to see in Frege a sort of neo-Kantian epistemologist.

The orthodoxy of the two most active schools of Fregeanism have originated another sort of extreme position among some important scholars, namely, that of not doing justice to the great value of Frege's writings – I mean Frege, not 'Frege' – both for the development of contemporary logic and for philosophy. That perfectly comprehensible reaction can be seen in the above mentioned history of mathematical logic of Grattan-Guinness, as well as in William Tait's paper 'Frege versus Dedekind and Cantor' and even in some writings of my friend – and coauthor of our *Husserl or Frege?: Meaning, Objectivity and Mathematics* – Claire Ortiz Hill, for example, in her book *Rethinking Identity and Metaphysics*. Although I am sympathetic to some of their criticisms of Frege, I think that the balance between criticism and recognition of the importance of Frege's views gets lost. As a Fregean scholar who is not a Fregean, I hope that I have attained the proper balance in the present writing.

This book has a long history, and even a predecessor. After teaching for the first time a graduate course on Frege some twenty-five years ago, and writing some reviews of books on Frege, I wrote a small book on Frege's philosophy during a sabbatical in 1982-83. I committed two decisive errors with respect to that book: firstly, I wrote it in my mother tongue, Spanish, and published it privately in 1985. Due to my own carelessness, the book had many misprints and some imprecise references. Moreover, due to the fact that it was a private publication on such an exotic theme – at least for culturally underdeveloped Puerto Rico – the book had no distribution, and I was limited to sending copies as a gift to different scholars. Nonetheless, the book received three pleasant reviews by Mauricio Beuchot, by Lourdes Valdivia, and by my friend Matthias Schirn.

Almost a decade ago, while participating in a congress in Brazil, my friend, the late Michael Wrigley, urged me to publish an English version of my old Frege book. I told him that I would have not only to translate the book, but also to revise and update it. Due to my commitment to other projects, the project remained unfulfilled for almost a decade. However, I now teach the graduate course on Frege's philosophy more or less every four to five semesters, and my views on Frege's philosophy have been maturing in the meantime. Thus, especially in my last two Frege courses I have had the opportunity to develop and polish my assessment of Frege's philosophy. The success of my joint book with Claire Ortiz Hill mentioned above – published in 2000 and reprinted in a paperback edition in 2003 – has clearly also served as an encouragement. Although in comparison to my old Frege book in Spanish, the expository core of this book has not suffered great changes, my assessment of Frege's philosophy having attained its maturation, the present book is not only somewhat longer – though still a short one – but also and foremost qualitatively superior to its ancestor, and not simply a sort of second edition. Moreover, though some of the Fregean issues discussed in the present book also have been considered in some of my papers included in my joint book with Claire Ortiz Hill, my assessment of Frege here is of his whole philosophy, not of particular issues. In fact, the present book is my most mature and complete assessment of Frege's philosophy as a whole.

The book is divided into seven chapters. The first chapter deals with Frege's philosophical views in his 1879 *Begriffsschrift*. A good understanding of the philosophical views of the young Frege – not only his views on identity statements, but also and especially his distinction between the notions of conceptual content and judgeable content – is essential for an adequate assessment of some later issues. Chapters 2 and 3 are concerned with Frege's philosophical masterpiece, *Die Grundlagen der Arithmetik*, and could very well serve as a commentary to that work. Nonetheless, they are not simply a commentary, but also an assessment of some Fregean views and even of a very influential recent criticism of Frege's views by Paul Benacerraf. The remaining chapters are concerned with Frege's post 1890 philosophical views. Chapters 4 and 5 are concerned mostly with Frege's two fundamental distinctions between sense and referent – made independently by Husserl as early as 1890 and present in the latter's review of Ernst Schröder's *Vorlesungen über die Algebra der Logik I* of 1891 – and that between concept and object, which permeates the whole Fregean philosophy from *Begriffsschrift* onwards. Chapter 6 is concerned with some important philosophical issues of *Grundgesetze der Arithmetik*, whereas the last chapter is concerned with three related important issues, namely, the Zermelo-Russell Paradox (as it should be called), Frege's views on Hilbert's axiomatization of geometry, and the old Frege's attempt at a geometrical foundation of arithmetic. In view of the origin of the work in a graduate course, some repetitions, digressions and cross-references have not been completely avoided. That is the case, e.g., of the issue of the presence or disappearance of the Context Principle from Frege's mature philosophy, as well as of his distinction between concept and object, which are considered already in the first part (Chapters 1-3), but their definitive treatment occurs in Chapters 4 and 5, respectively.

In the present book, I have always referred to Frege's works in their original language: German. Although in the references some English translations of Frege's works are included, I find that in good scholarship there is no substitute for the works in their original language. Notwithstanding the fact that my mother tongue is neither German nor English, I have translated all the passages quoted from Frege's writings, inserting the German original in the corresponding footnotes. Incidentally, to avoid interrupting the flow of the exposition, I have included quotations only when I am trying to make a point in the interpretation of Frege's writings that could seem controversial to orthodox Fregean scholars. In the bulk of the book references in the footnotes to the pertinent Fregean writings are more than enough.

To be a Fregean scholar and, in general, a scholar in very hard philosophy in a country so culturally deprived as Puerto Rico is not an easy matter. It means not only partial isolation from similar scholars around the world, but also total isolation from other academicians at your university and in your country. Thus, my graduate courses on Frege's philosophy, on Husserl's *Logical Investigations*, on the philosophy of mathematics or Logical Empiricism, on recent semantic theories of truth or classical model theory usually have had small audiences. Probably the greatest enduring joy that I have had in three decades of teaching is that there is always a very small but non-empty set of very capable students with philosophical acumen, interested in learning hard philosophy and its logical tools. Three of them – who wrote their MA Theses on Frege under my supervision – are mentioned in the references. Two of them, Dr. Wanda Torres Gregory and Mr. Pierre Baumann, have been extremely helpful in reading a preliminary version of the whole book and correcting my English. I have followed their advice most of the time, but not always, opting sometimes for a third option or, in a few cases, obstinately grasping to my original formulation. Thus, all the remaining errors in the book are my sole responsibility. My wife, Dr. Tinna Stoyanova and our friend, Dr. Joel Donato, Director of the LABCAD of the University of Puerto Rico at Río Piedras, have assisted me with the more technical aspects of the computer, by making the manuscript camera-ready. I am most grateful to all of them. Finally, I want to thank Prof. Jan Szrednicki for his encouragement and support during the final stages of the preparation of the book, as well as Paul Coulam, Sarah Charters and the editorial staff of Ashgate for their patience, and very especially Anthea Lockley for thoroughly reading the whole manuscript and having the patience to wait for my corrections.

In some sense, this book is dedicated to the joy of a productive life and to the sorrow of death. Thus, in the first place, I dedicate this book to my mother, Asia Haddock, in her 100th birthday in June 2005. I also want to dedicate this book to my late friend Michael Wrigley, former editor of Manuscrito, whose untimely death deprived philosophy, especially research on Wittgenstein's philosophy of mathematics, of an excellent scholar and all who knew him of an even more excellent human being. Last, but not least, I want to dedicate this book to all those former students, on whose lives my teachings have had some effect, and who have maintained in me the joy of doing hard philosophy in an extremely inappropriate environment and the hope in their future scholarly work in philosophy or in any other discipline of their choice. Besides the two mentioned above and the three referred to in the book, I want especially to mention Pedro Javier and Carlos Rubén, Luis Domingo and David, Marco Antonio and Freddie.

Guillermo E. Rosado Haddock
San Juan, March 2005, updated May 2006

Chapter 1

Philosophy in *Begriffsschrift*

Begriffsschrift is not a philosophical but a logical treatise. In fact, its publication in 1879 can be considered a turning point in the history of logic, the birth of contemporary logic, sometimes called 'symbolic' or 'mathematical' logic. Of course, Frege was not a logical Adam – nor was he a philosophical Adam – since many others, including his contemporaries Ernst Schröder and Charles S. Peirce, had already made important contributions to the new logic that represented a break with twenty-three centuries of tradition.[1] Even his invention and use of a concept-script did not come out of the blue, but had its roots in Leibniz and some predecessors in his immediate academic and personal entourage.[2] But though *Begriffsschrift* is a logical work, its Preface and Introduction contain interesting philosophical discussions by the young Frege, and an acquaintance with them is indispensable for a thorough understanding of the views of the mature Frege. Some of these views are already clearly expressed in *Begriffsschrift*, whereas others appear in that early work either in an embryonic state or under a different light. Even some of the obscurities and difficulties of Frege's mature philosophy can be traced back to this early work.[3]

1 An Epistemological Distinction

At the very beginning of the Preface of his *Begriffsschrift* Frege makes an important but frequently ignored distinction, which was to be decisive for his philosophy, namely, the distinction between the genetic-psychological origin of a statement and its foundation. Thus, he distinguishes between the genetic path by which we acquire knowledge of a statement and the way in which we can found it most securely.[4] The first question, to which, as Frege correctly observes, different people would give different answers, asks for a genetic or historical-individual

---

[1]See almost any history of logic, for example, Ivor Grattan-Guinness' recent *The Search for Mathematical Roots, 1870-1940* (Princeton, 2000), or Corrado Mangione and Silvio Bozzi's *Storia della Logica* (Milano, 1993).
[2]See on this issue Lothar Kreiser's recent book *Gottlob Frege: Leben-Werk-Zeit* (Hamburg 2001), pp. 153-70, or his previous paper '*Freges außerwissenschaftliche Quellen seines logischen Denkens*', in Ingolf Max and Werner Stelzner (eds), *Logik und Mathematik* (Berlin, 1995), pp. 219-25.
[3]See section 5 of this chapter, as well as Chapter 4 of this work.
[4]*Begriffsschrift*, p. IX.

explanation of how we obtained the statement. On the other hand, the second question, which in no way should be confused with the first one, is not only clearly more precise, but is more intimately related to the nature of the statement. It concerns the epistemological foundation of the statement.

Frege underscores from the very beginning[5] that a logical proof is the most secure foundation, since it does not take into account the peculiar nature of things, and is based only on the laws on which any knowledge is founded. Thus, Frege divides all statements that require a foundation in two groups, namely: (i) such whose proof can be obtained in a purely logical way, and (ii) such whose proof has to be based on experience. Thus, in this classification of statements in his early work, there is no place for the synthetic *a priori* introduced a century earlier by Kant. Nonetheless, when discussing *Die Grundlagen der Arithmetik*[6] in the next chapter, we will see that Frege offered there a much finer classification of the different sorts of statements. In particular, he will coincide with Kant's view that geometrical statements are neither empirical nor derivable in a purely logical way, and should be considered synthetic *a priori*.[7] This, however, is a long stretch away from any justification of the nowadays very popular interpretation of Frege in Anglo-American circles as a sort of neo-Kantian.

Finally, it should be clear that on the basis of Frege's distinction between the genetic-psychological origin of a statement and its epistemological foundation, it is perfectly possible, as Frege underscores, that a statement belongs to the group of statements derivable by purely logical means, but that it could only be known by humans on the basis of experience. As Frege stresses,[8] his classification is not based on any psychological origins but on the most perfect possible foundation for the statement.

2 On the Nature of Arithmetical Statements

Frege's main interest is not so much the general epistemological question, but its application to arithmetical statements. Thus, in *Begriffsschrift* Frege is interested in examining how much arithmetic can be derived on the basis of the laws of logic, which in this early work he called 'laws of thought'.[9] It is precisely in order to fulfil this objective that Frege invented his concept-script, which should allow him to determine with utmost certainty whether a given inference is conclusive or not,

[5]Ibid.

[6]*Die Grundlagen der Arithmetik* 1884, Centenary Edition with an Introduction by Christian Thiel (Hamburg, 1986). When referring to *Die Grundlagen der Arithmetik*, I will always follow the pagination in Christian Thiel's Centenary Edition, where the original pagination is indicated at the inner side of each page. Moreover, when referring to works with many essentially different editions, I will also refer to the section, which remains invariant with respect to the different editions

[7]On this issue, see Chapter 2.

[8]*Begriffsschrift*, pp. IX-X.

[9]Ibid., p. X.

and would allow us to discover any assumption on which the inference is based and trace it to its ultimate roots. To attain this objective, the concept-script should ignore anything that is irrelevant for the inference. Frege called 'conceptual content' precisely that part of the content of statements that is relevant for inferences.[10]

Probably to make the concept-script more palatable to future readers, Frege tries to justify the use of such a cumbersome artificial language. First of all, he compares the relation between the concept-script and our natural languages with the relation between the microscope and the human eye. Thus, though the microscope is not useful for non-scientific activities of our eyes, it is much more adequate for scientific use because of its much greater sharpness. In the same way, the concept-script is inadequate for most non-scientific activities of our natural languages, but supersedes by far natural languages for scientific usage. Moreover, Frege correctly argues that a great part of scientific development has its origin in a methodological change. Finally, Frege makes use of the authority of Leibniz, who had recognized some two centuries before the advantages of an artificial language more adequate for scientific purposes than our natural ones, without being totally conscious of its difficulties. Moreover, Frege considers[11] that arithmetical, geometrical and chemical symbolisms are partial fulfilments of Leibniz's conceptual calculus. Thus, Frege sees his concept-script in some sense as a step in the same direction, but with the peculiarity that it concerns the central region of knowledge, namely, logic, which is connected with each and every other region of knowledge. By the way, Frege envisions the possibility of extending the usage of his concept-script to geometry and physics.[12]

3 Concept-Script versus Natural Language

Later in the Preface Frege expresses a general philosophical conviction to which he was going to adhere during his whole life, and which could be considered as the starting point of what is sometimes called 'the analytical way of philosophizing'. Thus, Frege considers that it is the task of philosophy to free the human spirit from the power exercised on it by words, by discovering the unavoidable deceptions caused on us by natural language, thus, liberating our thought from the chains of our usual linguistic means of expression.[13] Hence, Frege hopes that the concept-script can be especially useful to philosophers for the fulfilment of that task.

Frege adds that natural language – he usually prefers the expression 'language of life' – often hides from us what is logically important and forces us to consider logically relevant what is not. Traditional logic has usually followed the guidance of natural language grammar, and has wrongly believed that the

---

[10]Ibid.
[11]Ibid., p. XII.
[12]Ibid.
[13]Ibid., pp. XII-XIII.

distinctions and concepts under its study are also important for logic. As an example of such a deception, Frege mentions the case of the notions of subject and predicate, which he is going to replace by those of argument and function, understood – as we will see – in a much broader way than was usual in the mathematics of his day.[14] Frege considers that such a replacement will be justified by its results, one of which would be that the conception of a content as a function of an argument creates new concepts.

At the end of the Preface, Frege asserts that in his logical system he is going to use only one rule of inference, namely, Modus Ponens, and justifies that choice arguing that it is very convenient for expository purposes to make use of the most simple primitives in the foundation of the concept-script. However, Frege tacitly makes use of a substitution rule in his logical systems. But we are not going to dwell on this issue.

4 Judgeable Content

At the beginning of Chapter 1 Frege makes a distinction between two sorts of signs, namely, (i) those under which we can represent different things, and (ii) those with a completely determined meaning. Although expressed in a somewhat cumbersome manner, this distinction is none other than the familiar distinction between variables and constants. Each sign of the concept-script belongs to one and only one of these groups of signs.

In sections 2 and 3 Frege introduces two notions of the utmost importance for understanding many of the difficulties of his later philosophy, namely, the notions of judgeable content [*beurteilbarer* (Frege writes: *beurtheilbarer*) *Inhalt*] – which presumably is the mother cell, whose division originated Frege's distinction between sense and reference – and the notion of conceptual content [begrifflicher Inhalt] – which officially disappeared after *Begriffsschrift*, but which constantly reappears, as a sort of philosophical ghost in many later writings. Interestingly, almost no Fregean scholar has given these two notions their due importance. In particular, they have not seen the almost omnipresent philosophical ghost of the defunct notion of conceptual content. Let us consider first the less mysterious notion.

In section 2 of Chapter 1 Frege explains the use in the concept-script of a special sign that will precede each and every theorem, a symbol composed of a vertical line followed by a horizontal line: $\vert$—. Frege calls the horizontal line the 'content line' and the vertical line the 'judgement line'. Not any sequence whatever of signs of the concept-script can follow either the complex sign built from the vertical and the horizontal lines, or the horizontal line standing alone. A judgeable

---

[14]Frege's use is even broader than in current set-theoretical mathematics, in which functions are special cases of relations. In categorial mathematics, however, the notion of 'morphism', which is a sort of generalized function, is at least as broad and fundamental as Frege's notion of 'function'.

content is precisely a sequence of signs that can be preceded either by the horizontal line alone or by the combination of the vertical line and the horizontal line. Thus, Frege makes a distinction between judgeable and non-judgeable contents. The horizontal line brings together the signs standing at its right. The vertical line expresses the assertion of the judgeable content and, thus, can never occur without the horizontal line at its right side. Hence, if S is a judgeable content, $|$—S expresses the assertion of the judgeable content S. On the other hand, when S is preceded only by the horizontal line, —S, we do not have a judgement, but only an interlocking of signs, which Frege suggests should be verbalized as 'the circumstance that S' or 'the proposition that S'.[15]

Before continuing with the exposition of the philosophical views of the young Frege in *Begriffsschrift*, it is convenient to mention that in his *Grundgesetze der Arithmetik*[16] Frege modified his interpretation of the compound sign ' $|$—'. The vertical line continues to be the judgement line, but the horizontal line is no longer called the 'content line' and it is applicable not only to judgeable contents – as in *Begriffsschrift* – but also to non-judgeable ones. Moreover, in *Grundgesetze der Arithmetik* Frege interprets the horizontal line as the name of a function of one argument, whose value is always a truth-value. Thus, in the terminology of the mature Frege '—' is a conceptual word, that is, a name for a concept. When applied to an argument that refers to the True, that conceptual word will have the True as value, and when applied to any other argument, it will have the False as value. Hence, only the True will fall under the concept referred to with '—'. In other words, when the argument Δ refers to a truth-value, —Δ will have as referent the same truth-value, namely the True when the referent of Δ is the True, and the False when the referent of Δ is the False, But if Δ does not refer to a truth value – in which case Δ would not be a 'judgeable content' – —Δ refers to the False.[17]

5 Conceptual Content

At the beginning of the extremely important section 3 of *Begriffsschrift*, and as a sort of justification for not distinguishing a subject and a predicate in a judgement, Frege asserts that two judgements S and S* can differ only in two ways, namely: (i) either in such a way that, if one fixes any determinate set of judgements Σ, the same consequences can be derived from S combined with Σ as from S* combined with Σ; or (ii) that is not the case. Thus, using the symbol '$\cup$' for the union of two sets of sentences and the symbols '{' and '}' to enclose (unit) sets, we can express (i) as follows: For any sentence S', $\Sigma \cup \{S\} |$—S' if and only if $\Sigma \cup \{S*\} |$—S'. When (i) holds, Frege says that S and S* have the same conceptual content. As an example of a pair of statements with the same conceptual content, Frege offers the

---

[15]Ibid., p. 2.
[16]*Grundgesetze der Arithmetik I*, 1893 (reprint: Hildesheim, 1962), section 5, pp. 9-10.
[17]Ibid.

following pair, consisting of a statement in the active mode and its correspondent statement in the passive mode: (a) 'In Platea the Greeks defeated the Persians', and (b) 'In Platea the Persians were defeated by the Greeks'. Frege says that between (a) and (b) there is a difference in sense but that concordance prevails.[18] What is identical in (a) and (b) is the conceptual content. But since the conceptual content is the only part of the content of a statement that is relevant for the concept-script, this sort of language does not have to distinguish between two statements with the same conceptual content. Only what can have some influence in the consequences of a statement is important for the concept-script. Thus, it will express exactly what is necessary for a correct inference, whereas what is not necessary for such an inference will not be expressed at all.[19]

Frege does not sufficiently clarify his notion of conceptual content, and even less those of judgeable content and of content. Nonetheless, as we will later see, those notions played a decisive role both in the genesis of his distinction between sense and reference, and in the difficulties that surround the distinction. In any case, Frege's explanation of the notion of conceptual content does not clarify much, since then not only statements like $p \to q$ and $\neg p \lor q$, or $\neg(\forall x)A(x)$ and $(\exists x)\neg A(x)$ would have the same conceptual content, but also statements like Zermelo's Well-Ordering Principle, Zorn's Lemma, the Axiom of Choice and even Tychonoff's Theorem would have the same conceptual content, since they have the same logical consequences. However, it is not only especially convenient, but indispensable that a concept-script distinguish between them, and a language that does not would be completely inadequate for mathematics.

Finally, it should be mentioned that Fregean scholars, regardless of how much their interpretations differ on other issues, have agreed to ignore the notions of conceptual content and judgeable content, as well as their difference. Moreover, in verbal communication, some otherwise fine Fregean scholars have argued that in his *Begriffsschrift* Frege considered both notions either identical or, at least, equivalent. Such interpretation, however, is not only totally unwarranted but on the verge of being absurd. To consider that a philosopher and logician so careful, precise and accurate in his mode of expression, and so conscious of the dangers of natural language would introduce in successive sections of a logical treatise the same notion, but using different words and different explanations, and, moreover, without explicitly mentioning that they are equivalent explanations of the same notion, is completely untenable.

6 The Universal Predicate of all Statements

Still in section 3 Frege discusses in a very ingenious way the already mentioned issue of the little relevance for logic of the distinction between subject and predicate. Frege mentions that a language is possible, in which the statement

---

[18]*Begriffsschrift*, p. 3.
[19]Ibid.

'Arquimedes died in the conquest of Syracuse' would be expressed in the following way: 'The violent death of Arquimedes in the conquest of Syracuse is a fact'. We can distinguish in the last statement a subject and a predicate if we wish, but clearly all the content is expressed in the subject, whereas the predicate has only the role of asserting that content as a judgement. But in a strict sense we cannot speak here of a subject and a predicate. Frege conceives the concept-script as such a language, in which the complex sign ' |—' is the only predicate, a common predicate applied to all judgements.[20]

As we will later see, Frege's interpretation of the grammatical predicate 'is true' in his mature work is similar to his analysis of the predicate 'is a fact' in such a possible language. The grammatical predicate 'is true', added to a complete statement, expresses the same content as the statement alone, and simply asserts the statement, which in any case is already asserted by the form of the statement. In the same way, to add the predicate 'is a fact' to a statement does not add anything to the content or assertion of the statement. Nonetheless, there is a small but important difference between those two natural language predicates and Frege's judgement sign, since though the latter does not add any content to the combination of the content sign and the judgeable content occurring at its right, it does add the assertion; whereas the two natural language predicates do not. Thus, the analogy between ' | ' and 'is a fact' or 'is true' in natural language should not be pressed. On the other hand, Frege would say that the statements (a) 'Arquimedes died in the conquest of Syracuse', (b) 'Arquimedes died in the conquest of Syracuse is a fact' and (c) 'The violent death of Arquimedes in the conquest of Syracuse is a fact' have the same conceptual content. Since 'is a fact' does not add anything to the content of a statement, (a) and (b) clearly have the same sense, as conceived by Frege in *'Über Sinn und Bedeutung'* and *Grundgesetze der Arithmetik*. But (c) can only have the same sense as (a) and (b) if we conflate the notion of judgeable content, from which the official notions of sense and reference were obtained, and which is especially close to the official notion of sense of a statement, with the notion of conceptual content. And, as we will later see, that is essentially what the mature Frege does, namely conflate his official notion of the sense of a statement with his old notion of conceptual content.

7 Abandonment of some Traditional Distinctions

In section 4 Frege underscores that the traditional distinction between general and particular judgements is really a distinction between the contents of judgements, since such properties belong to the contents of sentences already before they are asserted in a judgement. To prefix the judgement line ' | ' to —S, where S is a judgeable content, does not add any generality or particularity to that content. A similar situation occurs with negation. It adheres to contents of sentences,

---

[20]Ibid., pp. 3-4.

regardless of whether that content is judged or not. For Frege, negation is a trait of a judgeable content. To try to conceive negation, generality or particularity as belonging to the judgement, and not to the judgeable content, would be to conflate the content of a judgement, namely, —S, with the recognition of its truth, namely, |—S.

Frege will maintain this important distinction between the content of a judgement and the judgement, that is, the recognition of the truth of the judgement content, throughout his whole career. After 1890 he will express that distinction as one between apprehending a thought – thinking – and recognizing its truth – judging.

On the other hand, Frege dismisses the distinction made in traditional logic between categorical, hypothetical and disjunctive judgements as purely grammatical, but does not offer any sort of argument on which to base that rejection. Seen from our vantage standpoint, Frege was right in abandoning that distinction, but for most of his potential contemporary readers such a schematic rejection was not palatable.

Much more interesting is Frege's exclusion of the modalities. For Frege the distinction between apodictic and assertoric judgements consists only in that in the first case somehow there is an appeal to the existence of general statements from which the sentence asserted as apodictic can be derived, whereas in the case of assertoric judgements there is no indication of the existence of such general statements. When we call a statement necessary we somehow refer to the statements on which the judgement is based. But this does not touch the conceptual content of the judgement. Now, since for the concept-script only the conceptual content is relevant, the form of the apodictic judgement has no importance, and the distinction between apodictic and assertoric judgements should not be expressible in it.

It is not necessary to underscore that Frege's treatment of the distinction between apodictic and assertoric judgements is very unsatisfactory, and it is so regardless of our misgivings concerning the modalities. The notion of possibility does not fare any better. Frege asserts that when a sentence is presented as possible, then the speaker refrains from any judgement and indicates that he ignores the laws on which its negation could be based, or he asserts that the negation of the sentence is not generally true. In this latter case, possibility reduces to a particular affirmative judgement. Frege expounds his views on possibility as concisely as he does with apodictic judgements. He simply tries to reduce the attribution of the modality of possibility to the content of judgements to either of the following two cases, neither of which includes any reference to modalities: (i) either we are indicating that we ignore the laws on which the negation of the sentence is based, in which case the importance of the attribution of possibility is epistemological, not logical; or (ii) the possibility judgement is assimilated to the particular affirmative judgements. In either case, the ontological nature of the distinction between necessity, factual existence and possibility, which seems to found the traditional distinction between apodictic, assertoric and problematic judgements, is lost.

8 Identity Statements in *Begriffsschrift*

In section 8 of *Begriffsschrift* Frege introduces what he there calls 'content equality', which is one of the most relevant issues for the study of the evolution of his thought. As we will see in Chapter 4, his disappointment with the solution given to this problem in his early work was one of the most important reasons – if not the most important one – for the introduction of the distinction between sense and reference.

Thus, at the beginning of that section Frege says that content equality, in contrast with the conditional (introduced in section 5) and with negation (introduced in section 6) concerns [*sich bezieht auf*] names and not contents. For Frege in *Begriffsschrift*,[21] though names usually serve only to represent their content – and, thus, any link in which they enter expresses only a relation between their contents – as soon as they are brought together by the sign for content equality, they bring to the forefront their own being, since this is the way in which we designate the circumstance that two names have the same content. Thus, for Frege,[22] with the introduction of the content equality sign a double duty in the meaning – Frege uses the word *Bedeutung* – occurs, since signs would sometimes represent their contents and sometimes themselves.

Frege's attempt to elucidate the notion of content equality helps very little to understand what his view really is. Sometimes it seems as if what he is trying to say is that an identity statement expresses a relation between names (or symbols) conceived merely as traces on paper or on the blackboard, without any connection with anything else. But such a conception is very difficult to sustain, since in such a case each time that we have two different signs, for example, 'a' and 'b', a statement of the form 'a=b' is false. In fact, such a rendering of Frege's views in *Begriffsschrift* would very probably be incorrect, since, as we have seen, he later says that the content equality relation is a relation between signs having the same content. Thus, the correct interpretation of Frege's views on identity statements in his early work is that they express a sort of congruence between the signs at the left and at the right hand sides of the identity sign modulo identity of content. There still remains an obscurity, since Frege never made the notion of content precise. Moreover, as we will see in Chapter 4, this conception of identity statements, though not so distant from his mature views on the subject, has also its difficulties. An ingredient is still missing, namely, the notion of sense.

Later in the same section Frege justifies the use of different signs for the same content, and this justification also serves to clarify his views. Thus, Frege says that both the use of different signs for the same content and the use of the identity sign are clearly justified by the fact that very frequently only after the introduction of the different names do we learn that they have the same content. In this case, a different name corresponds to each of the different ways used to determine the same content. Moreover, the requirement of having a sign for the

---

[21]Ibid., p. 13.
[22]Ibid., pp. 13-14.

equality content is based on the fact that the same content can be determined in different ways. Precisely the judgeable content of an identity statement is that the same is given by two different ways of determination. But before we learn that the same is determined in two different ways we need two different names associated with the two different ways of determination. Now, for the expression of such a judgement a sign for the content equality is required, which connects the two names. In this manner, Frege considers that the sign for the content equality is completely justified.[23] Our contention that, besides the obscurity of the notion of 'content', the only difference between Frege's conceptions of identity statements in *Begriffsschrift* and in his writings after 1890 is the introduction of the notion of sense, is clearly supported by his justification of the use of different names for the same content.

Moreover, Frege underscores[24] that the use of different names for the same content is not a cosmetic device but concerns the essence of what is under consideration when two names are connected with different ways of determination. He even goes so far as to sustain that a judgement that concerns the content equality is a synthetic one according to Kant's terminology.[25] We are not going to dwell on this issue, though we are conscious that Kant had an extremely narrow view of analytic statements. In any case, such remarks could have contributed to mislead some Fregean scholars, who have sustained that for Frege all true statements of the form 'a=b' are synthetic.[26]

My contention, already mentioned above, that Frege in *Begriffsschrift* conceived identity statements of the form 'a=b', where 'a' and 'b' are names introduced by different ways of determination, as expressing a congruence relation between names modulo sameness of content, seems now well justified. But, as I also underscored, the relation is not completely clarified, due to the fact that the notions of content and equality of content remain obscure. Nonetheless, it seems that in this context when Frege talks about the content of a sign, he is talking about what he later would call the 'referent of the sign' and, thus, the expression 'content equality' should be interpreted as sameness of reference.

Now, if the relation expressed is one between names with the same content, since the link of a name to an object is always arbitrary, each and every identity statement of the form 'a=b', where 'a' and 'b' are different names, would be not only synthetic according to Kant, but also synthetic and even empirical according to Frege's later views, since in its foundation one should have to include the empirical statement describing the fact that the names 'a' and 'b' – arbitrarily associated with the two different ways of determining a content – determine the same content. (Thus, though the signs '6' and 'vi' determine their content as a result of arbitrary stipulations, it is an empirical fact that they determine the same

---

[23]Ibid., pp. 14-15.
[24]Ibid., p. 15.
[25]Ibid.
[26]See, e.g., Hans Sluga's 'Semantic Content and Cognitive Sense', in L. Haaparanta and J. Hintikka (eds), *Frege Synthesized* (Dordrecht, 1986), pp. 58 and 60.

content.) This consequence of Frege's treatment of identity statements in *Begriffsschrift* would make identity statements like '2 is the smallest prime number' or '5+2=7' not only synthetic but empirical statements, according to Frege's definitions in *Die Grundlagen der Arithmetik*.[27] Moreover, if Frege had ever thought, as tacitly accepted by Fregean scholars, that the notions of judgeable content and conceptual content introduced by totally different means in sections 2 and 3, respectively, had the same content, by the light of Frege's treatment of identity statements in his early work, such a contention would have to be empirically established. Of course, as we have already mentioned, it is almost an insult to Frege's acuteness and search for the maximum precision to attribute to him such an unwarranted view.

Frege mentions an additional, but less important reason, for the introduction of the content equality sign, namely, that it is sometimes convenient to introduce abbreviations instead of a longer expression.[28] Thus, one should have to be able to express the content equality between the abbreviation and the original longer expression.

9 Functions in *Begriffsschrift*

In *Begriffsschrift* Frege introduces functions as follows.[29] When we conceive an expression as changing, we conceive it as divided into two parts, one of which changes, whereas the other remains constant. The constituent that remains constant represents the totality of the relations present in the expression, whereas the first part is conceived as replaceable by other signs and means – Frege uses the word *bedeuten* – the object that is in such a relation. Frege calls the unchanged constituent 'the function' and the replaceable one 'the argument'. According to Frege, this distinction does not have anything to do with the conceptual content, but concerns only our way of conceiving it. Thus, he expounds his views by considering a content like 'd is taller than b', in which we could take 'd' as the argument and 'taller than b' as the function, or 'b' as the argument and 'shorter than d' as the function. Thus, 'd is taller than b' and 'c is taller than b' can be conceived as the same function, but with two different arguments 'd' and 'c', or as two different functions 'shorter than d' and 'shorter than c' with the same argument 'b'. Frege sums up his views as follows.[30] When in an expression, which does not need to be a judgeable content – that is, does not need to have the form of a statement – there is a simple or compound sign in one or more places, and we conceive it as replaceable by another sign in some or all of those places, but always by the same sign, we call 'function' that part of the expression that remains

---

[27]*Die Grundlagen der Arithmetik* 1884, Centenary Edition, 1986, section 3.
[28]*Begriffsschrift*, p. 15. This last point concerns definitions, which will be thoroughly treated in Chapter 7.
[29]Ibid.
[30]Ibid., p. 16.

constant and call 'argument' the replaceable part. But since the same sign can appear in an expression as (a replaceable) argument and also in other places, in which it is not thought as replaceable, Frege makes it clear that in a function one has to distinguish the argument places from the remaining places.[31]

Before continuing our exposition of Frege's views on functions in his early work, it is convenient to underscore two important points. Firstly, it should be emphasized that Frege's treatment of functions is syntactical, it concerns a sort of signs, in contrast with other signs, the argument signs. There is no trace of semantic or ontological aspects of functions in that treatment. As we will see in Chapter 4 and beyond, Frege will later ontologize both functions and their arguments, which he will then call 'objects'. He will then refer to the syntactical side as including proper names and function symbols, which will be connected to their ontological counterparts by means of the fundamental semantic relation of reference via their respective senses. Secondly, it is important to underscore that Frege in some sense relativizes the distinction between function and argument to what he calls 'conception'. Thus, though the distinction between argument and function in a conceptual content is fundamental, different conceptions that determine diverse ways of subdividing a conceptual content in function and argument can correspond to the same conceptual content.

Later on, Frege makes some especially interesting remarks that deserve attention not only because of their intrinsic importance, but also because they can very well serve as examples of how natural language misleads us and blurs the logical structure of statements.[32] Frege underscores that it would be mistaken to conceive the statements 'Number 20 can be represented as the sum of four square numbers' and 'Every positive integer can be represented as the sum of four square numbers' as differing only because in the two cases the same function 'can be represented as the sum of four square numbers' has different arguments, namely, 'number 20' in one case, 'every positive integer' in the other. This view is mistaken, since 'number 20' and 'every positive integer' are not expressions of the same level. As Frege observes,[33] what is said about the number 20 cannot be said in the same sense about every positive integer, or at least can be said of every positive integer only under special circumstances. Contrary to the expression 'number 20', the expression 'every positive integer' is incapable of an independent representation, but obtains its meaning – Frege uses the word *Sinn* – by means of the sentential context.[34]

---

[31]Ibid.
[32]Ibid., p. 17.
[33]Ibid.
[34]This last remark of Frege has made Hans Sluga think that Frege is here anticipating the Context Principle of his *Die Grundlagen der Arithmetik*. See on this issue his book *Gottlob Frege* (Routledge, 1980), p. 94. But precisely on the basis of the context in which such a remark was made, I think that our rendering in the next paragraph is much more plausible. On this issue, one should not forget that the Context Principle of *Die Grundlagen der Arithmetik* applies to all constituent parts of statements and not only to conceptual words.

A thoughtful reading of Frege's views expounded in the last paragraph shows that Frege is pointing, however confusedly, to the distinction between concept and object. What he tried to express in *Begriffsschrift* would have been expressed in his mature work approximately as follows: The statements 'Number 20 can be represented as the sum of four square numbers' and 'Every positive integer can be represented as the sum of four square numbers' have very different logical structure. The first statement expresses that the object referred to by the proper name 'number 20' falls under the concept referred to by the conceptual word 'can be represented as the sum of four square numbers'. The second statement does not say anything about numbers, but expresses the subordination of the concept referred to by 'positive integer' to the concept referred to by 'can be represented as the sum of four square numbers'. What is said about 'number 20' cannot be said of 'every positive integer', since those expressions refer to fundamentally different entities. Contrary to the expression 'number 20', the expression 'every positive integer' does not refer to a saturated (or complete) entity, an object, but to an incomplete one, that requires saturation. In fact, the statement 'Every positive integer can be represented as the sum of four square numbers' could be rendered more clearly as follows: 'For all x, if x is a positive integer, then x can be represented as the sum of four square numbers'. Although this statement has a saturated referent, namely, an object, its constituent parts are unsaturated and, thus, cannot refer to objects.

Later in section 9 Frege argues[35] that what is of relevance here is that function and argument be completely determined and distinguished from each other, whereas the different possible ways in which we can conceive a conceptual content as a function of this or that argument are of no importance. However, when the argument is indeterminate – in current terminology: is a variable – the distinction between function and argument becomes relevant for the content. On the other hand, it can also be the case that the function is indeterminate, whereas the argument remains fixed. We can, for example, fix the argument '2' and consider a variable function '*f*' of '2', where the indeterminate function '*f*' can be successively replaced by the determinate functions 'the square of _', 'the successor of _', 'the predecessor of _', and so forth. In both cases, as Frege points out,[36] the whole is divisible into function and argument by contrasting what is determined with what is completely or, at least, partially indeterminate with respect to its content, not merely as a matter of the conception. Frege is here already taking into account the possibility of second level functions, to which he will return more emphatically at the end of section 10.

But, as Frege stresses,[37] functions need not be of one argument. If in a function, we consider replaceable a sign that until now had been considered as determined, we obtain a new function of both the old and the new argument, that is, a function of two arguments. Thus, if in the function '2+x=x+2', we conceive

---

[35]*Begriffsschrift*, p. 17.
[36]Ibid.
[37]Ibid., pp. 17-18.

'2' as replaceable, we obtain a function of two arguments 'x+y=y+x'. In this way we can obtain functions of two or more arguments.

At the end of section 9 Frege says[38] that in statements analysed in the traditional manner, as containing a subject and a predicate, the subject is usually conceived as the most important argument, whereas the second most important argument occurs as a predicate. However, language is free to let appear as most important argument this or that constituent of the statement by choosing between the active and the passive mode, or between expressions like 'taller than' and 'shorter than', or between verbs like 'to give' and 'to receive'.

Frege uses the symbol sequences $\Phi(A)$ and $\Psi(A,B)$ to express, respectively, a function of argument 'A' and a function of the two arguments 'A' and 'B', in which nothing else is determined. In $\Phi(A)$ and in $\Psi(A,B)$ the signs 'A' and 'B' represent the argument places of A and B in the functions, regardless of whether there are none, one or many. In the case of functions of two arguments, the order of the arguments is important since $\Psi(A,B)$ and $\Psi(B,A)$ are, in general, different or, more precisely and using, Frege's terminology in *Begriffsschrift*, they have different conceptual content. Thus, the functions 'x<y' and 'y<x' have different conceptual content.

It should be stressed that Frege's readings of the functions of one and two arguments are somewhat misleading, if not inadequate. In section 10, Frege renders $|\!\!-\!\Phi(A)$ as 'A has property Φ' and $|\!\!-\!\Psi(A,B)$ either as 'B is in the relation Ψ with A' or as 'B is the result of the application of the procedure Ψ to A'. First of all, we should observe that Frege's notion of a function is wide enough to include what we nowadays would call 'monadic predicates' and 'relational (or polyadic) predicates'. Frege is perfectly conscious of his use of the word 'function' and at the end of section 10 underscores that his notion of function is much wider than what is current in mathematical analysis. However, even accepting that extension of the use of the word 'function', Frege's examples and renderings are of almost no help for assessing what he tries to convey. If $\Phi(A)$ is read as 'A has property Φ', it is in no way clear in which sense that is a function, or what is the value of the function Φ for the argument A. In his writings after 1890, when he ontologizes functions, he will say that the value of such a function is a truth-value, that is, either the true or the false. In fact, after 1890 he will conceive concepts as functions of one argument, whose value is a truth-value. Nonetheless, a concept would be only a special sort of function, and it does not seem to be appropriate to clarify the notion of a function of one argument by using as an example what is clearly a very special and in no way representative case of the notion of function.

With respect to the two renderings of $\Psi(A,B)$, it should firstly be said that they are not equivalent. According to the first reading, $\Psi(A,B)$ is a dyadic relation (with inverted arguments). Besides such inversion of the order, the difficulties of this reading are similar to those of $\Phi(A)$. If $\Psi(A,B)$ is a function of two arguments, it is not clear what is the value of the function for the ordered pair <A,B>. After

[38]Ibid., p. 18.

1890, when Frege ontologizes relations, he would conceive (dyadic) relations as functions of two arguments, whose value is a truth-value, that is, either the True or the False. However, relations would be a very special case of dyadic functions and, as in the case of concepts, their use as representative examples of all dyadic functions is inappropriate. On the other hand, according to the second reading, Ψ(A,B) is clearly a function of one argument A, whose value is B, thus, not a function of the two arguments A and B.

Frege concludes section 10 with a brief but important additional remark to his discussion in section 9 of determinate and indeterminate components of conceptual contents. He observes that in an expression of the form Φ(A) we could conceive the sign 'Φ' as replaced by other signs 'Ψ', 'Γ'and, thus, obtain other functions of the argument 'A'. In this case, we can conceive Φ(A) not as a function of the argument A, but as one of the argument Φ. We have here the first decisive step for the introduction of a hierarchy of functions.

In section 11 Frege introduces quantification – or, more precisely, universal quantification – both of individual and of functional variables. Frege's rendering of quantification in *Begriffsschrift* and, especially, his treatment of the relation – in non-Fregean symbolism – between $\mid$— (∀x)Φ(x) – to be read as 'Φ(x) is a fact', regardless of what its argument x is – and judgements like $\mid$—Φ(A) is clearly substitutional. In fact, when explaining the meaning of $\mid$— (∀x)Φ(x) Frege does not make any reference to objects for which the function is to hold, but only to the possible substitutions of the variable ξ in the function Φ(ξ).

In the same section 11, Frege discusses what is now called 'the scope of a quantifier', as well as multiple quantification. It should be stressed that section 11 contains some of Frege's most important contributions to contemporary logic, contributions made in a small and philosophically somewhat immature book, but of gigantic importance for the development of logic.

10 Axiom Systems

The remaining two chapters of *Begriffsschrift* are of a technical logical nature, and we will say very little about them in this introductory book to Frege's philosophy. Nonetheless, it should be mentioned that at the beginning of Chapter 2,[39] Frege makes interesting remarks on an issue on which he will say much more in his later work, namely, the axiomatic formulation of a set of laws. First of all, Frege distinguishes between the knowledge of the laws and the knowledge of the logical relations between them. When we have this second sort of knowledge, we are in possession of a small number of laws that include, though without its deployment, the content of the remaining laws. An important feature of the method of derivations is precisely that it allows us to get acquainted with this nucleus of laws. Moreover, since it is impossible to enumerate all the laws that should be displayed,

---

[39] Ibid., p. 25.

the completeness of a system can only mean the obtaining of all those laws that include the content of the remaining laws of the system. Now, there is more than one way in which this goal can be attained, that is, there are many possible systems of laws that include the remaining laws of the system. That means, however, that one mode of presentation of the complete set of laws of the system is incapable of clarifying all the logical relations present in what Frege, in this early work, called the 'laws of thought'.[40] There is most surely another set of laws, from which all the laws of thought could be obtained. Thus, Frege not only acknowledges the importance of an axiomatic formulation of the logical laws, but also is conscious that such a presentation cannot do justice to all derivability relations between laws. A different axiomatic system could very well derive all the laws of thought. But in such a different presentation of those laws some derivability relations would occur, which do not occur in the first axiomatic system, whereas some derivability relations would not occur, which are present in the first axiomatic system.

---

[40] The use of the expression 'laws of thought' to designate the logical laws will be rejected by Frege from 1890 onwards, since it opens the door to a psychologistic interpretation of logical laws. See on this issue Chapter 6. In *Die Grundlagen der Arithmetik*, however, such unfortunate terminology is still present.

Chapter 2

Die Grundlagen der Arithmetik: First Part (§§1-45)

Five years after *Begriffsschrift*, and probably following Carl Stumpf's advice[1] to write a philosophical book expounding his views on logic and logicism, Frege published his philosophical masterpiece *Die Grundlagen der Arithmetik*. This small book is very probably the most studied work in the philosophy of mathematics. In this chapter and the next I will expound most of its fundamental views. In this one I will be concerned (i) with Frege's goals, with the methodological considerations and fundamental distinctions he introduces to attain such goals – all of which is presented in the Preface and the Introduction to the book; and (ii) with Frege's criticisms of other's views, especially of naturalistic, psychological and Kantian views on arithmetic. In Chapter 3 I will complete my exposition of *Die Grundlagen der Arithmetik* by considering Frege's views on numerical predication, his conception of arithmetic and, especially, his three attempts at defining the notion of natural number.

1 The Need for a Clarification of the Nature of Mathematics

At the very beginning of his Introduction to *Die Grundlagen der Arithmetik*[2] Frege points out that there is a lack of clarity among mathematicians about the nature of the number one and, moreover, he stresses that having such a confused conception of a notion so familiar and apparently simple is a shame for the whole of mathematics. Of course, if there is no clear notion of the number one, it is impossible to have a clear notion of number, in general. Now, if a notion so fundamental to a science like mathematics offers so many difficulties it is an unavoidable task to investigate it precisely and to eliminate confusions, that would obviously generate difficulties in other important mathematical concepts based on such a fundamental one.

    Immediately, Frege asserts that thought is everywhere the same and, thus, that the laws of thought[3] do not change according to the objects studied. Frege

---

[1] On this point, see the letter from Carl Sumpf to Frege in *Wissenschaftlicher Briefwechsel*, pp. 256-7, especially p. 257.
[2] *Die Grundlagen der Arithmetik*, p. 4.
[3] See the last footnote of Chapter 1.

considers that the differences in the applications of the laws of thought to the
different sciences are based on the lesser or greater purity and independence of any
psychological influences, as well as on external devices like language and
numerical signs, and also on the finesse of the conceptual construction. But, as
Frege emphasizes,[4] in this last aspect mathematics supersedes any other science,
and even philosophy.

Hence, for Frege, the same laws of thought are valid for all disciplines,
and there is only one science that studies them: logic. In fact, Frege explicitly
mentions that his book will show that every mathematical inference, especially the
apparently so peculiar inference that allows us the transit from n to n+1, is based
on general logical laws.[5] Though Frege's formulation is inadequate – since he
takes as a conclusion what is part of the premises – it is clear that he has in mind
the Principle of Mathematical Induction.

Now, as Frege stresses,[6] a profound investigation of the concept of
number will always be of a philosophical nature, and is, thus, a common task for
mathematics and philosophy. According to Frege, the dominance in philosophical
investigations, and even in logic, of psychological considerations has impeded the
cooperation between mathematics and philosophy, since psychology cannot
contribute anything to the foundation of mathematics. Internal images, their origin
and transformation are of no interest to the mathematician. It is a mistake to take a
description of how an idea originates for a definition, or the psychological or
physiological conditions required for becoming conscious of a statement, for its
demonstration. Moreover, it would be an error not to distinguish the truth of a
statement from its being thought. Using Frege's comparison: in the same way in
which the sun is not destroyed when we do not see it, a statement does not cease to
be true when it is not thought by us.[7] Thus, we have here already in a very concise
form the nucleus of Frege's criticism of psychologism as well as his views on the
objectivity of logic and, especially, his conception of the non-temporality of truth.

However, not only psychologism, but also historicism is the subject of
brief critical remarks in the Introduction. This may seem somewhat strange, since
there is no criticism of historicism in the main text and since there was no serious
attempt worth considering of giving mathematics a 'historicist foundation'.
Nonetheless, it should be remembered that in the nineteenth century different sorts
of historicisms had been propounded both in the sciences and in philosophy, from
Comte and Marx to some applications of Darwin's theory of evolution. Thus,
probably Frege was anticipating any such unfounded 'historicist foundation' of
mathematics. In any case, Frege makes some brief but important remarks on what
can be called 'the historical point of view'. Thus, the historical point of view,

---

[4]*Die Grundlagen der Arithmetik*, p. 5.
[5]Ibid. It should be observed that at the end of the book – see section 87, p. 99 – Frege says
that in *Die Grundlagen der Arithmetik* he has made plausible that arithmetic is derivable
from logic.
[6]Ibid., p. 6.
[7]Ibid., p. 7.

which, as Frege points out,[8] studies the process or becoming of things and attempts to learn about the essence of things by these means, clearly has its justification. But it also has its limits. If in the continuous flux of becoming nothing would remain unchanged, says Frege,[9] we would not be able to have knowledge of any objects and total confusion would prevail. Moreover, Frege rightly adds that what is usually called 'history of concepts' is just either the history of our acquaintance with those concepts or a history of the meanings of words.[10] Although the history of discoveries is perhaps in some cases important for other investigations, it should never replace such investigations.

These last remarks made by Frege, probably motivated by the historicist trends in the nineteenth century, are still of the utmost importance for all science, but very especially for the most rigorous, namely, logic, mathematics and physics. We have already seen attempts in the second half of the twentieth century to replace the logical-epistemological study of physical science with historical analyses by Thomas Kuhn[11] and many others. But those studies, even if correct, can only have a complementary role, and will never replace the studies of the structure of science or of scientific theories. And, of course, sociological, historical-materialist or psychological studies of science are not even complementary, but irrelevant for the understanding of science and scientific theories – as they are also for philosophy.

Continuing with Frege, he underscores[12] that we should not only block any intervention of psychology in the realm of mathematics, but at the same time acknowledge the strong bonds between logic and mathematics. For Frege, it is not possible to separate those two areas of knowledge. The study of the correctness of proofs and the justification of definitions belongs to the province of logic, but mathematics cannot afford to ignore those issues, since only when we finally obtain a satisfactory answer to them is it possible to attain the needed security of the mathematical methods and results.

2 The Methodological Principles

Of special – but somewhat unequal – importance are the three fundamental methodological principles introduced by Frege in the Introduction and which serve him as guiding principles in his investigation. They are the following:[13]

---

[8] Ibid., p. 7.
[9] Ibid.
[10] Ibid., pp. 7-8.
[11] See, for example, his *The Structure of Scientific Revolutions* (Chicago, 1962, revised edition 1970).
[12] Ibid., p. 9.
[13] Ibid., p. 10.

(1)   We should clearly distinguish the psychological from the logical, the subjective from the objective.

(2)   We should ask for the meaning of words only in the context of sentences.

(3)   We should always have present the difference between concept and object.

In order not to violate the first principle, Frege will always use the word 'representation' [in German: *Vorstellung*] in a psychological sense, and he will clearly distinguish representations both from concepts and objects. Frege justifies the second principle by stating that if we ignore it, we will almost surely take as the meaning of words internal images or actions of our subjectivity, what would also make us violate the first principle.[14] With respect to the third principle Frege simply says, without further elaboration, that we cannot replace an object by a concept without transforming it.[15]

It should be stressed here that both in *Die Grundlagen der Arithmetik* and in his later writings principles (1) and (3) have a clearer role than principle (2), which I – following other authors – will call the 'Context Principle' from now on. The radical separation between the logical and the psychological, between what is objective and what is subjective is one of the most basic aspects of all of Frege's writings, including – as we have seen – his early work *Begriffsschrift*. In particular, that principle is omnipresent in *Die Grundlagen der Arithmetik* and is the basis of Frege's criticism of psychologism in mathematics and logic. The radical separation between concept and object is also a fundamental component of Frege's philosophy from 1884 onwards, and – as we have seen – its nucleus was already present in his *Begriffsschrift*, though it was not expounded as clearly as in later writings. In *Die Grundlagen der Arithmetik* the distinction between concept and object plays a very important role, though it had not attained its full articulation. In his writings after 1890, however, the centrality of the distinction between concept and object in Frege's philosophy is even clearer, being now as fundamental as that between the logical and the psychological.

Something very different happens with the Context Principle. This principle is explicitly mentioned only a few times more in the book, namely, in sections 60, 62 and 106. Its presence is less noticeable than that of the other two principles, being explicitly used in the preliminary clarification of the notion of

---

[14]This remark by Frege on the role of the Context Principle seems to support David Shwayder's contention that Frege abandoned this principle from 1891 onwards, since its role had become unnecessary after the introduction of the distinction between sense and reference. On this issue, see Shwayder's paper 'On the Determination of Reference by Sense', in M. Schirn (ed.), *Studies on Frege III* (Stuttgart, 1976), pp. 85-95. See also both my critical review of Schirn's book in *Diálogos* 38, (1981a): 157-83, my paper 'Remarks on Sense and Reference in Frege and Husserl', in *Kant-Studien* 73/4, (1982): 425-39, reprinted in Claire Ortiz Hill and Guillermo E. Rosado Haddock, *Husserl or Frege?* (Chicago, 2000, 2003), pp. 23-40, as well as below in this same section and in Chapter 4.
[15]*Die Grundlagen der Arithmetik*, p. 10.

number and in the second attempt to define that notion precisely, and mentioned also in the summary at the end of the book. However, as we will see, the definition of number finally adopted by Frege does not seem to have need of that principle. Much more important, however, is the fact that this principle – so dear to many followers of Wittgenstein, and not only to them – seems to have been abandoned some years later, probably because it is difficult to reconcile with some Fregean views from 1891 on. But some ideas die hard, and though the Context Principle disappeared from central stage in Frege's philosophy after 1890, there is still a residue in *Grundgesetze der Arithmetik*,[16] which caused Frege unnecessary problems that he could not satisfactorily solve. In any case, there has been an interesting discussion about Frege's possible abandonment of the Context Principle after 1890. Sluga, Tugendhat, Currie and Schirn[17] – among others – have argued that Frege never abandoned the Context Principle, whereas Resnik, Shwayder and the present author have argued that he did.[18] I believe that, though there is a residue in Frege's argumentation in sections 29-31 of his *Grundgesetze der Arithmetik*, he abandoned the principle after 1890. Once the distinction between sense and reference (or referent) was made, one would first of all have to ask whether the principle is applicable to the sense, to the reference, or to both. Now, both with respect to the notion of sense and to that of reference the Context Principle is not easily reconcilable with Frege's theses that the sense of a compound expression is a function of the senses of its component parts and that the referent of a compound expression is a function of the referents of its component parts. Moreover, in the case of the reference, if we combine the Context Principle with Frege's particular selection of the truth-values as the referents of statements, the situation is even less comfortable. Since in a language like the concept-script there are as many statements that refer to the True and as many statements that refer to the False as there are natural (or rational) numbers, thus, infinitely many, if Frege had applied his Context Principle to his notion of reference he would have had to clearly show how the referents of the extremely varied component parts of the infinitely many

---

[16]*Grundgesetze der Arithmetik I*, sections 29-31.

[17]See H. Sluga's book *Gottlob Frege*, as well as Currie's book *Frege: An Introduction to his Philosophy* (Totowa, N.J., 1982), E. Tugendhat's paper 'Die Bedeutung des Ausdrucks "Bedeutung" bei Frege' in M. Schirn (ed.), *Studies on Frege III*, pp. 51-69, and also M. Schirn's Editor's Introduction to his *Frege: Importance and Legacy* (Berlin, 1996), pp. 1-42.

[18]See Shwayder's paper already mentioned, M. Resnik's paper 'Frege's Context Principle Revisited', in M. Schirn (ed.), *Studies on Frege III*, pp. 35-49, and my review article of Schirn's book *Frege: Importance and Legacy* in *History and Philosophy of Logic* 19/4, (1998a), pp. 249-66. Michael Dummett has been somewhat ambivalent on this issue. See his *Frege: Philosophy of Language* (London, 1973, 1981a), p. 645, as well as *The Interpretation of Frege's Philosophy* (London, 1981b), Chapter 19, especially pp. 371-2 and 374ff, and *Frege: Philosophy of Mathematics* (London, 1991a), Chapter 16. More recently, in his 'The Context Principle: Centre of Frege's Philosophy', Dummett rejects his earlier misgivings and sustains very emphatically the permanence of the Context Principle in *Grundgesetze der Arithmetik*. See Ingolf Max and Werner Stelzner (eds), *Logik und Mathematik*, pp. 3-19, especially pp. 13-16.

statements that refer to the True – or to the False – are obtained only from the referent of a given statement in which they occur. Furthermore, since a component part of a true statement can also occur as a component part of a false statement, the difficulties for a Fregean application of the Context Principle to the reference are even worse. It is difficult to believe that Frege was not conscious of the insurmountable difficulties of a theory that would combine the application of the Context Principle with his thesis that the referents of statements are truth-values. In fact, in the second volume of *Grundgesetze der Arithmetik*[19] Frege argues that we cannot obtain the referents of the component parts of statements even if we know not only the referent of the whole statement, but also the referent of the remaining component part. On the other hand, the Context Principle does not seem to be easily reconcilable with some remarks made by Frege on our capability to understand sentences that we had not heard before.[20] Finally, as already mentioned – and probably stated for the first time by Shwayder – after Frege made the distinction between sense, reference and representation, the role of the Context Principle in *Die Grundlagen der Arithmetik* of blocking a conflation between meaning and representation, became unnecessary.[21]

3 The Classification of Statements

In section 3 of *Die Grundlagen der Arithmetik* Frege discusses the problem with which he began the Preface of *Begriffsschrift*, namely, that of the classification of judgements. Frege first observes that both the distinction between *a priori* and *a posteriori* and that between analytic and synthetic concern not the content of judgements but the justification for making a judgement. Moreover, when we say, for example, that a statement is analytic, or that it is *a posteriori*, we are not making judgements about any psychological, physiological or physical circumstances that could have made it possible for the content of the statement to be formed in our conscience. Nor are we judging how someone ever came to consider that statement true. Rather, we are concerned only with the justification of our considering it true. In this way Frege intends to free the epistemological problem of the classification of statements from everything psychological.[22]

To answer the question about the nature of a true statement we have to find its proof and follow it regressively until we arrive at the ultimate truths on

---

[19] *Grundgesetze der Arithmetik II*, section 66.
[20] See, for example, the letter to Philip Jourdain in *Wissenschaftlicher Briefwechsel*, pp. 126-9, especially p. 127, where Frege explicitly mentions that we can understand sentences that we had never heard before because we build the sense of sentences from the senses of their component words. For more details on this issue, including relevant quotations, see Chapter 4, section 2 of this book.
[21] See on this issue Frege's 'Gedankengefüge', in his *Kleine Schriften*, edited by Ignacio Angelelli (Hildesheim, second edition 1990), pp. 378-94.
[22] *Die Grundlagen der Arithmetik*, section 3, p. 15.

which it is based. If in this way we find only general logical laws and definitions in its foundation, the statement is analytic. If that is not the case and it is not possible to prove the statement without making use of truths that are not of a general logical nature, but belong to a special sphere of knowledge, then the statement is synthetic. On the other hand, a statement is *a posteriori* if its proof requires that we refer to facts, that is, to truths that lack generality and contain assertions about particular objects. If, on the contrary, it is possible to prove the statement on the basis only of general laws, not reducible to any other statements, its truth is *a priori*.[23] It should be mentioned here that the Fregean definitions above are meant to include proofs of length one and, thus, that it does not make any sense to raise the artificial problem of the nature of the logical axioms. If Frege did not consider the truths of logic as analytic, he would not have dared to try to prove the analyticity of arithmetical statements by deriving them exclusively by logical means from logical statements.

Frege's main concern, however, is not of a general epistemological nature, but with the application of the definitions to the study of arithmetical statements. Thus, Frege stresses[24] a point already made in *Begriffsschrift* and which will also be underscored in *Grundgesetze der Arithmetik*, namely, that it is necessary to derive the arithmetical axioms with the greatest rigour, since only if we have avoided each and every gap in the inference chain can we know on which original statements is the derived statement based and, hence, answer the philosophical question as to the nature of arithmetical statements.

4 The Naturalist Conception of Mathematics

In general, the views on mathematics that are the main targets of Frege's criticisms in *Die Grundlagen der Arithmetik* can be classified as either variants of naturalism or of psychologism. However, there are also present both criticisms of Kant's views on arithmetic and coincidences with Kant's views on geometry, though only in the main thesis of the synthetic *a priori* nature of geometrical knowledge, not in the argumentation on behalf of that thesis. Frege's views on geometry occur when discussing the naturalist conception of mathematics, and I will consider them in the next section. Firstly, I will expound Frege's criticism of some naturalist conceptions of mathematics.[25]

It is not easy to bring together in a homogeneous whole the diverse naturalist conceptions of mathematics. Without attempting to be totally exact, we can say that the naturalists targeted by Frege's criticisms conceived mathematics as

---

[23]Ibid., section 3, pp. 14-15.

[24]Ibid., section 4, pp. 15-16.

[25]I prefer the expression 'naturalism' instead of 'empiricism' to designate such views, because psychologism is also a sort of empiricism, but one clearly different from the views we are presently considering. It should, however, not be confused with its grandson of the same name propounded by Quine and others in recent Anglo-American philosophy.

an empirical natural science and its objects of study as completely similar to the objects and properties of the real physical world. Probably the most important representative of this naturalist conception in the philosophy of mathematics was John Stuart Mill, who considered arithmetical truths as empirical propositions obtained by induction, in the same fashion, in which, according to him, natural scientists obtained the laws of the remaining natural sciences. For the very influential Mill the difference between mathematics and other natural sciences was not a qualitative one but only one of gradation, mathematical truths being just natural laws of a higher degree of generality and more entrenched in our psyche than those of other natural sciences.

Mill believed that the definitions of numbers, for example, 3=2+1, did not merely determine the meaning [Frege: *Bedeutung*] of a number, but somehow contained some observed physical facts. Thus, according to Mill, the calculations with numbers would be based not merely on the definitions of numbers but also on empirically observed facts. Frege ridicules Mill's views, firstly, by considering very big numbers and asking about the physical facts we have to take into account to add such big numbers.[26] Moreover, Frege argues that, if the Millian were to assert that only small numbers are linked to the observation of physical facts, then such a distinction between small and big numbers would be arbitrary, since if definitions and calculations beginning with a determined number – be it 10, 25 or whatever – had no need of empirical observations, the same could be said of definitions and calculations concerned with the smaller numbers.[27]

Moreover, Frege stresses a point already made, namely, that when we call a statement 'empirical' because we needed to use our senses to become conscious of its content, we are not using the word 'empirical' in a sense that contradicts Frege's definition of '*a priori*'.[28] Furthermore, Frege argues that Mill conflates arithmetical statements with their applications, some of which are physical and presuppose the observation of facts.[29]

Another important critique of naturalist views made by Frege concerns the inductive method. Thus, Frege points out that the inductive method in the empirical sciences presupposes a uniformity of the cases considered as data that is completely absent in arithmetic, since between numbers there is a hierarchical order, and each number has not only its determined position in that order, but also its peculiar properties.[30] On the other hand, if we do not conceive the inductive procedure as merely based on habit – as Hume did – it seems justifiable only by arithmetical statements. But habit cannot serve as a foundation of any knowledge. Thus, if induction is going to be legitimized at all, it has to be founded on the doctrine of probability, since it cannot confer the general statement obtained anything more than probability. But the mathematical theory of probability

---

[26]*Die Grundlagen der Arithmetik*, section 7.
[27]Ibid., section 8, p. 21.
[28]Ibid., pp. 21-2.
[29]Ibid., section 9, p. 23.
[30]Ibid., section 10, p. 24.

presupposes the general arithmetical laws. Hence, the attempt to found arithmetical statements on the inductive procedure would be guilty of a vicious circle.[31]

On the basis of such arguments, in section 12 Frege concludes[32] that the arithmetical statements cannot be empirical. They are, thus, either analytic or synthetic *a priori*.

5 The Nature of Geometry

The rejection of the naturalist-empiricist conception of arithmetic is followed in section 13 by some extremely important observations on the difference between arithmetic and geometry. This contrast serves to assess not only Frege's conception of arithmetic, but also and especially his views on geometry. First of all, Frege observes that we should not overestimate the analogy between arithmetic and geometry. The geometrical points – as well as the lines and planes – when considered for themselves, that is, isolated from any other points – respectively, lines or planes – are indistinguishable from any other geometrical entity of the same sort. They do not have any intrinsic properties that could differentiate them, but we can distinguish one from the other only if we compare them, for example, two straight lines with respect to their length. Something very different occurs with numbers, since each and every number has its peculiarities, its special properties that distinguish them from any other. Thus, the number 2 is the smallest even number, the smallest prime number and the only even prime number; whereas the number 3 is the smallest odd prime number, and the number 4 the smallest square number that is not its own square. Hence, it is not easy to determine to what extent a given number can represent all other natural numbers, that is, when its peculiarities are irrelevant, and when relevant. Thus, from the fact that geometrical statements are – as Frege thinks – synthetic *a priori*, nothing can be inferred with respect to the nature of arithmetic.[33]

Some decades ago there was a very influential criticism of Frege by Paul Benacerraf, challenging not only Frege's views on the peculiarities of the different natural numbers, but also his views on arithmetic, in general.[34] Thus, Benacerraf argued (i) that the sequence of the so-called natural numbers is just a special case of a ω-sequence, (ii) that arithmetic studies the properties of such sequences, (iii) that any peculiar properties of the natural numbers are irrelevant for arithmetic, and (iv) that natural numbers do not exist as entities. Since Benacerraf's views have been extremely influential on the philosophy of mathematics in recent decades, a few critical remarks should be made here. The starting point of Benacerraf's argumentation is the fact that in the set theoretic representations of numbers given

---

[31]Ibid., p. 25.
[32]Ibid,, section 12, p. 26.
[33]Ibid., section 13, p. 28.
[34]'What Numbers Could Not Be', 1965, reprinted in Paul Benacerraf and Hilary Putnam, (eds), *Philosophy of Mathematics* (second edition, Cambridge, 1983), pp. 272-94.

by Zermelo and von Neumann the natural numbers seem to have different properties. However, Benacerraf confuses natural numbers with their representations – understood in a non-Fregean objective usage. It is the set-theoretic representation of the natural numbers given by von Neumann that has different properties than the one given by Zermelo, not the natural numbers being represented. The situation is similar to that of referring to an object by means of expressions having different senses, as well as to that of looking at the same object by means of different telescopes. Using Frege's comparison in 'Über Sinn und Bedeutung',[35] Benacerraf confuses the properties of the images in the lenses of the different telescopes used by Zermelo and von Neumann to see the moon with the moon itself. If something is to be learnt from Benacerraf's example is simply that set-theoretic representations of numbers are always somewhat artificial.

Secondly,[36] it is true that the sequence of prime numbers, as well as the sequence of even numbers, that of odd numbers, and many others are also ω-sequences and, as ω-sequences, have the same structure as that of the natural numbers (they are all order-isomorphic). However, if we take into account the additive and multiplicative properties of the natural numbers, as well as the properties of being prime, or of being odd, they get lost or have to be redefined when we consider other ω-sequences. Thus, for example, in the ω-sequence of even numbers, none has the property of being equal to its own product. Moreover, though in the ω-sequence of positive integers there is only one even prime number, in the ω-sequence of odd positive integers there is, of course, none, whereas in the ω-sequence of all positive integers with the exception of 2 – that is, in the sequence <1,3,4,5,...> – there are infinitely many even primes, namely, 4, 8 and all those numbers – like 6, 10, 14, 18, 22, 26, 34, and 38 – which in the sequence of natural numbers could only be factorized by an odd prime number and 2. Moreover, in the different ω-sequences arithmetical operations like addition or multiplication would have to be redefined, and even then the additive (respectively, multiplicative) arithmetic of such a sequence would not be isomorphic to that of natural numbers. Thus, for example, both the sequence of odd numbers and that of prime numbers are not closed under addition. Hence, such structures order-isomorphic to the arithmetic of natural numbers are not exactly similar to the latter with respect to other structural properties. Moreover, even the sequence of negative integers is in some sense similar to that of the positive integers, being a sort of mirror image of the latter. However, the sequence of negative integers is not closed under

---

[35] 'Über Sinn und Bedeutung', pp. 146-7.
[36] In contrast to the first and third arguments, the second argument presupposes that when we talk about the members of ω-sequences, for example, about the sequence of odd numbers, its third member is the number 5, which is the sixth member of the sequence of natural numbers, and does not occur in the sequence of even numbers, thus, not a mere geometrical mark on paper.

multiplication, as is the sequence of positive integers. More importantly, in Cantor's terminology, they are not even sequences of the same order type.[37]

Thirdly, to infer from the order-isomorphism, as Benacerraf does, the inexistence of arithmetical entities is totally unwarranted. As I have argued elsewhere, let us make the true assumption that I have two copies of the centenary edition of Frege's *Die Grundlagen der Arithmetik*, edited by Christian Thiel. They are structurally identical, though I can distinguish very well between them – one was kindly sent to me by the editor. More importantly, they exist, as well as any other copies of the same book in the shelves of other scholars. In the same way, according to the accepted physical theory of the macro-world, namely, general relativity, our physical world has the structure of a four-dimensional pseudo-Riemannian manifold of variable curvature, and we can conceive so many manifolds structurally similar to it as we wish. But that does not mean that our physical world does not exist. Finally, in this century of cloning, it is not excluded that some scientists are able to clone Einstein or Frege. But that does not mean that scholars of the next century would not be able to distinguish between Frege and his clone, born maybe in 2040, nor would they believe that it was Frege's clone who wrote *Die Grundlagen der Arithmetik*, nor would they dare to question Frege's existence because there is one or many clones of Frege. Benacerraf's application of his questionable argument on structural similarity to the natural numbers, their properties and their existence, if applied to structurally similar entities of our physical world, would have absurd consequences – like the denial of his own existence (*malgré* Descartes) if there happened to be a clone of Benacerraf himself – and serves only to disclose its shaky basis of anti-Platonist prejudices.[38]

Continuing with Frege's arguments, the comparison of arithmetical, geometrical and empirical truths with respect to the regions to which they apply speaks against either the empirical or synthetic a priori nature of arithmetical statements. Empirical truths are valid only for physical or psychological reality, geometrical truths apply to the region of what is spatially intuitive, which clearly includes our physical reality, but is not confined to it and includes also what is the product of our imagination.[39]

According to Frege, conceptual thinking can free itself from the geometrical axioms only when it presupposes, for example, a space of four

---

[37]In some sense, one could think that those two 'one-dimensional' mathematical objects could be considered to be in a relation similar to that of Kant's famous example of the left and right hand, and could cover one another by means of a displacement in two-dimensional (non-orientable) space. However, such a view would miss the important difference between the two sequences of being of different order type – what the left and right hand clearly are not. See Bertrand Russell's treatment of related issues in *The Principles of Mathematics* (London, 1903, 1942), p. 320, as well as pp. 417-18.

[38]On this point, see my paper 'On Antiplatonism and its Dogmas' in *Diálogos* 67, 1996: 7-38, reprinted in Claire O. Hill and Guillermo E. Rosado Haddock, *Husserl or Frege?*, pp. 263-89. See also my review of Anastasio Alemán's book *Lógica, Matemáticas y Realidad* in *Philosophia Mathematica* 11/1, 2003: 109-20.

[39]*Die Grundlagen der Arithmetik*, section 14, p. 28.

dimensions, or of positive or negative curvature.[40] Frege considers that, though such considerations are not completely fruitless, they abandon the realm of intuition. When we appeal to intuition we always consider Euclidean space, since this is the only one of which we have figures. When we try to make intuitive non-Euclidean geometries, we take intuition not for what it is, but symbolically for something else. Thus, for example, we call straight what we intuit as curved. In fact, for conceptual thinking it is always possible to presuppose the negation of one or another axiom without arriving at any contradictions when we extract conclusions from hypotheses that conflict with intuition. Frege correctly argues[41] that this possibility shows that geometrical axioms are both independent from each other and independent from logic. In this sense, we can say with Frege[42] that the consistency proofs of non-Euclidean geometries are at the same time independence proofs of all geometries and, in particular, of Euclidean geometry from logic. Thus, geometrical statements are essentially different from arithmetical statements. Arithmetical laws are restricted neither to the real nor to the intuitive. They are valid for the realm of the numerable, and everything thinkable is numerable. Hence, the realm of arithmetical statements is the same as that of logical laws: the realm of the thinkable.[43] Contrary to Kant's views, arithmetical statements are in no way restricted by intuition.

On the other hand, it is of special interest to observe here the similarity of Frege's conception of geometry with Kant's views, even though their arguments are different. Both philosophers consider (i) that geometrical statements are synthetic a priori, (ii) that they are intimately related to our intuition of space, (iii) that intuitive space is Euclidean, and (iv) that non-Euclidean geometries are a mere conceptual possibility, being consistent, but at the same time completely disconnected from intuition.

6 Numbers and Properties of Objects

To complete his attack on what I have called 'the naturalist conception of arithmetic', Frege discusses in Chapter II[44] the thesis that numbers are properties of objects, as are also colour or hardness. Clearly, such a conception of numbers seems to gain support from some uses of words for numbers in natural language. Numbers usually appear in adjectival form and as attributes, in a very similar fashion as red, heavy or tall, all of which mean[45] properties of external objects.

---

[40]Ibid.
[41]Ibid.
[42]Ibid., pp. 28-9.
[43]Ibid., p. 29.
[44]Ibid., sections 21-5, pp. 34-8.
[45]Since in *Die Grundlagen der Arithmetik* Frege had still not distinguished between sense and reference, when possible, we sometimes use the words 'meaning' and 'to mean' to prevent any misinterpretation in terms of the later distinction.

Thus, as Frege says,[46] it seems natural to ask whether we are to conceive natural numbers in the same fashion, that is, whether numerical words mean properties of things.

This case can very well serve to illustrate Frege's contention that natural language often deceives us, hiding from us the prevailing logical relations and, thus, we have to free ourselves from the chains of natural language in order to clearly see such logical relations. Behind the presumed similarity between the use of numerical words and the use of words expressing properties, lies an essential difference. Although we cannot change the colour – or any other property – of an external object by conceiving the object differently, we can attribute different numbers to a book, depending on whether we conceive it as one book, or as composed of, say, twenty-four chapters, or of one hundred thousand words. The colour and hardness of the cover of the book do not depend on our conception, whereas the attribution of the number one and not the number twenty to a book of twenty essays does depend on our conception. Moreover, when we say that the leaves of a tree are green, we mean that each and every leaf in the tree is green, but when we say that there are one thousand leaves in the tree, we do not attribute the number one thousand to each and every leaf, but only to the whole tree.[47] Thus, when we attribute a colour to a tree and when we attribute a number to the same tree we are clearly making essentially different attributions. In the first case, the attribution does not depend on our will, but in the second case it does, it depends on how we want to conceive the object. Now, Frege concludes[48] that the fact that we can attribute different numbers to the same object clearly shows that objects are not the genuine bearers of numbers.[49] Moreover, Frege rejects Mill's view, according to which a number designates a property belonging to the aggregate of things we are naming, and such that this property is the characteristic fashion in which the aggregate can be formed or divided in parts. For Frege, it is an error to talk about 'the characteristic fashion' in which an aggregate can be divided, since there are always different ways in which an aggregate can be divided and there is no basis for saying that one of them is more characteristic than any other.[50] Another important reason offered by Frege for not assimilating numbers to properties like redness or rigidity is the much wider applicability of numbers.[51] Furthermore, as Frege points out,[52] sometimes we make numerical distinctions to which nothing physical corresponds. Thus, with respect to the same visual perception, we can speak of a pair of boots and of two boots, though a pair and two

---

[46]*Die Grundlagen der Arithmetik*, section 21, p. 34.
[47]Ibid., pp. 34-5.
[48]Ibid., p. 35.
[49]Of course, with the same right, one could also have concluded that numbers are subjective or at least dependent on transcendental subjectivity, but Frege will also reject psychologism and Kantianism.
[50]*Die Grundlagen der Arithmetik*, section 23, p. 36.
[51]Ibid., section 24, p. 37.
[52]Ibid., pp. 37-8.

are not the same. Thus, if Frege's wife told him that she had found the missing pair of socks, she very probably meant that the socks were identical and belonged to the same pair, whereas if she told Frege that she had found the two missing socks, she probably meant that the socks were not identical and belonged to different pairs. In the same way, as Frege stresses,[53] two concepts are not the same as three concepts, though we cannot differentiate them physically.

In Chapter III – where Frege attempts to clarify the notion of unity – Frege offers additional arguments, concerned especially with the concept of unity, as opposed to the conception of numbers as properties of objects. It seems convenient to reproduce the two most decisive.

Firstly, it should be observed that if unity were a property, everything would have that property, and it would not be understandable why we are explicitly attributing such a property. It is only because there exists the possibility that some object does not have a given property, that it makes sense to predicate it of some other objects. Appealing to a thesis from traditional logic, Frege says[54] that the content of a concept diminishes as its extension is enlarged, and if the latter includes everything, the content is lost. Hence, adds Frege,[55] it does not seem clear how it is that a language has a word expressing a property that cannot serve to determine an object more precisely.

On the other hand, adds Frege,[56] if the word 'one' expressed a property in the same sense in which the word 'wise' does, then it could be used as a predicate. However, though we can very well understand what is meant by the statement 'Plato was wise', 'Plato was one' is not understandable when standing alone. Moreover, though from the statements 'Plato was wise' and 'Aristotle was wise' we can build the statement 'Plato and Aristotle were wise', even if 'Plato is one' and 'Aristotle is one' were intelligible, we could not say 'Plato and Aristotle were ones'.

I will now consider Frege's criticism of the psychologistic conception of mathematics. After all, psychologism is Frege's main target not only in *Die Grundlagen der Arithmetik* but also in most of his critical writings. However, it is in his philosophical masterpiece that the critique of psychologism is more compelling and less tainted by misinterpretations and a certain blindness to see valuable points in the writings of those whom he considered his adversaries.

7 Psychologism in Mathematics

Psychologism in mathematics and, especially, in arithmetic holds that to attain the ultimate foundation of our judgements about numbers – as of all judgements – both

---

[53]Ibid., section 25, p. 38.
[54]Ibid., section 29, p. 44.
[55]Ibid.
[56]Ibid., p. 45.

numbers and arithmetical statements should be submitted to an investigation of the mental processes that precede the utterance of such a judgement.

Frege correctly argues against psychologism that the description of the mental processes preceding the utterance of an arithmetical judgement, regardless of how correct the description may be, can never replace a genuine determination of the concepts involved, nor can it serve as a proof of any arithmetical statement. With its help we do not learn any new property of numbers. Numbers are not objects of study of psychology, and they are as little the result of any psychological processes as are the objects of our physical world. It would, thus, be as incorrect to carry out a psychological investigation of what numbers are as it would be to investigate the Atlantic Ocean by such means. The first is as objective as the second.[57]

In the argumentation expounded above, Frege is making a distinction, which is crucial for the understanding of his philosophical views, namely, the distinction between what is objective and what is spatial, perceptible, physically real. As he expressed with great lucidity in one of the last of his writings published during his lifetime, namely, 'Der Gedanke', what is physically real is objective, but not everything objective is physically real.[58] Thus, for example, says Frege,[59] the earth's axis and the central point of mass in the solar system are objective, but they are not real in the sense in which the earth is real. Moreover, the equatorial line is also objective, but it cannot be perceived by our senses as physically real objects can. The equatorial line is not an invented line, a product of our thought, the result of any psychological process, but is only known to us, apprehended by us, by means of our thought.[60]

Furthermore, argues Frege,[61] it is not only possible that other rational beings can have a very different representation of space from that of human beings, but we cannot even know if the representations that different human beings have of space coincide, since we cannot put the representation of space of one human being together with the representation of space of another human being, in order to be able to compare them.[62] Nonetheless, there is something objective present in our concept of space, since we all recognize the same geometrical axioms. What is objective there is what is submitted to laws, what is conceptual and capable of being judged, what can be expressed in words, and we do not conflate it with our subjective representations.[63]

---

[57]See ibid., section 26, p. 39.
[58]'Der Gedanke', 1918, reprinted in *Kleine Schriften*, pp. 342-62, especially p. 360.
[59]*Die Grundlagen der Arithmetik*, section 26, p. 40.
[60]Ibid.
[61]Ibid.
[62]Ibid. This is a recurrent Fregean argument, though it would strictly apply only against subjectivists, or individual relativists, in case philosophers of such a sort existed. Moreover, they would most probably not care. See on this issue the discussion below in this same section, as well as that of psychologism in logic in Chapter 6.
[63]Ibid.

Two points should be emphasized concerning the last argumentation. Firstly, it should be stressed that Frege's use of the word 'representation' in the above argument and in his whole work is restricted to designate what is subjective, psychological and incommunicable. I have already mentioned the second point, namely, that Frege was very traditional with respect to his views on geometry. Although non-Euclidean geometries already had half a century of existence, he still maintained that we all accept the same geometrical axioms, namely, those of Euclid. An interesting related problem merely touched upon by Frege's remarks is the following. How is it that we have objective geometrical knowledge, if geometry is based on spatial intuition, intuition is a form of representation, in Frege's use of this term, and our representation of space is subjective and incommensurable with that of other human beings? Problems of this sort are the fundamental epistemological ones, and there is not even an attempt at an answer for them in Frege's writings. Thus, contrary to a very popular school of Fregean scholarship, Frege was not an epistemologist.

Frege makes it clear that he understands by objectivity an independence of our feelings, intuitions, representations, or internal images in our memory of previous sensations. That does not mean, adds Frege[64] in a somewhat enigmatic way, independence of reason. He considers that to answer the question about what is independent of reason would mean to judge without judging.[65] Although such a remark by Frege reminds us superficially of an all embracing Hegelian Reason, and others have rendered it as a commitment to a sort of Kantianism, I consider that Frege just wants to stress that nothing objective is outside the realm of reason and of the laws of logic, which is *par excellence* the science concerned with everything objective or, as he would later say, with the laws of truth.

Frege then discusses what he considers the absurd consequences of the psychologistic thesis. Thus, he observes that if numbers were representations, arithmetic would simply be part of psychology. But arithmetic is as little psychological as astronomy. In the same way in which astronomy is concerned with the planets, not with our representations of planets, the objects of study of arithmetic are not representations. Frege adds,[66] however, that if the objects of study of arithmetic were the representations of numbers, not the numbers themselves, such representations would be only mine, since the representation that another person has is as such different from mine. Thus, in that case there would be millions of twos, since there are millions of representations of twos. But since the number of representations had by the whole of humanity is finite, then – contrary to what is usually believed – there could not be infinitely many numbers.[67]

Frege's argumentation is one of his favourites, and is repeated in other works, for example, in his attack on Erdmann's psychologism in logic. The whole argument, however, is not as solid as we may at first sight believe. Its first part is

---

[64]Ibid., p. 41.
[65]Ibid.
[66]Ibid., section 27, pp. 41-2.
[67]Ibid., p. 42.

perfectly correct: if numbers were representations and representations are psychological activities, then arithmetic would be a part of psychology. But it is a non sequitur to conclude that then arithmetic would be subjective. First of all, such a conclusion presupposes Frege's special rendering of the word 'representation', which is clearly not the only use given to this word by other philosophers contemporaries of Frege.[68] Furthermore and most importantly, Frege conflates what Husserl called 'specific relativism', that is, relativism to a species, of which not only psychologism, but also Kant and his followers were guilty, with individual relativism or subjectivism, which probably did not have any defenders. Psychologism in some sense presupposed that we are all similar enough as to have the same representations, and probably none of them thought that their theses would be rendered in Frege's fashion. This in no way means that I consider psychologism as not having been refuted, but just that the second part of Frege's argumentation is not compelling, and that a less subjective rendering of the views of psychologism and more sophisticated arguments were needed, for example, like those given by Husserl.[69] Thus, I agree with Frege's conclusion, which follows immediately, but find his refutation of psychologism in mathematics – and also in logic – not completely compelling.

Continuing with Frege, on the basis of the varied difficulties that surround both the psychologistic conception of number as well as the naturalistic discussed above, Frege concludes that numbers are neither spatial and physical nor subjective, like representations. They are at the same time not perceptible by our senses, and objective. Hence, the basis for objectivity cannot be found in sensible impressions – which are affections of our psyche and, thus, subjective – but only in reason.[70]

8 Numbers and the Process of Abstraction

In section 38, in which Frege stresses the necessity of distinguishing between the unities and the number one, the distinction already made in *Begriffsschrift* between concept and object is expounded with the utmost clarity. Moreover, Frege uses one of the linguistic criteria that helped him to distinguish between genuine proper names, which allow no plural form, and conceptual words, which admit of a plural form. Thus, Frege stresses that when we say 'the number one' our use of the definite article serves to indicate that we are speaking about a determinate singular object of scientific research. There are not many numbers one but only one. We

---

[68]See on this issue Husserl's enumeration in *Logische Untersuchungen II* (1900-1901, Dordrecht 1975-84), U. V, section 44 of thirteen different meanings of the word 'representation' [*Vorstellung*] in the philosophical writings of their contemporaries.

[69]*Logische Unteresuchungen I*, especially Chapter 7, where the distinction between specific and individual relativism is made.

[70]Ibid. Essentially the same argument is used in 'Der Gedanke', with respect to thoughts, on behalf of a third realm of Platonic entities. Numbers clearly would belong to such a realm.

have in the sign '1' a proper name, incapable as such of having a plural. Only conceptual words can have a plural. Hence, when we speak of unities we are not using that word as a synonym of the proper name 'one', but as a conceptual word.[71]

Before discussing Frege's views, it may be convenient to mention his critique of the conception of numbers as obtained via some sort of process of abstraction from concrete things, a conception that seems to combine both naturalist and psychologistic components. Firstly, Frege points out[72] that to indicate the way in which we abstract something from things is not and should not be considered a definition of that something. On the other hand, if a definition of number were to be correct, it would have to be adequate, in particular, for the numbers '0' and '1'. Now, Frege asks, from what are we going to abstract to obtain the number '1' using, for example, the moon as the basis of the abstraction? Frege observes that if we abstract from the object 'the moon', we obtain the following series of concepts: 'companion of the earth', 'companion of a planet', 'celestial body without proper light', 'celestial body', 'body', 'object'; but the number '1' cannot be obtained in that series, not being any concept under which the moon could fall. With respect to the number '0' the situation is even worse. There does not even exist an object that can be used as the basis for such a process of abstraction of the number '0'. Moreover, it does not make any sense to argue that '0' and '1' are not numbers in the same sense as '2', '3' and the remaining natural numbers, since numbers are the possible answers to the question 'How many?'. Thus, if someone asks 'How many moons does this planet have?', to answer 0, or 1, is as legitimate as to answer 2, or 3, or 1,000. Certainly the numbers 0 and 1 have their peculiarities, but each and every number has them, though in the case of the bigger numbers their peculiarities are not so visible. Hence, it is totally unwarranted and arbitrary to make any essential distinction between the numbers 0 and 1, and the remaining numbers. As Frege puts it:

> What is not applicable to the numbers 0 and 1 cannot be essential to the concept of number. [73]

I agree with Frege on this point against the young Husserl of *Philosophie der Arithmetik*.[74]

After having expounded the critical first part of *Die Grundlagen der Arithmetik*, I will now discuss its extremely influential constructive part.

---

[71]For this whole discussion, see ibid., section 38, p. 52.
[72]Ibid., section 44, p. 58.
[73]Ibid. 'Was nicht auf 0 oder 1 passt, kann für den Begriff der Zahl nicht wesentlich sein.'
[74]See *Philosophie der Arithmetik* (1891, Den Haag 1970), p. 134.

Chapter 3

Die Grundlagen der Arithmetik: Second Part (§§46-109)

1 Predications about Concepts

In the important section 46 of *Die Grundlagen der Arithmetik* Frege considers numbers in the context of judgements, in order to assess the way numbers are applied in all its generality. Firstly, Frege offers an example similar to those used to show that numbers are not properties of objects, but for a slightly different purpose. He points out that with respect to the same visual appearance we can with the same right say 'here are four companies' and 'here are 500 men'. What is different in each of the two cases is not what we perceive, whether the singular objects nor the aggregate, but our designation of what is perceived. This is a sure sign for Frege that we have replaced a concept with another concept. Frege concludes[1] that it seems as if predications involving numbers assert something about concepts. Thus, adds Frege,[2] when we say, e.g., 'Venus has 0 (that is, no) moons', there is no moon or aggregate of moons about which something is being said. However, something is being attributed in such a statement to the concept 'moon of Venus', namely, that nothing falls under such a concept. Moreover, if we say that the Pope has ten assistants, we are not attributing any property to the Pope, but asserting something about the concept 'assistant to the Pope', namely, the number 10 is attributed to such a concept.

Frege then considers a possible objection, which serves him to introduce another important point that permeates his mature philosophy. He considers the possibility that, if numerical attributions were properties of concepts, someone could object that concepts have their properties changed with time, though some traits of the concepts remain fixed. Thus, e.g., the concept 'citizen of Canada' changes each year, and even from day to day, since each day some Canadians die, while others are born or adopt the Canadian citizenship. Frege answers this possible objection by reminding us that objects change their properties with time, but that does not prevent us from recognizing those objects as being the same objects. Moreover, one could argue that though the presumed concept 'citizen of

---

[1] *Die Grundlagen der Arithmetik*, section 46, p. 60.
[2] Ibid.

Canada' has a temporal component, to the concept 'citizen of Canada at noon of the 1st of January 2005' there corresponds the same number for eternity.[3]

The above argument is essentially the same, though expressed more briefly, as the argument used by Frege thirty-four years later in 'Der Gedanke' on behalf of his thesis that a thought is eternally true or eternally false.[4] Thus, completing Frege's argumentation in *Die Grundlagen der Arithmetik* to make it completely parallel to that in 'Der Gedanke', we have to consider 'citizen of Canada' not as a concept, but as an incomplete concept, which requires the addition of a temporal coordinate to be a proper concept. Incidentally, we should not conflate this incompleteness of a presumed concept like 'citizen of Canada' with another sort of incompleteness of all legitimate concepts, namely, their predicativity or unsaturatation, of which I will have much to say in Chapter 5.

For Frege, concepts are something objective and radically different from representations, which are always subjective. Thus, e.g., when we subordinate a concept under another concept, we assert something objective. Frege adds that if concepts were subjective, the relation of subordination would also be subjective – in the same fashion in which a relation between representations is irremediably subjective.[5]

In section 47 Frege applies the results of section 46 to the study of the traditional universal affirmative statements of the form 'All As are Bs'. Firstly, Frege points out that though at first sight a statement like: (*) 'All tigers are felines' seems to express something about animals, not about concepts, if we ask which animals is the statement talking about, none could be mentioned. Moreover, even on the assumption that there are tigers, the statement does not say anything about them. We cannot infer from that statement that an existing animal is a feline without an additional hypothesis that says, that such an animal is a tiger, of which (*) does not say anything. In general, Frege considers it impossible to say something about an object without somehow designating or naming it. But the word 'tiger' does not name any particular object. Moreover, says Frege,[6] the fact that a statement – like 'All tigers are felines' – can only be justified by observing how things in the world are does not establish anything about its content. With respect to the question about the content of a statement, both its truth-value and the grounds for considering it true or for considering it false are irrelevant. Thus, if concepts are objective, there is no problem if a statement about this concept contains something factual.[7] The statement 'All tigers are felines' expresses the subordination of the concept of tiger under the concept of feline, in the same fashion as the statement 'All ultraproducts are reduced products' expresses the subordination of the concept of 'ultraproduct' under the concept of 'reduced product'. That, in fact, there are tigers and felines in our empirical world, but there

---

[3]See ibid., p. 60.
[4]See 'Der Gedanke', in *Kleine Schriften*, pp. 348-9.
[5]*Die Grundlagen der Arithmetik*, section 47, pp. 60-61.
[6]Ibid., p. 61.
[7]Ibid.

are neither ultraproducts nor reduced products makes no relevant difference: both statements express the subordination of a concept under another concept.

Frege considers that when we acknowledge that numbers occur in predications about concepts, the difficulties that surround other views on numbers disappear. Thus, the presumed fact that different numbers can correspond to the same thing was based on the mistaken assumption that objects are the bearers of numbers. Now that we have acknowledged that the legitimate bearers of numbers are concepts, we see that numbers are as exclusive as colours. Now it is also easier to see how we obtain numbers presumably as the result of the abstraction process from things. What is really obtained by abstraction is a concept, in which we then discover the number.[8]

However, abstraction from one or more objects is not the only way in which a concept can be obtained. Frege underscores[9] that one can obtain a concept from traits; and precisely because of this sort of concept formation, there exists the possibility that nothing falls under a concept. Thus, beginning with the concepts of triangle and equilateral, one can build the concept of an equilateral triangle, and beginning with the concepts of round and rectangle, one can build the concept of round rectangle. The concepts of triangle and equilateral are traits of the concept of equilateral triangle, whereas the concepts of round and rectangle are traits of the concept of round rectangle. All equilateral triangles fall under the first compound concept, whereas nothing falls under the second compound concept. Incidentally, as Frege stresses,[10] if we could not form concepts from traits, that is, by combining different concepts to form a compound one, we could never negate existence and, thus, the assertion of existence would loose its content.

2 Concept and Object in *Die Grundlagen der Arithmetik*

The fundamental distinction between concept and object is presented in a very detailed fashion in section 51. A conceptual word designates a concept. Only if it is preceded by a definite article or a definite pronoun can a conceptual word have the role of a proper name of something; but in that case it has been transformed and has ceased to be a conceptual word. On the other hand, the name of an object is a proper name. An object does not occur repeatedly, but instead different objects fall under the same concept. A concept does not have to be obtained by means of abstraction from things. Moreover, a concept remains a concept, even when only one object falls under the concept, in which case that object is completely determined by the concept but is still essentially different from the concept under which it falls. To such a concept (e.g., to the concept 'Pope in January of 2004') there corresponds the number 1, which is a number in the same sense as any other natural number greater than 1. Thus, in the case of concepts we ask whether

---

[8]Ibid., section 48, p. 61.
[9]Ibid., section 49, p. 62.
[10]Ibid.

something falls under it and, moreover, what falls under it. In the case of proper names such questions are complete nonsense – or using more recent terminology, are a categorial mistake, or, even a confusion of types. One should be careful not to be misled by natural language, which sometimes uses a proper name, e.g., moon, as a conceptual word – e.g., when we talk about Jupiter's moons, instead of Jupiter's natural satellites – and also the other way around, e.g., when a European says 'The American does not enjoy learning foreign languages', but is not talking about any singular American and simply sustains that the concept of 'being an American' is subordinated to the concept 'does not enjoy learning foreign languages'. Hence, those uses notwithstanding, the essential difference between concept and object is maintained. Now, to recognize a conceptual word, Frege uses the following criterion: if a word is used with the indefinite article or in the plural form without article, it is a conceptual word.[11]

After clearly distinguishing between concept and object, Frege makes a clear distinction between properties that apply to concepts – what we would now call 'second order properties' – and traits of those same concepts. The traits are not properties of the concept, but of the objects that fall under the concept.[12] Thus, 'German' is a trait of the concept 'German philosopher' and a property of Gottlob Frege, of Immanuel Kant and of many others.

Such distinctions motivate Frege to examine very briefly the ontological proof of God's existence. Although at first sight that problem seems to be completely alien to Frege's philosophical interests, it should be mentioned, however, that what Frege says about the ontological proof of God's existence is just an application of the distinction between traits and properties that I expounded immediately above.[13]

Frege conceives the attribution of existence – as he does with numerical attributions – as a second order predication. To assert the existence of something is nothing other than to deny the attribution of the number 0 to a concept. Thus, when we say that there are Germans, we are just saying that the number 0 does not correspond to the concept of 'being a German', that is, we negate the content of the statement that nothing falls under that concept. Hence, since existence is not a trait but a property of a concept, the ontological proof of God's existence is not valid. In the same fashion, unity is not a trait but a property of concepts. Hence, neither the existence nor the uniqueness can be used to define the concept of God. Immediately afterwards Frege states that those remarks on the ontological proof by no means are to be rendered as establishing the impossibility of deriving existence, uniqueness or any other property of a concept from its traits, but only that it cannot occur in such a direct way as is done in the presumed proof under discussion.[14]

---

[11]Ibid., section 51, p. 64.
[12]Ibid., section 53, p. 64.
[13]Ibid. For a more detailed discussion of this issue, see Frege's 'Dialog mit Pünjer über Existenz', in *Nachgelassene Schriften*, pp. 60-75.
[14]See *Die Grundlagen der Arithmetik*, p. 64.

On the other hand, it would be clearly mistaken to conclude that existence or uniqueness can never be traits of concepts. What Frege sustains is that they are not traits of concepts under which objects can fall, that is, of first order concepts. However, we can very well combine in one concept all concepts under which only one object falls, and such a compound second order concept would have the second order concept of uniqueness as one of its traits. As Frege puts it,[15] concepts like 'moon of the earth', 'even prime number', and 'author of *Die Grundlagen der Arithmetik*' would fall under such a compound concept, but neither the celestial body that we call moon nor the number 2, nor Gottlob Frege would fall under such a concept. Thus, a concept can fall under a concept of a higher order, in this case under a second order concept or, as Frege would later express it,[16] in a second order concept. On the other hand, the relation of a concept falling in a concept should be clearly distinguished from the subordination of a concept to another concept. In the latter relation the two concepts are of the same order. The falling of a first order concept in a second order concept is similar to the falling of an object under a first order concept, though it should not be conflated with the latter.

3 First Attempt at a Definition of Number

Once it is known that numerical attributions contain an assertion about a concept, Frege considers – in Chapter IV – the following three definitions, which together would represent a definition of natural number. Thus, we could try to define number as follows:[17]

(1)   To a concept F corresponds the number 0, if in general, regardless of what b is, the statement that b does not fall under F is true.

(2)   To a concept F corresponds the number 1, if the statement that b does not fall under F is not true in general, regardless of what b is, and if from the pair of statements 'b falls under F' and 'c falls under F' follows that b and c are the same thing.

(3)   To the concept F corresponds the number n+1, if there is an object b such that to the concept 'falls under F but is different from b' corresponds the number n.

Although Frege acknowledges the naturalness of the explanations (1)-(3), he does not consider such explanations sufficient. First of all, Frege points out that (3) is not free of difficulties, since, strictly speaking the meaning of the phrase 'to the concept G corresponds the number n' is as unknown as the meaning of the

---

[15]Ibid., p. 65.
[16]See his 'Über Begriff und Gegenstand', in *Kleine Schriften*, pp. 167-78, and his 'Ausführungen über Sinn und Bedeutung', in *Nachgelassene Schriften*, pp. 128-36. See also Chapter 5 below.
[17]See *Die Grundlagen der Arithmetik*, section 55, p. 66.

phrase 'to the concept F corresponds the number n+1'. Of course, says Frege,[18] on the basis of (2) and (3), we can understand the meaning of the phrase 'to the concept F corresponds the number 1+1', and then, on the basis of the meaning of that phrase and (3), we could obtain the meaning of the phrase 'to the concept F corresponds the number 1+1+1', and so forth. However, on such a basis, we cannot decide in general whether a given purported number is or is not a number, e.g., if someone would ask us if Julius Caesar is a number, we could not be able to answer that question on the basis of (1)-(3).[19] In other words, adds Frege,[20] by means of (1)-(3) we really do not apprehend what a number is, since we do not even have a criterion that would allow us to decide whether a purported number is a number or not – and, of course, since the set of natural numbers is infinite, we cannot sit and watch long enough to see if, by applying the process of obtaining the number n+1 from the number n, Julius Caesar is or is not obtained in a finite number of steps. It should be mentioned here that this is the first time that Frege discusses the problem nowadays referred to by Fregean scholars as the Julius Caesar Problem.

Moreover, on the basis of (1)-(3), we cannot establish that when to a concept F corresponds both the number b and the number c, then b=c. The phrase 'the number that corresponds to the concept F' – specifically, the use of the definite article – could not be justified and, thus, it would be impossible to prove an identity between numbers, since we could not apprehend a determinate number. Furthermore, it only looks as if we had explained the numbers 0 and 1. According to Frege, we have really just fixed the meaning of the phrases 'the number 0 corresponds to' and 'the number 1 corresponds to', which is not sufficient to allow us to apprehend the numbers 0 and 1 as independent objects.[21] Thus, the concept of number is not given by means of the explanations (1)-(3).

It should be briefly mentioned here that the purported definition of number under consideration by Frege is essentially an attempt at a recursive definition of number. Only the last clause of current recursive definitions is missing, which is the one that precludes the intromission of unwanted objects like Julius Cesar or the pen in Frege's pocket after finishing *Begriffsschrift*. In his writings from 1890 onwards, Frege is going to reject recursive definitions in general – as well as other sorts of non-traditional definitions – allowing only traditional explicit definitions. However, his rejection of the above definition in *Die Grundlagen der Arithmetik* does not have such a wide scope.

Frege considers then the following possible objection. Someone could argue against Frege that we cannot have a representation of numbers as independent objects. Frege clearly concedes that numbers cannot be represented either as independent sensible objects or as properties of external objects, since they are neither sensible objects nor properties of external objects.[22] On the other

---

[18]Ibid., section 56, p. 67.
[19]Ibid.
[20]Ibid.
[21]Ibid.
[22]Ibid., section 58, p. 68.

hand, even if it were correct that each and every word produces in us some representation, such representations do not have to correspond in any near way to the content of the word, and even if they did correspond they could vary considerably from one human being to another. Moreover, even if we do not have any representation of the earth's separation from the sun, that is no ground to question the correctness of the calculations made by physicists of such a distance, nor is it an impediment for them to base other inferences on the result of such calculations.[23]

Frege concludes his argumentation as follows:[24] By means of our thought, we are sometimes driven beyond the frontier of what is representable, without in this way losing the ground for our designations. Although it seems that we, as human beings, are unable to think without some sort of representation – and Frege is inclined to believe that it is mostly so – the connection between the representations and what is thought by us is not only completely external but also arbitrary and conventional. Thus, the non-representability of the content of a statement is no reason to deny it any meaning or to avoid its usage. The resemblance of the opposite thesis is the result of considering words in isolation, so that when we ask about their meanings, we are prone to take their representations instead. Thus, if we fail to produce an internal image of what corresponds to the word, we think that the word does not have any content. Now – and this is the first explicit application of the Context Principle in the book – one has to consider always a complete sentence. Only in a sentence do words have any meaning. Moreover, the internal images that we use as supports do not have to correspond to the logical components of judgements. It is enough that the sentence as a whole has a sense, since by this means all its parts obtain their content. Hence, the independence that Frege attributes to numbers does not mean that words for numbers are designative in isolation, that is, without the context of a sentence, but he simply wants to exclude their usage as predicates or attributes, in which case their meaning would be somewhat transformed.

This last point made by Frege is not clear enough, on the basis of the preceding remarks. It is not clear how Frege connects the requirement expressed in the Context Principle of looking for the meaning of a word only in the context of a sentence, so as to avoid taking as the meaning of the word a subjective image or representation, sometimes even completely alien to the content of the word, with the exclusion of the usage of words for numbers as predicates or attributes. Two possible explanations are the following: (i) Frege is using the words 'predicate' and 'attribute' in this context only in the restricted sense of predicate or attribute of objects, and he is trying to connect in some unclear way the violations of the Context Principle with the error, to which Frege repeatedly alludes, of taking the number as a property or attribute of things. (ii) Frege is anticipating his conclusion that, though numerical attributions are predications about concepts, the number is properly the extension of such a second order concept. Although the passage is not

---

[23]Ibid., section 59, p. 69.
[24]Ibid., section 60, p. 69.

clear, precisely the context in which Frege's expressions occur seems to support the second rendering.[25]

In section 61 Frege places numbers in what he later – in 'Der Gedanke'[26] – will call a 'third realm of entities', in contraposition to both the realm of external physical objects and to the realm of our representations and decisions. Firstly, Frege points out that numbers have no spatial coordinates. However, from this it does not follow that they are not objects, but simply not spatial objects. Incidentally, not all objects have spatial coordinates. E.g., spatial predicates are not applicable to representations: a representation is neither at the right side nor at the left side of another representation; nor can their separation be expressed in the metrical or any other measurement system. When we say that representations are in us, we simply mean that they are subjective. Thus, there is no contradiction between the objectivity and the non-spatiality of numbers. Numbers are exactly the same for everyone who considers them. But such objectivity has nothing to do with spatiality: not every object has spatial coordinates.[27]

Frege's argument needs some repairing, since the notions of objectivity and objectuality (that is, the quality of being an object) are not always clearly separated in it. Representations – in Frege's usage – are in any case objectual (two physicians can have Frege's headache as an object of study), but not objective. Hence, the analogy with representations – in Frege's usage – allows us only to conclude that not everything objectual is spatial, but it does not allow us to conclude that there is something objective that is not spatial nor, thus, that there exists a non-empty third realm of entities. Now, the fact that numbers are the same for each and every one of us – as are also the laws that govern them – is what allows us to conclude that numbers (and their laws) are not only objectual – without being spatial – but also objective in the sense of being intersubjective, that is, the same for each of us.

4 Second Attempt at a Definition of Number

In section 62 Frege refers to the Context Principle for the third time in the book and for the second in the main text. He begins the section reminding the reader that, as seen in section 60, words have meaning only in the context of sentences and, thus, in order to determine the nature of numerical attributions we have to clarify the sense of statements, in which there is such an attribution.

According to Frege, the preceding discussion has established that words for numbers designate independent objects. Now, says Frege, if the sign 'α' is going to designate an object, there should exist some distinguishing mark that would allow us to decide in each case whether the object designated by 'β' is the same as that designated by 'α', even if we are not always capable of applying it.

---

[25]On this issue, see the preceding paragraph.

[26]See 'Der Gedanke', in *Kleine Schriften*, pp. 342-62, especially pp. 353-4 and 360-61.

[27]For this discussion, see *Die Grundlagen der Arithmetik*, section 61, p. 70.

More specifically, we have to explain the sense of the statement: 'The number that corresponds to the concept F is the same as the number that corresponds to the concept G'. In other words, we have to formulate the content of that statement without using the phrase 'the number that corresponds to the concept F'. In this way, adds Frege, we would be giving a general distinguishing mark for the content equality.[28]

At the beginning of section 63, Frege refers to Hume's explanation of equality between numbers,[29] namely: If two numbers can be related in such a fashion that to each unity of one there corresponds a unity of the other, we say that the two numbers are one and the same. In this principle – baptized by Fregean scholars as 'Hume's Principle' – equality between numbers is explained by means of bijective correspondence. As is well known, some illustrious contemporaries of Frege, like Cantor and Schröder, maintained that we have to define equality between numbers by means of such a correspondence. However, Frege correctly considered[30] that the relation of equality occurs not only between numbers, but is capable of a much wider application. Although Frege does not say it explicitly, what he means is that equality is not an arithmetical but a logical notion, and as such should be explained in the logical system before any consideration of arithmetical notions. Thus, it seems, says Frege,[31] that we do not have to explain equality especially for the case of numbers, but assume that we already have such a concept. We can then use such a general relation, together with the concept of number, to obtain when two numbers are equal, without requiring a special definition. Nonetheless, we face an immediate difficulty, namely, that the concept of number has not been defined. It is precisely the concept of number that has to be determined by means of such an explanation.[32]

Frege's objective is to form the content of a judgement that can be conceived as an equation, each of whose sides designates a number. He does not intend to explain equality for this special case, but to obtain what is going to be considered equal by means of the already known notion of equality. Now, such an unusual sort of definition requires some illustration. Frege offers two examples that can help to illustrate what he is looking for. He considers first the following judgement, on which most of the discussion is based:[33] 'The straight line α is parallel to the straight line β', in symbols $\alpha/\!\!/\beta$, can be conceived as an equation. In this way we obtain the concept of direction and could express the same content as follows: The direction of the straight line α is equal to the direction of the straight line β.

---

[28]Ibid., section 62, p. 71.
[29]Ibid., section 63, p. 71.
[30]Ibid., p. 72.
[31]Ibid.
[32]Ibid.
[33]Ibid., section 64, p. 72.

Frege points out[34] that to be able to serve for the introduction of a definition of such a sort, the relation R – in the example: ∥ – has to be transitive. As a matter of fact, to transform a statement containing R in an equation, it is required that R be not merely transitive, but at least an equivalence relation, that is, also reflexive and symmetric, or even a congruence relation in the sense of universal algebra. What Frege does in the example consists in obtaining the concept of direction from the concept of parallelism, introducing directions as equivalence classes modulo parallelism. In other words, what we have is a partition of straight lines in a given space, e.g., in a plane, in equivalence classes, in such a fashion that the straight lines α and β will belong to the same equivalence class if and only if they are parallel to each other. Thus, directions are introduced as equivalence classes of straight lines on the basis of such a partition.

In the same fashion, the concept of form can be obtained from the concept of geometrical similarity. Thus, e.g., instead of saying 'The triangles A and B are similar', we could say either 'The triangles A and B have the same form', or 'The form of triangle A is the same as that of triangle B'. In a way similar to what happens in the first example, the forms are introduced as equivalence classes of triangles modulo similarity in this example. Frege's discussion, which we will follow, considers mostly the first example. It should be clear, however, that we could replace that example by the second, or by the corresponding statement about numbers – which I will formulate below – without affecting in any sense the argumentation.

To go from the concept of parallelism to the concept of direction – or from the concept of similarity to the concept of form – we can try to define the latter as follows: 'The direction of the straight line α is equal to the direction of the straight line β' is going to have the same meaning as 'The straight line α is parallel to the straight line β'. Frege acknowledges[35] that such a definition is very unusual, since it seems to introduce the concept of equality, whereas it really introduces the phrase 'the direction of the straight line α'. Although Frege does not say it explicitly, the definition under discussion is a contextual definition.

Of course, someone could ask whether such a stipulation does not contradict the well-known laws governing equality. Frege answers this possible objection by asserting that the usual laws of equality can be inferred from the concept of equality.[36] With respect to this issue, it should be stressed that on the basis of Frege's definition of analyticity, his assertion is possible only if the concept of equality is a logical concept – and that is precisely what he presupposes in this whole discussion.

Frege accepts Leibniz's definition of identity, namely: '*Eadem sunt, quorum unum potest substitui alteri salva veritate*', that is, '[Those things] are the same, which can be substituted one for the other without affecting the truth', and

---

[34]Ibid., p. 73.
[35]Ibid., section 65, p. 73.
[36]Ibid.

applies it to equality. In this way, all laws about equality are included in general substitutability.[37] Thus, to legitimize the definition of the direction of a straight line, Frege has to show that if the straight line α is parallel to the straight line β, then we can replace everywhere the direction of α by the direction of β. Frege explains that this requirement is simplified by the fact that at this point we know of no statement about the direction of a straight line that does not express its concordance with the direction of another straight line. Thus, we only need to establish the substitutability in such cases of equality and in compounds, which have such equalities as components, whereas in the case of any remaining statements about directions, we would first try to explain them and then stipulate that for such statements the substitutability of the direction of a straight line for the direction of another parallel straight line has to be allowed.[38]

It should be mentioned here that in his early *Philosophie der Arithmetik* Husserl criticized Frege for conflating the notions of identity and equality when using Leibniz's Principle, which concerns identity, not equality.[39] Thus, Husserl rightly observes that equality is a weaker relation than identity, and that two objects can be equal in some aspects without being equal in each and every aspect. In more recent mathematical terminology of universal algebra, one could restate what Husserl is trying to express by saying that though both identity and equality are equivalence relations, identity is a congruence relation but equality is not. Hence, the use of Leibniz's Principle of Substitutability to assess what is meant by equality really seems suspicious at least. However, though Husserl's distinction is correct, I doubt that it would alter much in Frege's analysis, since what the latter is considering in this context is not merely equal but also identical. Husserl also correctly argues[40] that Frege inverts the logical relations, since it is because two contents are identical that they are everywhere intersubstitutable, not the other way around.

Continuing with my exposition of Frege, after having shown how to introduce new (abstract) objects – namely: the direction of a straight line and the form of a triangle – and the equality of two (abstract) objects of similar sort by means of a contextual definition based on a congruence relation, and after having argued that equality is going to obey exactly the laws of general substitutability, the terrain has been adequately paved for a similar definition of number and their equality. Such a definition would read: The number that corresponds to the concept F is the same as the number that corresponds to the concept G if and only if the concept F is equinumerous with the concept G.

However, such definitions face another difficulty.[41] In the statement 'The direction of the straight line α is equal to the direction of the straight line β' the direction of the straight line α appears as an object – the phrase naming it is a

[37]Ibid., p. 74.

[38]Ibid.

[39]*Philosophie der Arithmetik*, pp. 97-8.

[40]Ibid., p. 97.

[41]*Die Grundlagen der Arithmetik*, section 66, pp. 74-5.

proper name, not a conceptual word – and the definition allows us to recognize this object when it appears designated by another proper name of the form 'the direction of the straight line β'. But such a definition does not allow us to decide all possible cases, in particular, the explanation does not allow us to decide in the case of statements like 'The direction of the straight line α is the same as γ', if γ does not have the form 'the direction of the straight line β'. Thus, once more the so-called Julius Caesar Problem comes to the fore. We simply do not have any concept of direction, since such a concept has not been clearly delimited by the contextual definition. If we really had fixed the concept of direction, we could stipulate as follows: if γ is not a direction, we have to deny the statement; if γ is a direction, the above explanation decides. This is an especially unpleasant situation for Frege, since, as we will later see,[42] he requires that any concept be defined for each and every object.

Although someone could try to solve the quandary by saying that 'γ is a direction when there is a straight line β such that γ is the direction of β', Frege argues[43] that such a move would be circular, because to be able to apply such an explanation, we would already have to know in each case, whether the statement 'γ is equal to the direction of the straight line β' is to be asserted or denied. Thus, the quandary remains as before, since we have no means to decide, whether γ is equal or not to the direction of the straight line β.

On the other hand, if we were to say 'γ is a direction if it is introduced by means of the above definition', we would be considering the way in which an object is introduced as a property of that object. But according to Frege, a definition of an object does not state anything about that object. Only after the definition has been made, it is transformed in a judgement. But then it does not introduce the object anymore and is at the same level of the other statements about the object.[44] Moreover, if someone would choose such a way out, argues Frege,[45] he would be tacitly presupposing that an object could be given in only one way, since from the fact that γ has not been introduced as a direction of a straight line it does not follow that it could not be introduced in that way. Hence, under such a presupposition, all true equations would simply consist in recognizing as the same what is given as the same, e.g., 'a=a'. Of course, that is so obvious and fruitless that it does not need to be mentioned explicitly, and we could not infer anything even slightly different from what is presupposed. But Frege was perfectly conscious at least since the time he wrote *Begriffsschrift*, that the importance and utility of equations is based precisely on the fact that one can recognize as the same what is given in different ways.[46]

---

[42]See Chapters 5 and 6.
[43]*Die Grundlagen der Arithmetik*, section 66, p. 75.
[44]Ibid., section 67, p. 75. See on this issue Chapters 6 and 7.
[45]*Die Grundlagen der Arithmetik*, section 67, p. 75.
[46]Ibid.

Since a contextual definition of number as given above would face the same insurmountable difficulties as the definition of direction discussed in detail by Frege, and, thus, would not be capable of delimiting the concept of number, he decides to abandon such a sort of definition.

Frege's rejection of his second attempt to define the concept of number is of special importance and requires some comments. Firstly, once more the so-called Julius Caesar Problem appears as the main reason for rejecting the definition. We are not able to decide whether a presumed number that is not designated by a phrase like 'the number that corresponds to the concept G' is or is not a number. Frege's requirement that we should be able to recognize whether Γ is a number, though it is not introduced as the number assigned to a determinate concept, is legitimate, since there is no reason to admit only one sort of designation for entities. However, Frege not only considers justified, but also indispensable that one should decide, for any object, whether it is equal to a number given as 'the number that corresponds to the concept F'. In other words, he acknowledges only one domain of objects, for which each and every predicate is defined. Such a strong requirement – which could be called the 'Julius Caesar Dogma' – is not only very unintuitive – to require an answer to the question whether Julius Caesar is or is not a number is as unintuitive as to require an answer to the question whether my computer will be the next Pope – but it opens the door to paradox. As we will later see, the infamous Principle V of *Grundgesetze der Arithmetik* that is responsible for the so-called Russell Paradox – which should better be called 'Zermelo-Russell Paradox', since Zermelo probably discovered it first[47] – has the same form as Frege's contextual definition of number. Principle V essentially says – if, for simplicity's sake, we restrict ourselves to the special case of concepts and their extensions – that the extension of the concept F is the same as the extension of the concept G if and only if for all x, F(x) if and only if G(x). Such a principle in its full extent introduces Frege's purportedly generalized extensions, which he called 'value ranges', in a very similar way as the rejected contextual definition of number. At this point, however, it seems appropriate to limit this digression to extensions and concepts. Thus, since extensions (and their purported generalizations) are objects, they can and should fall under their own concepts and, thus, the Zermelo-Russell Paradox makes its way into Frege's logic. Due to the similarity between the contextual definition of number and Principle V, if the latter alone could derive the paradox, then if Frege had not rejected such a purported definition, it would seem that the system sketched in *Die Grundlagen der Arithmetik* would probably have been inconsistent. However, the problem does not reside in contextual definitions or principles, but in the combination of Frege's requirement that concepts (and functions) be defined for all objects, with Principle V and his view of extensions as objects. If Frege had opted for a division of objects into levels, as he did for functions, the Zermelo-Russell Paradox would not have entered his system of logic. Thus, had he assigned the level 0 to objects to which

---

[47]On this issue, see Gregory H. Moore's *Zermelo's Axiom of Choice* (New York, 1982), p. 89.

first level (or order) concepts apply, and assigned the extensions of such concepts the level 1, then such extensions could not be possible arguments of their corresponding concepts, though they could be possible arguments for concepts of a second level. Such second level concepts would also have extensions, but these could not be possible arguments of their corresponding concepts, and the question whether extensions are or not their own members would simply have to be considered a category mistake, or a type-confusion. Another way out would have been the introduction of the current notion of a universe of discourse, excluding extensions of concepts from the universe of discourse. However, such a notion was completely foreign to Frege, who stubbornly adhered to the Julius Caesar Dogma. But I have been anticipating too much. In any case, we will later see that in *Grundgesetze der Arithmetik* and later Frege rejects contextual definitions in general, though in his purported logical masterpiece he postulates Principle V without seeing its resemblance to the rejected contextual definition of number. The consequences of such a postulation, combined with his view of value ranges as objects and, especially, his requirement that functions be defined for all objects – that is, the Julius Caesar Dogma – could not be worse.

Anticipating a little, it should be mentioned that neither Frege's second attempt to define the concept of number or the notorious Principle V could be adequately interpreted using the semantic tools of his mature philosophy. Contrary to what Frege says in 'Funktion und Begriff',[48] it is clearly not the official notion of sense – in this case, the thought – that the two sides of Principle V, or the two sides of the purported second definition of number, have in common, since only trivial translations between languages, like 'London is the capital of England', 'Londres es la capital de Inglaterra' and 'London ist die Hauptstadt Englands' express the same thought. On the other hand, since the two sides of Principle V, or of the purported second definition of number, are statements, if what they had in common were their referent, that is, according to Frege, their truth-value – we are here ignoring the Zermelo-Russell Paradox – there would be infinitely many statements both of Frege's logical system and of natural language sharing the same referent with them. Thus, both statements would be completely indeterminate. *A fortiori*, the sides of each of the two notorious statements did not have in common the judgeable content, from which the sense and referent of statements were obtained. What the two sides of the purported second definition of number had in common, as well as what the two sides of Principle V would have had in common, if it had been true, is the conceptual content, the elusive notion of *Begriffsschrift*, presumably extinct like a dinosaur since the beginning of the 1880s. But once more I have digressed too much.[49] Let us return to the exposition of Frege's philosophical masterpiece.

---

[48]'Funktion und Begriff', in *Kleine Schriften*, pp. 125-42.
[49]See the more detailed discussion in Chapter 5, section 4.

5 Third Attempt at a Definition of Number

In sections 68 and 69 Frege offers a third and definitive definition of number. Firstly, we should observe with Frege[50] that if the straight line α is parallel to the straight line β, then the extensions of the concepts 'straight line parallel to the straight line α' and 'straight line parallel to the straight line β' are the same. That is so because the relation of parallelism between straight lines is an equivalence relation defining a partition in the set of all straight lines in space. The equivalence classes that are thus determined are the extensions of concepts of the form 'straight line parallel to the straight line α'. Hence, if the straight line α is parallel to the straight line β, these two straight lines belong to the same equivalence class, that is, to the same extension. Such an equivalence class can be designated with the same right as the extension of the concept 'straight line parallel to the straight line α' or as the extension of the concept 'straight line parallel to the straight line β'.

Furthermore, if the extensions of the two concepts mentioned above are the same, then the straight line α is parallel to the straight line β. In other words, if the extension of the concept 'straight line parallel to the straight line α' is the same as the extension of the concept 'straight line parallel to the straight line β', then α and β belong to the same equivalence class and, thus, α is parallel to β. Hence, the straight line α is parallel to the straight line β if and only if the extension of the concept 'straight line parallel to the straight line α' is the same as the extension of the concept 'straight line parallel to the straight line β'

On the basis of the preceding discussion, Frege offers an explanation of the concepts of direction and form. Thus, Frege says:[51]

(*) The direction of the straight line α is the extension of the concept 'parallel to the straight line α'
(*') The form of triangle δ is the extension of the concept 'similar to triangle δ'.

To apply this new sort of explanation to the case with which Frege is concerned, namely, the notion of number, he will replace 'straight line' or 'triangle' with 'concept', and the notion of 'parallelism' or 'similarity' with an expression that can convey the possibility of establishing a bijective correspondence between the objects that fall under a concept and the objects that fall under another concept. With that goal in mind, Frege introduces the expression 'equinumerosity'. Frege observes[52] that when it is possible to establish a bijective correspondence between the objects that fall under a concept F and those that fall under a concept G, one can say that the concept F is equinumerous with the concept G. To avoid the misunderstanding of considering that the word 'equinumerous' presupposes the word 'number' in a non-etymological sense and,

---

[50]See *Die Grundlagen der Arithmetik*, section 68, p. 76.
[51]Ibid.
[52]Ibid.

thus, that the use of such a word in the definition of number would make that definition circular, Frege states[53] that the word 'equinumerous' [in German: *gleichzahlig*] should be considered an arbitrarily chosen mode of designation, whose meaning is going to be given exclusively by such a stipulation, not by the linguistic composition of the word.

Thus, Frege defines number as follows:[54] The number that corresponds to the concept F is the extension of the concept 'equinumerous to the concept F'. There is still, however, a long way to go until we can obtain sufficient clarity about the notion of number. The notion of 'equinumerosity' has not been explained, except negatively by saying that it should not be understood on the basis of its etymology, nor has the notion of extension been explained. The latter notion seems to worry Frege the most.

In a very famous footnote of section 68,[55] Frege asserts that we could simply replace the phrase 'extension of the concept' with the word 'concept' in the definition of number just given, without affecting its content. However, at first sight such a modification of the definition faces the following difficulties mentioned by Frege himself:[56] (i) It is difficult to reconcile with Frege's previous assertions, according to which numbers are objects and numerical words – Frege sometimes says simply: numbers – are only part of the predicate in an attribution of number; and (ii) various concepts can have the same extension without being the same concept. Frege treats these difficulties somewhat lightly, and simply says that they are not insurmountable. Nonetheless, on the basis of Frege's ontological principles, the difficulties that could impede such a replacement of the phrase 'extension of the concept' by the word 'concept' do not seem so light as Frege would like us to believe. In fact, we have not found any similar remark in his other writings.

The first of the two difficulties is, however, solvable, if we take into account precisely the grammatical strictures invoked by Frege on behalf of his ontology and his later semantics. The definite article in the singular is a distinctive sign of the designation of an object, and extensions are, for Frege, objects. Thus, if we make the replacement mentioned by Frege in the famous footnote under consideration, we obtain the following definition of number: The number that corresponds to the concept F is the concept 'equinumerous with the concept F'. Although concepts are not objects and concept words designate concepts, the use of the definite article before the word 'concept' indicates that the word designates in this context not a concept but an object. Moreover, this object is none other than the extension of the concept 'equinumerous with "the concept F"'. Thus, 'the concept' and 'the extension of the concept' are two different names for the extension of the concept. Some important Fregean scholars – e.g., Matthias

---

[53]Ibid.
[54]Ibid.
[55]Ibid.
[56]Ibid.

Schirn[57] – do not agree with the interpretation that the expression 'the concept F' designates the extension of the concept F, and prefer to postulate some mysterious *deus ex machina* objects. Their arguments, however, are not compelling for either the rejection of our interpretation or the introduction of such *ad hoc* entities.

The other difficulty seems more compelling. Even if we were to acknowledge Frege's later view of concepts and functions as the referents (or denotations) of concept words, and respectively, of function words, that is, even if we were to ontologize them and interpret them extensionally, the fact of the matter is that the relation between concepts and their extensions is a many-one relation – e.g., the (ontological) concepts of 'a smallest prime number' and of 'a smallest even number' would have the same extension. Thus, the replacement of 'extension of the concept' by 'concept' would seem to generate an unavoidable ambiguity. However, our solution of the first difficulty, on the basis of Frege's grammatical strictures, would exclude the possibility of such an ambiguity, and the second difficulty would also artificially disappear. Nonetheless, Frege's grammatical strictures are by no means unobjectionable, and if we do not presuppose them the second difficulty reappears with all its force. It could be said that the first difficulty also reappears, but such a difficulty is an offspring of the same Fregean grammatical strictures, which at the same time create the quandary and allow us to solve it the way we did in the preceding paragraph. The second difficulty, namely, that the relation between concepts and their extensions is many-one, is completely independent of Frege's writings.

At the end of the footnote, Frege says that in this whole discussion it is presupposed that we know what is the extension of a concept. If we take into account his logicist programme in *Die Grundlagen der Arithmetik*, Frege's assertion should be rendered as a clear indication that for him the notion of 'the extension of a concept' is a logical notion or, more precisely, that extensions are logical objects.

At the beginning of section 69, Frege considers the possibility[58] that someone could maintain that under the extension of a concept one usually understands something different from what he understands. In other words, one could try to question what Tarski has called[59] 'the material adequacy of a definition', since if we question the material adequacy of the expression 'extension', which is a fundamental part of the *definiens* of the definition, we are questioning the definition altogether. Frege answers this possible objection by

---

[57]See, e.g., Matthias Schirn's 'Frege's Objects of a Quite Special Kind', *Erkenntnis* 32, (1990): 27-60, 'On Frege's Introduction of Cardinal Numbers as Logical Objects', in M. Schirn (ed.), *Frege: Importance and Legacy*, pp. 114-73, and 'Fregean Abstraction, Referential Indeterminacy and the Logical Foundations of Arithmetic', *Erkenntnis* 59 (2003): 203-32. For a view similar to mine, see Richard Mendelsohn's paper 'Frege on Predication', *Midwest Studies in Philosophy VI* (Minneapolis, 1981), pp. 69-82, as well as my former student and now colleague Dr. Ivette Fred's MA thesis *Concepto y Objeto en la Filosofia de Gottlob Frege*, 1989, written under my supervision.

[58]*Die Grundlagen der Arithmetik*, section 69, p. 76.

[59]See Alfred Tarski's 'The Concept of Truth in Formalized Languages', in A. Tarski, *Logic, Semantics, Metamathematics*, pp. 152-278, especially, pp. 152 and 209.

saying that what is understood by the extension of a concept can be made clear by considering the most basic statements about extensions of concepts. They concern either (i) the equality between extensions, or (ii) the fact that an extension comprises more than another extension. Here there seems to be a third – somewhat implicit – appeal to the Context Principle.

With respect to (i), Frege points out[60] the following: The statement 'The extension of the concept "equinumerous to the concept F'' is the same as the extension of the concept "equinumerous to the concept G''' is true if and only if the statement 'To the concept F corresponds the same number as to the concept G' is also true.

On the other hand, one does not usually say that a number comprises more than another number in the sense in which the extension of a concept comprises that of another concept. Moreover, Frege stresses[61] that in the particular case of numbers, the following is true: When all concepts that are equinumerous with the concept F are equinumerous with the concept G, then all concepts that are equinumerous with the concept G are equinumerous with the concept F. Of course, this is so because equinumerosity is an equivalence relation. Thus, the possibility that the extension of the concept 'equinumerous with the concept F' could comprise more than the extension of the concept 'equinumerous with the concept G' is excluded in the particular case of numbers. One should not conflate the relation of 'comprising more than', which is not a relation between numbers, with the relation of 'being greater than', which is a relation between numbers.

The possibility is not excluded, however, that the extension of the concept 'equinumerous with the concept F' comprises more or less than another extension, which, on the basis of the preceding observations, cannot be a number. Thus, e.g., the extension of the concept 'equinumerous with the concept F' comprises more than the extension of the concept 'equinumerous with the concept F but different from F', which is not a number, and comprises less than the extension of the concept 'equinumerous with the concept F or identical to Gottlob Frege', which also is not a number.

The impossibility for a number to comprise more than another number is a consequence of the statement that 'equinumerous with the concept F' determines an equivalence class. We should not forget that the extensions under discussion are equivalence classes resulting from a partition and, thus, are pairwise disjoint, that is, do not have any common members. Hence, it does not make any sense to talk about one of them comprising more than another, since the intersection of any two of them is empty. On the other hand, two extensions that are not numbers – or, as already mentioned, two extensions, one of which is a number but the other is not – can very well be in the relation of one comprising more than the other, being this the case each time one of the corresponding concepts is subordinated to the other, without the subordination being mutual subordination. As we also already mentioned, all this does not exclude the possibility of applying the relation of

---

[60] *Die Grundlagen der Arithmetik*, p. 77.
[61] Ibid.

'being greater than' to numbers. But that is a very different relation from the relation of 'comprising more than'.

According to Frege,[62] definitions are justified by their fruitfulness. Moreover, those that could have very well been omitted without having any effect on proofs should better be discharged as useless. To justify his definition of number, Frege is going to derive well-known properties of numbers from his explanation of the number that corresponds to the concept F. For this purpose, Frege considers it convenient to clarify a little more the notion of equinumerosity. First of all, he observes that such a notion was introduced as a sort of bijective correspondence. Thus, Frege has to clarify the notion of bijective correspondence. But a bijective correspondence is, on the other hand, a relation and, thus, before discussing the notion of bijective correspondence, he wants to be sure that the notion of relation is a logical notion.

Frege points out[63] that if we abstract α and β from a judgeable content about the object α and the object β – e.g., in 'α is larger than β' – we obtain a relational content that requires a sort of double completion. Let us consider the following statement: 'Fidel Castro is taller than George W. Bush'. If we abstract 'Fidel Castro' from such a statement, we obtain the concept 'being taller than George W. Bush'. On the other hand, if we instead abstract 'George W. Bush' from such a statement, we obtain the concept 'being shorter than Fidel Castro'. But if we abstract both 'Fidel Castro' and 'George W. Bush' from the same statement, we obtain the relation 'being taller than'. That relation (or relational concept) by itself – as well as the simple concepts – requires completion to be able to have a judgeable content as content. But in the case of relations, what is required is not a simple but a double completion. Clearly, in any of the three cases we can fill the blanks with other proper names than 'Fidel Castro' and 'George W. Bush', e.g., 'Vladimir Putin' or 'Pope John Paul II'.[64]

Thus, in *Die Grundlagen der Arithmetik* Frege not only clearly distinguishes objects from concepts and relations, but also underscores the most distinctive trait of concepts and relations, namely, their unsaturation – in the case of relations, their double unsaturation. Compared to *Begriffsschrift*, Frege's views on this issue have matured, since in that early work he spoke mostly of a syntactical distinction between saturated and unsaturated signs – though as shown in Chapter 1,[65] there is a passage in which one can already see that the distinction between concept and object is not merely syntactic.[66] On the other hand, if we compare Frege's treatment of the distinction in his philosophical masterpiece with

---

[62]Ibid., section 70, p. 77.
[63]Ibid., p. 79.
[64]Ibid., p. 78.
[65]See Chapter 1, section 9 above.
[66]*Begriffsschrift*, p. 17.

what he says about the same distinction in his writings after 1890,[67] some vagueness still subsists here, namely, the vagueness that surrounds the notion of judgeable content.[68]

The pairs of objects in correspondence are related in a similar fashion – we could say: as subjects – to the relational concept as the singular object to the usual concept under which it falls. But in a statement that has the form of a relation the subject is in some sense compound or, better, there are two subjects.[69] In some cases the relation is symmetric and the argument places can be interchanged, as, e.g., in 'George W. Bush is a friend of Osama bin Laden', which could also be expressed using the conjunction 'and' as follows: 'George W. Bush and Osama bin Laden are friends'. Of course, in other cases that is not possible, e.g., one cannot express the relation 'Fidel Castro is taller than George W. Bush' as 'Fidel Castro and George W. Bush are taller', which is nonsense, since 'taller than' is not a symmetric relation. In any case, as well as the simple concepts, relational concepts belong to pure logic. Of course, it should be clear that we are not considering here the particular content of a relation – which can obviously be empirical – but only its logical form. Thus, Frege states that what can be said about the logical form of relations, as well as about the logical form of usual concepts, if true, is analytically true and known *a priori*.[70]

At the end of section 70, Frege stresses[71] that the schema 'α is in the relation φ with β' is the general form of a judgeable content about the objects α and β, in the same sense as the schema 'α falls under concept F' is the general form of a judgeable content about an object α.

Now, says Frege,[72] if every object that falls under the concept F is in the relation φ with some object that falls under the concept G, and if for every object that falls under the concept G there is an object that falls under the concept F that is in the relation φ with it, then the objects that fall under the concepts F and G are in a correspondence by means of the relation φ. Nonetheless, Frege asks himself about the meaning of the statement (*) 'All objects that fall under concept F are in the relation φ with an object that falls under concept G', in case no object falls under concept F. Frege answers himself as follows: the statements 'α falls under F' and 'α is not in the relation φ with any object that falls under G' cannot coexist, that is, cannot both be true. Thus, regardless of what α stands for, one or the other, or both statements are false. Hence, appealing implicitly to our modern interpretation of the conditional originating with him, Frege concludes that all objects that fall under F are in the relation φ with some object that falls under G is

---

[67]This vagueness is due to the fact that, according to Frege himself in *Grundgesetze der Arithmetik*, p. X, in 1884 he had still not differentiated in the judgeable content the sense and the referent.
[68]See *Die Grundlagen der Arithmetik*, pp. 8-9.
[69]Ibid.
[70]Ibid., p. 79.
[71]Ibid.
[72]Ibid., section 71, p. 79.

true when there is no object that falls under F, since in such a case the statement 'α falls under F' is false, regardless of what α stands for.[73] It should be pointed out that Frege is interpreting (*) as the universal quantification of a conditional with the statement 'α falls under F' as antecedent, namely, as (**) 'For all x, if x falls under concept F, then x is in the relation φ with an object that falls under concept G'. In a similar fashion, the statement 'For every object that falls under G, there is an object that falls under F that is in the relation φ with it' means that the statements 'α falls under G' and 'No object that falls under F is in the relation φ with α' cannot coexist, regardless of what α stands for.[74]

We are now acquainted with the circumstances under which the objects that fall under F and those that fall under G are in the relation φ. Thus, Frege asserts,[75] a correspondence is bijective when the following conditions are met:

(1)   If δ is in the relation φ with α, and δ is in the relation φ with γ, then no matter what δ, α and γ are, α is the same as γ.

(2)   If δ is in the relation φ with α, and β is in the relation φ with α, then no matter what δ, β and α are, δ is the same as β.

In this fashion, says Frege,[76] it is shown that bijective correspondence is a sort of relation and belongs to pure logic. Thus, we can define:[77] The statement 'Concept F is equinumerous with concept G' means the same as the statement 'There is a relation φ that bijectively orders the objects that fall under concept F with the objects that fall under concept G'. Frege reminds the reader of the definition of number given before, namely: The number that corresponds to the concept F is the extension of the concept 'equinumerous with the concept F'. Moreover, he adds[78] that the statement 'n is a number' means the same thing as the statement 'There exists a concept such that n is the number that corresponds to it'. Frege concludes[79] that he has finally explained the notion of number, and that though it seems – in virtue of the etymology of the word 'equinumerous' – to have been explained by itself, it has really been adequately explained, without any sort of circularity, since the phrase 'the number that corresponds to the concept F' had already been explained.

Once again, a few words should be said about the difficulties of interpreting what Frege says without appealing to the notion of conceptual content. When Frege says that the statements 'Concept F is equinumerous with concept G' has the same meaning as 'There is a relation φ that bijectively orders the objects

---

[73]Ibid.
[74]Ibid., p. 80.
[75]Ibid., section 72, p. 80.
[76]Ibid.
[77]Ibid.
[78]Ibid.
[79]Ibid.

that fall under concept F with the objects that fall under concept G', what these two statements have in common cannot be – and on the same grounds as in the case of the purported second definition of number or Principle V – either the thought expressed or merely the truth-value. The conceptual content is what they have in common.

Continuing with the exposition, Frege will first establish that when the concept F is equinumerous with the concept G, the number that corresponds to the concept F is the same as the number that corresponds to the concept G. Frege underscores[80] that though someone could think that the above formulation is a tautology – in the traditional sense of the word – it is not so, since the meaning of the word 'equinumerous' follows not from its composition but from the explanation he has given. In virtue of the definition, one has to establish that the extension of the concept 'equinumerous with the concept F' is the same as the extension of the concept 'equinumerous with the concept G', when the concept F is equinumerous with the concept G. Thus, one has to establish that, under the assumption that the concept F is equinumerous with the concept G, the following statements are true:

(Γ) If the concept H is equinumerous with the concept F, then it is also equinumerous with the concept G.
(Δ) If the concept H is equinumerous with the concept G, then it is also equinumerous with the concept F.

Now, Frege observes[81] that (Γ) is obtained from the fact that there is a relation that makes the objects that fall under concept H bijectively correspond with the objects that fall under concept G, when there is a relation φ that establishes a bijective correspondence between the objects that fall under concept F and the objects that fall under concept G, and when there also exists a relation ψ that establishes a bijective correspondence between the objects that fall under concept H and the objects that fall under concept F. Thus, H ψ F φ G.[82] Expressed in words, the composition of two bijective correspondences is a bijective correspondence.

Such a relation, says Frege,[83] does not offer any difficulties. If we abstract from the content of γ and β – that is, if we consider them as mere reference points without any specific content – then the composition of relations is present in the statement: 'There exists an object with which γ is in the relation ψ, and which is in the relation φ with β' It is easy to show that such a relation is a bijection, and that it establishes a correspondence between the objects that fall under H and the objects that fall under G.[84] One can establish (Δ) in a perfectly similar way. Frege

---

[80]Ibid., section 73, p. 81.
[81]Ibid.
[82]Ibid.
[83]Ibid.
[84]Ibid., pp. 81-2.

concludes the general discussion with the hope that the above explanations have made it clear that we do not need to look for a foundation of arithmetic in intuition – as Kant had thought – and that definitions are by no means fruitless.

6 A Brief Sketch of the System

In the following pages, I will offer a brief exposition of Frege's sketch of the construction of the natural number series in *Die Grundlagen der Arithmetik*. Frege's sketch, which even touches superficially on the construction of other number systems, including the system of complex numbers, contains also interesting critical remarks on Cantor and on Kant that should not be ignored. Frege's sketch begins in section 74 with the definition of 0, namely: 0 is the number that corresponds to the concept 'different from itself'. In fact, at the end of that section Frege observes[85] that any other concept under which nothing falls could have served the same purpose, but that he opted for one, of which we can establish by purely logical means that no object falls under it.

To prevent a possible misunderstanding, Frege stresses[86] that the use of a concept that contains a contradiction – like 'being different from itself', which violates the reflexivity of identity – does no harm, so long as we do not presuppose that something falls under it. But the mere use of the concept does not involve any such presupposition. Moreover, it is not always obvious that a concept contains a contradiction; that frequently requires an investigation. In many cases, we have to use the concept and treat it logically as any other concept before any contradiction is discovered. Ironically, Frege reminds the reader here that the only thing that can be required by logical rigor is that each and every concept be so clearly delimited that for any object it can be determined whether the object falls or does not fall under the concept. As already explained, the seed of the Zermelo-Russell Paradox lies hidden precisely in this requirement. Continuing with Frege, he states[87] that concepts containing a contradiction trivially satisfy such a requirement, since it is clear for any object that it does not fall under such a concept.

In section 75 Frege establishes that all concepts under which nothing falls are equinumerous, and that the number 0 corresponds to all of them. In section 76 Frege explains the relation in which are two neighbouring members of the natural number series. On this issue he tells us[88] that the statement 'There exists a concept F and an object x falling under it, which are such that the number that corresponds to F is n, and the number that corresponds to the concept "falls under F but is different from x" is m' is going to have the same meaning as the statement 'n follows m immediately in the natural number series'. Frege remarks[89] that he

---

[85]Ibid., section 74, p. 83.
[86]Ibid., p. 82.
[87]Ibid.
[88]Ibid., section 76, p. 84.
[89]Ibid.

avoids the use of the expression 'n is the successor of m', since for the justification of the definite article one has first to prove two statements, namely, the existence and the uniqueness of the successor.

Now the stage has been set for the introduction of the number 1. Thus, Frege first shows that there is something that follows 0 immediately in the natural number series, namely, the number that corresponds to the concept 'equal to 0'. Under this concept falls exactly one object, namely, the number 0. Using the definition introduced before of 'n follows m immediately in the natural number series', Frege observes that the concept 'equal to 0' is related in the corresponding way to the concept 'equal to 0 but different from 0'. Under the latter concept nothing falls and, thus, as explained before, the number 0 corresponds to it. Hence, the number that corresponds to the former concept follows 0 immediately in the natural number series. Thus, Frege defines:[90] 1 is the number that corresponds to the concept 'equal to 0'. Hence, 1 follows 0 immediately in the natural number series. Frege has established the existence of a successor of 0 and has baptized it 1.

In section 78 Frege offers a list of arithmetical statements that can be proved on the basis of the definitions already introduced. Such statements are the following:[91]

(1)   If k follows 0 immediately in the natural number series, then k=1. (Uniqueness of the successor of 0).

(2)   If 1 is the number that corresponds to a concept, then there is an object that falls under the concept.

(3)   If 1 is the number that corresponds to the concept F, if the object x falls under the concept F, and if the object y falls under the concept F, then x=y.

(4)   If an object falls under a concept F and if, in general, from the fact that x falls under the concept F, and that y falls under the concept F, one can conclude that x=y, then 1 is the number that corresponds to the concept F.

(5)   The relation between m and n expressed by the statement: 'n follows m immediately in the natural number series' is bijective. (Here, Frege stresses,[92] it is still not said that for any number there exists another that either follows it or is followed by it.)

(6)   Every number except 0 follows another number immediately in the natural number series.

Frege observes[93] that to establish that for each number n in the natural number series there is another number that immediately follows it, we have to exhibit a concept to which this number corresponds. Frege explains that concept as

[90]Ibid., section 77, p. 85.
[91]Ibid., section 78, pp. 85-6.
[92]Ibid., p. 86.
[93]Ibid., section 79, p. 86.

follows: The statement 'If every object with which x is in the relation φ falls under concept F, and if from the fact that δ falls under concept F follows, in general, regardless of what δ is, that every object with which δ is in the relation φ falls under concept F, then y falls under concept F, regardless of what concept F is' means the same as 'y follows x in the series φ' and that 'x precedes y in the series φ'.[94] By means of such a definition, says Frege,[95] it is possible to reduce the presumably peculiar mathematical sort of inference from n to n+1 – though he really means mathematical induction – to the general laws of logic.

It should be briefly mentioned here that the details of such a derivation had already been worked out in Chapter III of *Begriffsschrift*.[96] In section 24 of that small book Frege introduces the notion of a hereditary property in a series generated by the iteration of an asymmetrical relation R. Thus, a property is hereditary in the series φ generated by R if and only if for all x, if x has property F, then each and every y such that R(x,y), that is, is related to x by R, also has property F.[97] By means of the notion of hereditary property, Frege then defines – see pp. 60-62 – the notion of following in a series. Thus, y follows x in the series φ generated by the relation R if and only if for all hereditary properties Φ and for all z, when R(x,z), and z has property Φ, then y has property Φ. In section 28, p. 71 Frege establishes the transitivity of the relation of following in a series, and in section 29, pp. 71-2 he defines the notion of 'belonging to a series that begins with x' (respectively, its dual relation of 'belonging to a series that ends at z'). As Frege shows on p. 74, the property of 'belonging to a series that begins with x' is hereditary. A decisive step is made on p. 77 with the definition of a relation uniquely determined in its last member, that is, what nowadays is called a function. From this Frege infers – see pp. 82-5 – that if x has property F, which is a hereditary property and, moreover, if y follows x in the φ series generated by the asymmetrical and functional relation R, then y has property F. In *Begriffsschrift* Frege does not go on to establish mathematical induction. The completion of the derivation of mathematical induction in the concept-script had to wait until the publication of the first volume of *Grundgesetze der Arithmetik*[98] in 1893. However, mathematical induction could have been obtained in *Begriffsschrift* simply by replacing x with 0 and the asymmetrical functional relation R by the successor

---

[94]Ibid.

[95]Ibid., section 80, p. 86.

[96]See *Begriffsschrift*, Chapter III sections 24-7. See also *Die Grundlagen der Arithmetik*, sections 43-6, pp. 58-60. On this issue, see also Bertrand Russell's *Introduction to Mathematical Philosophy* (London, 1919), Chapter 3, pp. 21 and 25-6, and *The Principles of Mathematics*, Appendix A, p. 420, as well as Michael Beaney's exposition in his 'Russell and Frege', in Nicholas Griffin (ed.), *The Cambridge Companion to Russell* (Cambridge, 2003), pp. 137-8, and Christian Thiel's footnote 102 on p. 168 of the Centenary edition of *Die Grundlagen der Arithmetik*.

[97]See *Begriffsschrift*, p. 55 for the symbolic version, and p. 58 for its rendering in German.

[98]See *Grundgesetze der Arithmetik I*, section 46, p. 60.

function in the above statement. And that is essentially what Frege does in section 46 of his logical masterpiece.

Continuing with Frege's exposition, in section 81 he offers the following definition: The statement 'y follows x in the series φ or is the same as x' means the same as 'y belongs to the series φ that begins with x' and 'x belongs to the series φ that ends with y'. Hence, in particular, k belongs to the natural number series that ends with n, if n follows k in that series or is identical with k.[99]

Frege then shows that – under conditions to be specified – the number that corresponds to the concept 'belonging to the natural number series that ends with n' follows n immediately in the natural number series. In this way, it will be established both that there is a number that follows n immediately in the natural number series, and that there is no last member of that series. We are not going to reproduce here Frege's sketch of a proof that in the series of natural numbers each number has an immediate successor. It should be mentioned, however, that such a proof presupposes – as Frege correctly observes[100] – some previous results. In particular, one first has to establish that no member of the natural number series that begins with 0 follows itself in such a series. In order to obtain the statement that the number that corresponds to the concept 'belonging to the natural number series that ends in n' follows n immediately in the natural number series that begins with 0, Frege then introduces the expression 'finite number', which is to mean the same as 'belonging to the natural number series that begins with 0'. More exactly, the statement 'n belongs to the natural number series that begins with 0' is going to have the same meaning as [*sei gleichbedeutend mit*] the statement 'n is a finite number'.[101] Thus, to complete the proof of the statement that the number that corresponds to the concept 'belonging to the natural number series that ends with n' follows n immediately in the natural number series, one first has to obtain the following result: No finite number follows itself in the natural number series.[102]

Finally, since no finite number follows itself in the natural number series, the number that corresponds to the concept 'finite number' is infinite, and Frege designates it by ∞_1. Frege observes[103] – but does not even sketch the proof – that one can show that ∞_1 follows itself and, thus, is an infinite number, since if it were finite, it could not follow itself in the natural number series. Hence, the statement: 'The number that corresponds to the concept F is ∞_1' means that there exists a bijective correspondence between the objects that fall under F and the finite numbers. Frege considers[104] that in this way the number ∞_1 has been introduced clearly and without any ambiguity, and thus a meaning has been given to such an expression.

[99]Ibid., section 81, p. 87.
[100]Ibid., sections 82-3, pp. 88-9.
[101]Ibid., section 83, p. 89.
[102]Ibid.
[103]Ibid., section 84, p. 89.
[104]Ibid., pp. 89-90.

The last remark serves as introduction to an attack by Frege on Cantor's theory of transfinite numbers in sections 85-6. Thus, in section 85 Frege criticizes Cantor because in his theory of transfinite numbers the independence from the order in the series is not preserved. On this critique, it should first be mentioned that what Frege says applies only to transfinite ordinal arithmetic, in which, e.g., addition is not commutative. It does not apply, however, to cardinal arithmetic, in which there is complete independence from order and, thus, addition is commutative. Cantor was perfectly conscious of the dependence from order in ordinal arithmetic, and also perfectly conscious of the independence from order in cardinal arithmetic. He simply wanted to develop and did develop both transfinite ordinal and cardinal arithmetic separately.

In section 86 Frege once more shows his lack of an appropriate understanding of Cantor's work. He says that Cantor's notion of following in a series is different from his', since it allows the possibility of a series, in which the number 0 would follow the number 13, by putting first all uneven numbers and then all even numbers. Frege's notion of following in a series does not allow such a possibility. Once more, it should be mentioned that Frege misunderstands Cantor. Frege is trying to establish that the arithmetic of natural numbers can be obtained from purely logical concepts and axioms, by defining all primitive arithmetical concepts and proving all primitive arithmetical axioms on the basis of logic alone. Cantor, however, is not especially concerned with the familiar natural number series, but with series in general. The level of abstraction of Cantor's treatment of numbers is much higher than Frege's and, thus Frege's objection is irrelevant. E.g., whereas for Cantor the notion of an order type of a number series is especially important, Frege does not seem to have even grasped the notion of an order type.[105]

It should be stressed here that such misunderstandings can occur and have occurred the other way around. Thus, as already mentioned,[106] Paul Benacerraf has argued that the natural number series is just an ω-sequence and that what counts for arithmetic is just that the natural numbers build such a sequence, and no ontological weight should be given to the natural numbers. This is, however, a misunderstanding. As already argued in Chapter 2, according to the general theory of relativity, our spatial-temporal universe is a special case of a four-dimensional pseudo-Riemannian manifold of variable curvature. That does not mean, however, that our spatial-temporal universe does not exist or that we should not inquire about the physical laws valid in our universe but should only be worried about the properties that all four-dimensional pseudo-Riemannian manifolds of variable curvature have in common. In the same fashion, though the natural number series is a special case of an ω-sequence, it does not follow that natural numbers do not exist, or that mathematicians (for example, number theorists) and philosophers

---

[105]It should be mentioned here that Cantor also seems to have failed to understand Frege. See on this issue Ernst Zermelo's footnote on p. 441 of Cantor's *Gesammelte Abhandlungen mathematischen und philosophischen Inhalts*, as well as Christian Thiel's Introduction to the Centenary edition of *Die Grundlagen der Arithmetik*, p. LII.
[106]In Chapter 2, section 5. See also the preceding footnote.

should not give its due importance to the properties of natural numbers – let us say, to the property of the number 1 of being equal to its product, or to that of the number 2 of being the only even prime number – which are not properties of the corresponding members of each and every ω-sequence – for example, of the number 3, which is the second odd number and the first odd prime, or of the number 5, which is the second odd prime number.

Finally, Frege also criticizes Cantor for appealing to the so-called internal intuition where it is feasible and desirable to use definitions and prove the statements. Although Frege does not say it explicitly, he is afraid that Cantor could be introducing psychological explanations in the foundations of arithmetic. I am not going to dwell on this issue, but shall just point out that Frege, because of his programme of avoiding any trace of psychologism in the foundations of logic and mathematics, sometimes goes too far in his attribution of even extreme psychologistic theses to authors that never sustained such radical views. His posthumously published sketch of a review of Cantor's writings on the transfinite – which is not only unjust but insulting – as well as his late review of Husserl's *Philosophie der Arithmetik* – though he should have already suspected that Husserl had in the meantime changed his views – are good examples of this peculiarity of Frege.[107] Later we will discuss still another example. Moreover, Frege seems to have had difficulties in understanding other authors of his generation, as attested by his treatment of Kerry's criticism, and by not taking seriously some of the young Husserl's criticisms.

7 Frege's Summary and his Assessment of Kant's Views

In Chapter V of *Die Grundlagen der Arithmetik* Frege summarizes the previous chapters, stressing at the same time the more important aspects. In particular, that chapter contains the most detailed comparison of Frege's views with those of Kant. It is appropriate to dwell a little on the last issue, since it can help us clarify the frequently misunderstood relation between Frege and Kant.

However, it should be mentioned first that at the beginning of the chapter Frege underscores that his book has made his logicist thesis plausible, that is, that arithmetical laws are analytic – that is, derivable exclusively from general logical laws – and, hence, also *a priori*. Thus, arithmetic would only be a development of logic, and every arithmetical statement a derived logical law.

In sections 88-89 Frege summarizes his divergences from Kant as well as his agreements. Thus, in section 88 he accuses Kant of having underestimated the importance of analytic statements, as a result of having based his discussion on a

---

[107]See 'Entwurf zu einer Besprechung von Cantor's Gesammelten Abhandlungen zur Lehre vom Transfiniten', in *Nachgelassene Schriften*, pp. 76-80. The version published during Frege's lifetime – see *Kleine Schriften*, pp. 163-6 – does not contain the most offensive passages. With respect to Husserl's early work, see his 'Rezension von: E.G. Husserl, *Philosophie der Arithmetik I*', in *Kleine Schriften*, pp. 179-92.

very narrow conceptual determination. Nonetheless, Frege mentions without further discussion that Kant seemed to have suspected his broader determination. On this point, Frege is probably referring to the fact that in his discussion of the supreme principle of analytical judgements in the *Kritik der reinen Vernunft*[108] Kant says that all analytical statements can be decided by the Principle of Non-Contradiction – which probably was meant to include also the Principle of Identity and the Principle of *Tertium non Datur*. Thus, Kant's second characterization of analyticity was a forerunner of Frege's characterization of analyticity as derivability from general logical laws. However, it should be mentioned that from the Principle of Contradiction – even with the help of the other two traditional principles – very little could be derived, except if one had enough logical inference rules, of which Kant seems not to have any clear notion. Frege correctly asserts[109] that on the basis of Kant's definition the classification of judgements in analytic and synthetic is not exhaustive. Kant seems to consider only general assertive judgements, in which case one can speak about a concept of the subject and ask whether, on the basis of his definition, the concept of the predicate is contained in it or not. However, adds Frege,[110] one can ask what would happen if the subject is a singular object, as is presumably the case in existential statements. In such a case, one cannot speak in the same sense about a concept of the subject. Before continuing with Frege's criticism of Kant, it should be mentioned that the above reading of existential statements is not easy to reconcile with Frege's official rendering of them as denying that the number 0 corresponds to the concept involved and, thus, as second order predications.

Continuing with Frege's assessment of Kant, he asserts[111] that Kant seems to presuppose that all concepts are built by coordinating distinctive marks, that is, combining properties of objects, which is one of the less fruitful conceptual formations. Frege stresses[112] that the most fruitful conceptual determinations trace division lines that were not available before. Thus, what can be inferred from such conceptual determinations cannot be seen at first sight. Such consequences clearly extend our knowledge and, thus, from Kant's perspective should be considered synthetic, though they can be proved by purely logical means and, thus, should be considered analytic. Sometimes, many definitions are required to prove a statement, which is, thus, not contained in any one of them, though it can be inferred by purely logical means from all of them.

Finally, Frege questions the generality of Kant's assertion that objects are given to us only by means of sensible intuition. In particular, he underscores[113] that numbers are not given to us by means of sensible intuition. Moreover, even if Kant understood by the word 'object' something different from Frege, and would

---

[108]*Kritik der reinen Vernunft*, A 150-52, B 190-91.
[109]*Die Grundlagen der Arithmetik*, section 88, p. 92.
[110]Ibid.
[111]Ibid.
[112]Ibid.
[113]Ibid., section 89, p. 93.

consider numbers to be concepts, not objects, Frege stresses[114] that the problem still remains, since for Kant even *a priori* concepts require that – the form of – sensible intuition be applied in mathematics and in the foundations of physics. But numbers, whether objects or concepts, are non-sensible and, as we saw in the preceding chapter, are not limited even by our imagination, but can very well be applied to anything thinkable. For Frege, numbers are given directly to reason without any intermediaries. The same occurs with all entities of what he later – in 'Der Gedanke' – would call 'the third realm'. Frege seemed not to allow for a sort of categorial intuition, though precisely in 'Der Gedanke' there is an enigmatic passage that could be rendered as being an acknowledgement of the role of a sort of non-sensible intuition in our acquaintance with the entities of the third realm.[115]

The above criticism notwithstanding, Frege asserts that we owe to Kant the distinction between analytic and synthetic judgements. This is not quite correct, since the distinction corresponds more or less to Hume's distinction between matters of fact and relations of ideas, and even to Leibniz's distinction between *vérités de fait* and *vérités de raison*.[116] What is new in Kant are both the terminology and the assertion of a third intermediate group of truths, the synthetic *a priori* truths, which are neither analytic nor empirical, since they, on the one hand, extend our knowledge, and, on the other hand, do not depend on the matter of experience, but only on their form, and this form is not the form of the object but the form of our sensibility. Frege underscores that he coincides with Kant on the synthetic *a priori* nature of geometrical statements, but differs from him on the issue of the nature of arithmetical statements, which for Kant are also synthetic *a priori*, but for Frege are derivable from general logical laws and, thus, analytic. Thus, Frege asserts[117] without any ambiguity that Kant was wrong with respect to the nature of arithmetic.

It should be pointed out here that, on the basis of Frege's references to Kant in *Die Grundlagen der Arithmetik* – or in any of his writings with the exception of those of 1924-25 – there is no ground to sustain that Frege was either a Kantian or a neo-Kantian. His agreement with Kant is essentially limited to their views on the synthetic *a priori* nature of geometry. But even on this issue the arguments used by Frege are clearly different from those of Kant, which he does not even mention. Although there is a big industry of Kantianizers of Frege – e.g., Sluga, Currie, Kitcher, Weiner and others – to consider Frege a Kantian is at least as unwarranted as to consider Leibniz a Cartesian or to consider Carnap a Humean or Quine a Millian. As a matter of fact, though there are one or two coincidences between the members of each pair, the differences are by far more numerous and

[114]Ibid.
[115]See *Kleine Schriften*, p. 360.
[116]For Hume, see his *Enquiry Concerning Human Understanding*, p. 25. For Leibniz, see, e.g., G.W. Leibniz, *Hauptschriften zur Grundlegung der Philosophie II*, edited by Ernst Cassirer, 1908 (3rd edn, Hamburg, 1966), pp. 500-502.
[117]*Die Grundlagen der Arithmetik*, section 89, p. 94. See on this issue the more detailed discussion in Chapter 2, section 5 above.

decisive than such coincidences for an adequate rendering of their respective philosophies.

Continuing with Frege, in section 90 he stresses once more that he has only made probable the analytical nature of arithmetical statements. To establish the logicist thesis with complete rigor, eliminating any possible doubt, one would have to derive arithmetical statements by means of an inference chain free from any gaps, and such that each step would be legitimized by purely logical means. Moreover, Frege adds[118] that since in mathematics one usually proceeds with less rigor, one has the impression that there is a multiplicity of mathematical inference forms, whereas they are really only combinations of more simple inference forms. Thus, it is of a decisive importance to avoid any gaps in the chain of inferences, though the derivations would become very lengthy. On this point, Frege stresses[119] the great utility of the concept-script for making such derivations shorter and more transparent.

In sections 94-5, Frege makes very valuable observations on the issue of the permissibility and consistency of concepts. According to Frege, a concept is permissible even when its traits contain a contradiction. What is not allowed is to presuppose that something falls under such a concept. But from the fact that a concept does not contain any contradiction one cannot infer that something falls under it. Thus, e.g., the concepts of sphinx and unicorn do not contain any contradiction, but that does not mean that there are objects that fall under them.[120] Moreover, from the fact that we do not see any contradiction in a concept it does not follow that there is no contradiction. The determinability of the definition of a concept and, thus, the exact determination of the conditions that an object would have to satisfy to fall under the concept, are no guarantee of the existence of such an object. On the other hand, Frege considers that the only way to prove the consistency of a concept is by exhibiting an object that falls under it. The converse, however, is incorrect. In other words, from the existence of an object that falls under a concept follows the consistency of that concept, but from the consistency of the concept does not follow that there is an object falling under it.[121]

In section 96 Frege continues his observations on consistency and applies them to the problem called by Husserl[122] of 'the imaginary', namely, to the problem of the extension of the number systems. Frege firstly stresses once more that mathematicians, as well as geographers, do not produce or invent their objects of study, but simply discover and name them. Moreover, the fact that one has not

---

[118]*Die Grundlagen der Arithmetik*, section 90, p. 94.

[119]Ibid., section 91, p. 95.

[120] This example of Frege is irrelevant, since it concerns purported physically real objects, for which it is clear that mere consistency is not sufficient. Requirements for mathematical existence are essentially different from those for physical existence, and, one could argue, it could very well be the case that for the former consistency were a sufficient condition.

[121]Ibid., section 95, pp. 97-8.

[122]See Appendix B, VI to his *Philosophie der Arithmetik*, pp. 430-51, or better, the corrected edition of Husserl's two lectures of 1901 to Hilbert's Circle in Göttingen, prepared by the late Karl Schuhmann and Elisabeth Schuhmann, in *Husserl Studies*, 17 (2001): 87-123.

found a contradiction when extending some mathematical operations or relations to new presumed entities – e.g., an extended number system – does not legitimize the acceptance of such new entities, since there remains the possibility of a hidden contradiction. Furthermore, as expounded above, for Frege consistency does not imply existence. Frege asserts that the popularity among mathematicians of the mistake of conflating consistency with existence is due to a deficient understanding of the difference between concept and object. To avoid such a confusion, Frege suggests that we not allow presumed definitions or equations in which at one side there occurs an indefinite article – which for Frege indicates that one is talking about a concept – and on the other side a definite article – which for Frege indicates that one is talking about an object. On the basis of the foregoing observations, in section 99 Frege makes a critical assessment of Hankel's formalist arithmetic. Frege considers that by means of a purely formal treatment of arithmetical operations with some determined properties and of some valid statements about them, one really fails to introduce the operations of addition and multiplication.[123]

In section 104, Frege observes, on the one hand, that if in a presentation of arithmetic we revert to intuition, we are introducing something alien into arithmetic; but if, on the other hand, we determine the concept of a number only by its traits, and only require that the number has some properties, there is no guarantee that something falls under the concept and satisfies our requirements. Such difficulties are of the utmost importance for Frege, since, as he expresses it, on such a basis one would then have to prove mathematical statements.[124]

I will finish the exposition of Frege's views in *Die Grundlagen der Arithmetik* by expounding some observations that he makes in section 105. Thus, according to Frege, in arithmetic we are concerned not with something alien and external, known to us by means of our senses, but with objects that are given immediately to reason, and such that reason can penetrate and apprehend them completely as belonging to it.[125] Nonetheless, such arithmetical entities are in no way subjective but, on the contrary, and precisely because they belong to reason, objective. Frege concludes that there is nothing more objective than arithmetic.[126]

---

[123]Ibid., section 99, p. 100.
[124]Ibid., section 104, p. 103.
[125]Ibid., section 105, p. 104. This last assertion of Frege has been used by Sluga in *Gottlob Frege*, p. 120, and by Currie in *Frege: An Introduction to his Philosophy*, p. 188, to support their Kantian interpretation of Frege. However, that is not the only possible rendering of Frege's words, and clearly not the most compatible with other assertions of Frege in this work. In fact, some pages before Frege had stressed that the task of mathematicians is to discover, not to produce, their objects of study.
[126]Ibid., p. 105.

Chapter 4

The Basic Distinctions I: Sense and Referent

Around 1891 Frege had completed the conceptual framework of his philosophy. This framework was presented in three especially important papers published between 1891 and 1892, namely, 'Funktion und Begriff',[1] 'Über Sinn und Bedeutung'[2] and 'Über Begriff und Gegenstand',[3] in a paper written as a sequel of those three – between 1892 and 1895 – but published only in 1969 under the title 'Ausführungen über Sinn und Bedeutung',[4] and in the first volume of *Grundgesetze der Arithmetik*,[5] published in 1893. In this book one can also appreciate the strict bond between Frege's conceptual framework and his logical system. Two distinctions made by Frege in the above mentioned papers are of such an importance for the understanding of his mature philosophy that from now on I will refer to them as the basic distinctions. One of these, namely, the semantic distinction between an expression, its sense and its referent, is distinctive of Frege's mature philosophy. The other, namely, the ontological distinction between function and object, is a generalization of his distinction between concept and object of *Die Grundlagen der Arithmetik*, present already even in his early *Begriffsschrift*. In this and the next chapter, I will expound and critically assess both important distinctions.

1 Sense and Referent

Frege uses the term 'proper name' not only for expressions such as 'Socrates', 'Napoleon', 'Adolf Hitler' or 'George W. Bush', but also for expressions such as 'the morning star', 'the teacher of Plato', 'the king of France in the year 2000', 'the theorem of Pythagoras', and even for assertive sentences, that is, for statements. In fact, for Frege any expression that refers univocally to a unique object is a proper

---

[1] 1891. See *Kleine Schriften*, pp. 125-42.
[2] 1892. See *Kleine Schriften*, pp. 143-62.
[3] 1892. See *Kleine Schriften*, pp. 167-78.
[4] See *Nachgelassene Schriften*, pp. 128-36.
[5] *Grundgesetze der Arithmetik I*, 1893, *II*, 1903, (reprint in one volume, Hildesheim, 1962).

name.[6] However, the preceding sentence is not clear enough, since we still do not know what Frege understands by the word 'object' or by the phrase 'an expression refers to'. In the following exposition I will try to clarify those expressions. Provisionally, we will understand by proper name just proper names in the strict sense (like 'Socrates' or 'Napoleon') and definite descriptions (like 'the morning star' or 'the theorem of Pythagoras').

Let us consider now the following two groups of expression pairs: (I) (i) 'Londres' and 'London', (ii) 'Spain's Capital' and 'die Hauptstadt Spaniens', (iii) '7' and 'VII'; (II) (i) 'the morning star' and 'the evening star', (ii) 'the teacher of Alexander the Great' and 'the most famous disciple of Plato', (iii) '3+4' and '5+2', (iv) 'the author of *Der logische Aufbau der Welt*' and 'the only member of the Vienna Circle who was both a student of Frege and of Husserl', (v) 'the Chang-Løs-Suszko theorem' and 'the Preservation Theorem under Unions of Chains of Models'. In each pair of expressions of group (I) the expressions differ only as signs, being simply names belonging to different languages, but referring in the same way to the same entity. If there were perfect synonyms in a language, they would also only differ as signs. In all such cases it is enough to know the language or languages to which the expressions belong to be aware of the fact that they speak about the same thing. They not only refer to the same thing, but also do so in the same fashion. Thus, '7' and 'VII' refer to the same number 7, and they do so in the same way.

The case of the expressions of group (II) is completely different. In each pair of expressions of this group the expressions also refer to the same thing, but they do so in a different fashion. To be aware of the fact that they refer to the same thing, it is not enough to know the language in which they are expressed. To know that the pair of expressions 'the morning star' and 'the evening star' name the same planet Venus, one needs some rudimentary knowledge of astronomy; to know that 'the teacher of Alexander the Great' and 'the most famous disciple of Plato' name the same person, namely, Aristotle, one needs some elementary knowledge of the history of Ancient Greece; to know that 'the Chang-Løs-Suszko Theorem' and 'the Preservation Theorem under Unions of Chains of Models' refer to the same model-theoretic result, one needs some advanced knowledge of logic. Someone lacking the rudimentary astronomical knowledge could very well believe that the expressions 'the morning star' and 'the evening star' are names of different objects, regardless of how good his knowledge of the English language may be. Something similar occurs with the remaining pairs of group (II). In fact, though the statements 'The morning star is the morning star' and 'The author of *Der logische Aufbau der Welt* is the author of *Der logische Aufbau der Welt*' do not have any cognitive value, the statements 'The morning star is the evening star' and 'The author of *Der logische Aufbau der Welt* is the only member of the Vienna Circle who was both a student of Frege and of Husserl' have much greater cognitive value. Incidentally, probably most scholars specialized in Rudolf Carnap's or the

---

[6]We will later see that statements refer univocally to a truth-value – that is, to 'the True' or to 'the False' – which for Frege are objects.

Vienna Circle's philosophy, do not know that Carnap was Husserl's student. Hence, the cognitive value of the last mentioned statement is no small matter.[7]

Thus, when we consider proper names, we have to take into account not only what is named by the proper name, its referent – some scholars prefer the words 'reference',[8] or 'denotation' – but also what Frege calls 'the sense of the proper name'. A proper name always refers to its referent by means of its sense, and it can even have a sense without having any referent. Thus, the proper name 'the ten feet tall basketball player' does not have any referent, whereas the proper name 'the greatest prime number' not only does not have, but also cannot have any referent, though both expressions have a very clear sense. For Frege the referents of proper names are objects.

Now the distinction between the pairs of expressions belonging to group (I) and those belonging to group (II) is even clearer. In each pair of expressions of the first group the members, though different as signs, have not only the same referent but also the same sense. On the other hand, in each pair of expressions of the second group, though the members have the same referent, they are not only different as signs but also express different senses. They refer to the same object by means of different senses. If we put aside equivocal proper names, we can say that the same sense may correspond to various signs, and the same referent may correspond to various senses.

However, proper names are not the only constituents of statements. There exists another constituent of statements that is essentially different from proper names, namely, what Frege called '*Begriffswörter*', and I will literally translate as 'conceptual words'. For Frege, each simple assertive sentence (that is, each statement) can be decomposed into a conceptual word and a proper name. This decomposition is not unique, however, since simple assertive sentences usually admit various decompositions into a conceptual word and one or two proper names.[9] As we will later see, for Frege, conceptual words are special cases of words for functions – briefly 'function words' – and proper names occur as arguments of conceptual words.

Conceptual words also possess a sense and a referent. The referent of a conceptual word is a concept, to which there corresponds a possibly empty extension. For Frege, the most fundamental logical relation is precisely that of an object falling under a concept. An object falls under a concept exactly when it belongs to the extension of the concept.[10] Thus, the extension of a concept is the

---

[7]On this issue, see Karl Schuhmann's *Husserl-Chronik* (Den Haag, 1977), p. 281. See also Ludwig Landgrebe's letter to Husserl of 11, XI, 1932 in Edmund Husserl, *Briefwechsel IV* (Dordrecht, 1994), p. 298.

[8]I prefer to use the word 'reference' for the act of referring to the referent. On the other hand, the word 'denotation', if it is ever used in this book, should be understood as a synonym of 'referent'.

[9]See, e.g., 'Einleitung in die Logik', in *Nachgelassene Schriften*, p. 209.

[10]See on this issue, e.g., 'Über Schoenflies: Die logischen Paradoxien der Mengenlehre', in *Nachgelassene Schriften*, pp. 191-9.

set of objects determined by the concept, whose members are all those objects that fall under the concept. The extension, however, is not a concept but an object.

On the syntactic side, conceptual words and proper names combine to form statements. Similarly, the senses of conceptual words combine with the senses of proper names to form the senses of statements. On the ontological side, the referents of proper names, that is, objects, combine with the referents of conceptual words, that is, concepts, to form the referents of the corresponding statements. Thus, the sense of a statement will be determined by the senses of its constituent parts, and the referent of a statement will be determined by the referents of its constituent parts. As Frege puts it in a letter to Russell:

> To the decomposition of the statement there corresponds a decomposition of the thought, and to this also something in the region of the referents, and I want to call this a logical original fact.[11]

It should be mentioned here that in his last years Frege seems to have abandoned his thesis that the referent of a constituent part of a statement or compound expression is a part of the referent of the statement or compound expression.[12]

Continuing with the views of the mature Frege, since to each expression there corresponds a unique sense – if we once more put aside equivocal expressions – and to each sense there corresponds a unique referent – in case it has one – the following statements seem to be true of Frege's semantics of sense and referent. The senses of the constituent parts of a statement determine both the sense of the statement and the referents of those constituent parts. Moreover, both the sense of the statement and the referents of its constituent parts determine the referent of the statement, and these two determinations need to have the same output. In other words, it is supposed that the following diagram is commutative, that is, if we follow the two different trajectories marked by the arrows, we arrive to exactly the same place:[13]

---

[11]'Der Zerlegung des Satzes entspricht eine Zerlegung des Gedankens und dieser wieder etwas in dem Gebiete der Bedeutungen, und dies möchte ich eine logische Ursache nennen.' [*Wissenschaftlicher Briefwechsel*, p. 224].

[12]See on this issue Frege's 'Aufzeichnungen für Ludwig Darmstaedter' of 1919, in *Nachgelassene Schriften*, pp. 271-7, especially p. 275, where he acknowledges that the referent of the proper name 'Sweden' is not a part of the referent of the compound proper name 'the capital of Sweden'. On the same page of that transitional writing Frege considers it incorrect to say that to the sense of a conceptual word (or function word) there corresponds as referent a concept, relation or function.

[13]I have considered only statements with one argument place, but the generalization to more complex statements offers no difficulty. On this point, see the similar analysis in David Shwayder's excellent paper 'On the Determination of Reference by Sense', in M. Schirn (ed.), *Studies on Frege III*, pp. 85-95.

$$\delta$$
$$<R_C, R_N> \rightarrow R_S$$
$$\rho \uparrow \qquad \uparrow \tau$$
$$<S_C, S_N> \rightarrow S_S$$
$$\sigma$$

In the diagram, S_N is the sense of a proper name, S_C is the sense of a conceptual word, S_S is the sense of the statement formed by combining the proper name with the conceptual word, R_N is the referent of the proper name, R_C is the referent of the conceptual word, and R_S is the referent of the corresponding statement. The map ρ assigns to the ordered pair $<S_C, S_N>$ the ordered pair $<R_C, R_N>$. The map σ assigns to the ordered pair $<S_C, S_N>$ the sense of the statement, namely, S_S. On the other hand, δ assigns to the ordered pair $<R_C, R_N>$ the referent of the statement, namely, R_S. Finally, τ assigns to S_S the same R_S. Hence, it is presupposed that we have the following equality: $\tau \otimes \sigma = \delta \otimes \rho$, where the symbol '$\otimes$' is used here for the composition of functions.

According to Frege,[14] both the sense of assertive sentences (statements), and that of interrogative sentences that require a yes or no as an answer, followed by the corresponding assertive sentence – which is frequently omitted – is a thought, whereas the referent of an assertive sentence – interrogative sentences do not have a referent – is a truth-value, namely, the True or the False. Although all statements in a scientific language should have a referent, this is sometimes not so in our usual non-scientific language. When a statement does not have any referent, one of its proper name constituents is also devoid of referent, since conceptual words always have a referent, namely, the corresponding concept. Of course, this concept could very well have an empty extension, as happens, e.g., in the case of absurd concepts. But in Frege's semantics that possibility does not deprive the corresponding conceptual word of having a referent.

The sense of a statement does not necessarily always coincide with the whole content of the statement. The thought is sometimes only a proper part of that content. This is the case when the statement contains words expressing sentiments, emotions or so-called states of mind. Expressions like 'sorry', 'happily' and other similar words, as well as expressions like 'still' and 'finally' do not contribute anything to the thought expressed by a statement. On the other hand, there are expressions with the same sense, which seem to differ in some sort of subjective evaluation. That is the case, according to Frege, of words like 'thoroughbred', 'horse', 'hack', 'jade', 'nag' and 'pony'. For Frege, the difference in content between such words does not belong to the sense of the word and, thus, when they occur in statements, their contribution to the thought expressed by the statement is the same. Their difference concerns only the colouration or illumination of the thought, which belongs to the content but not to the sense of the statement. Moreover, a language adequate for science, e.g., the concept-script, should,

---

[14]See 'Der Gedanke', in *Kleine Schriften*, p. 346.

according to Frege, completely avoid the expression of those components of the content of statements that do not contribute to its sense and, thus, to the determination of the truth or falsity of the thought expressed by the statement.[15]

Since the referent of a statement is for Frege a truth-value, and he acknowledges only two truth-values, namely, the True and the False, all statements that express true thoughts have the same referent: the True; whereas all statements that express false thoughts have the same referent: the False. For Frege, the True and the False are also objects. Thus, statements are correspondingly a sort of proper names, namely, proper names of the True or proper names of the False.

The case of compound statements obtained from simple ones by means of the (possibly iterated) application of extensional operators is completely similar to that of simple statements. The sense of such a compound statement is completely determined by the senses of its constituent statements, and the referent of such a compound statement is completely determined by the referents of its constituent statements.

However, not all compound statements are built from simple ones by means of the (possibly iterated) application of extensional operators. Frege acknowledges that in such other cases the referent of the compound statement is not determined by the referents of their constituent parts, in particular, their truth-value is not determined by the truth-values of their constituent statements. Thus, in the second part of 'Über Sinn und Bedeutung'[16] Frege examines in a detailed fashion different sorts of non-extensional compound sentences. Two especially important sorts of such sentences are the so-called 'direct discourse' and 'indirect discourse'. In the first case, we reproduce *verbatim* what another person said, and the referent of my discourse is not a truth-value but precisely the words of the other person. On the other hand, in the second case we do not reproduce literally what the other person said, but only the sense of the other person's words. My discourse refers neither to a truth-value nor to the other person's words, but to their sense. Cases similar to the last one are for Frege those of the belief contexts, in which words do not have their usual referent, and what is usually the sense of the constituent statement is now the referent of the complete statement.

2 The Context Principle and Frege's Semantics of Sense and Referent

As we saw in Chapter 2, according to the Context Principle, we have to look for the meaning of a word in the context of a sentence, thus, not in isolation. I already mentioned that such a principle seemed to have been abandoned by Frege from around 1891 onwards, though most Fregean scholars would not agree with this view. In any case, the arguments given by Resnik[17] and Shwayder[18] on the

---

[15]On this issue, see, e.g., 'Der Gedanke', in *Kleine Schriften*, pp. 347-8.

[16]'Über Sinn und Bedeutung', in *Kleine Schriften*, pp. 143-62, especially pp. 151-62.

[17]See his 'Frege's Context Principle Revisited', in M. Schirn (ed.), *Studies on Frege III*, pp. 35-49.

difficulties facing any attempt of inserting the Context Principle into the semantics of sense and referent seem sufficient to consider it extremely improbable that Frege could have persisted supporting his old principle. In fact, there does not seem to exist any writing of Frege after 1890, in which he explicitly propounded the Context Principle. Nonetheless, entrenched convictions die hard, and there is an apparent echo of the Context Principle in the discussion on referentiality, particularly in section 29 of *Grundgesetze der Arithmetik*.[19] The result of such a use was, in any case, not very illuminating and certainly unnecessary.[20]

If we were to apply the Context Principle to the semantics of sense and referent, we would first need to make it clear whether such a principle is going to apply to the sense, to the referent, or to both of them. We have seen, however, that for the mature Frege the sense of a statement is determined by the senses of its constituent parts – which ultimately are proper names and conceptual words – and the referent of a statement is determined by the referents of its constituent parts. Both in the case of senses and in the case of referents the determination is from the parts to the whole, not from the whole to the parts. Thus, we have to first know the sense of the constituent parts of a statement before we know the sense of the whole statement. Similarly, we have to first know the referent of the constituent parts of the statement before we know the referent of the whole statement. Moreover, only in this fashion can we explain the fact that we can understand the sense of statements – and sentences, in general – which we had never heard before, and determine its referent. On this point, it is convenient to quote Frege:

> The possibility for us to understand sentences that we had never heard before is clearly based on [the fact] that we construct [*aufbauen*] the sense of a sentence from parts that correspond to the words. When we find the same word, e.g., 'Aetna', in two sentences, we also recognize something common in the respective thoughts corresponding to that word. Without this [sic] a language properly understood would be impossible [.][21]
> It is marvelous what language is capable of doing, when it expresses interminably many thoughts with a few syllables, so that even for a thought that a world citizen

---

[18]In 'On the Determination of Reference by Sense', in M. Schirn (ed.), *Studies on Frege III*, pp. 85-95.
[19]*Grundgesetze der Arithmetik I*, section 29. There is also a passage on p. 273 of his 'Aufzeichnungen für Ludwig Darmstaedter', in *Nachgelassene Schriften*, pp. 273-7, which admits being rendered as a defence of the Context Principle for senses.
[20]Not only was Frege's argumentation far from convincing, but, if he had not been allergic to recursive definitions, he could have secured the referentiality by a recursive definition, as taught by Husserl and as is nowadays usual in logic textbooks.
[21]'Die Möglichkeit für uns, Sätze zu verstehen, die wir noch nie gehört haben, beruht offenbar darauf, dass wir den Sinn eines Satzes aufbauen aus Teilen, die den Wörtern entsprechen. Wenn wir in zwei Sätzen dasselbe Wort, z. B. 'Aetna' finden, so erkennen wir auch in den entsprechenden Gedanken etwas Gemeinsames, das diesem Worte entspricht. Ohnedies [sic] wäre eine Sprache im eigentlichen Sinne unmöglich[.]' [Letter to Jourdain, in *Wissenschaftlicher Briefwechsel*, p. 127].

has grasped for the first time, it finds a garment, in which someone else can recognize it, for whom it is completely new.[22]

The Context Principle is not easy to reconcile with those two quotations from Frege's mature period and, in general, with a semantic theory of sense and referent as that developed by Frege from 1891 onwards.

The difficulties for the Context Principle seem to be insurmountable, if we take into account Frege's particular choice – by no means the only possible one[23] – of a semantics of sense and referent, in which the referent of a statement is either one of two possible truth-values, the True or the False. Since in the languages of contemporary logic, as well as in natural languages, both the set of true statements and the set of false statements usually have the same cardinality as the set of natural numbers, it would be completely preposterous to try to obtain the referent of the constituent parts of a simple statement from the referent – the True or the False – that such a statement has in common with infinitely many other statements, whose constituent parts are completely different from those of the statement under consideration. In fact, Frege was perfectly conscious of the absurdity of applying the Context Principle to the referents. Thus, he observes both in 'Über Sinn und Bedeutung'[24] and, more forcefully, in the second volume of *Grundgesetze der Arithmetik* that given the referent of a compound expression – not necessarily a statement – and of one of its constituent parts, this does not determine, in general, the referent of its remaining part. This last passage deserves to be quoted:

> It is evident that by means of the referent of an expression and of one of its parts the referent of the remaining part is not always determined. Thus, one should not explain a sign or word by explaining an expression, in which it occurs, while the remaining parts are known. Since first an investigation would be necessary [to determine] whether a solution for the unknown...is possible, and whether the unknown would be uniquely determined.[25]

---

[22]'Erstaunlich ist es, was die Sprache leistet, indem sie mit wenigen Silben unübersehbar viele Gedanken ausdrückt, daß sie sogar für einen Gedanken, den nun zum ersten Male ein Erdbürger gefaßt hat, eine Einkleidung findet, in der ihn ein anderer erkennen kann, dem er ganz neu ist.' ['Gedankengefüge',1923, in *Kleine Schriften*, p. 378] On the same page, the first sentence of the next paragraph is also especially relevant.

[23]See the present author's paper 'Remarks on Sense and Reference in Frege and Husserl', 1982, reprinted in Claire Ortiz Hill and Guillermo E. Rosado Haddock, *Husserl or Frege?*, pp. 23-40.

[24]See *Kleine Schriften*, pp. 150-51.

[25]'Dass durch die Bedeutung eines Ausdrucks und eines seiner Theile die Bedeutung des übrigen Theils nicht immer bestimmt ist, leuchtet ein. Man darf also ein Zeichen oder Wort nicht dadurch erklären, dass man einen Ausdruck erklärt, in dem es vorkommt, während die übrigen Theile bekannt sind. Denn es wäre erst eine Untersuchung nöthig, ob die Auflösung für die Unbekannte...möglich sei, und ob die Unbekannte eindeutig bestimmt werde.' [*Grundgesetze der Arithmetik II*, section 66, p. 79.] See also 'Über Sinn und Bedeutung', in *Kleine Schriften*, pp. 150-51.

An additional and even more decisive argument against the contention of some Fregean scholars that Frege retained the Context Principle after 1890 can be obtained from the first part of the second of the two series of writings titled 'Über die Grundlagen der Geometrie'. Thus, Frege says:

> But letters are of a completely different kind from the numerical signs >2<, >3< etc. or from the signs for relations >=<, >><. They do not have to designate [*bezeichnen*] numbers, or concepts, or relations, or any function whatsoever, but they should only indicate [*andeuten*], to convey generality to the sentences in which they occur. Thus, only in the context of a sentence do they have a certain task to fulfill, do they have to contribute to the expression of a thought. But outside of this context they signify [*besagen*] nothing.[26]

In the last passage quoted Frege contrasts referring expressions, like proper names and functional expressions, with variable expressions, which only serve to indicate but do not refer. He asserts that, contrary to proper names and relational expressions, variables designate neither numbers nor relations, but only indicate them, that is, indicate that they are variables for numbers or for relations. Moreover, he adds[27] that only in the context of statements do variables have any meaning and, thus, contribute to the expression of a thought, whereas outside of this context they lack meaning. Thus, Frege advocates a sort of Context Principle for variables, while contrasting them with proper names and relational expressions, which do not need such a principle to denote and, thus, to have a sense. The Context Principle of *Die Grundlagen der Arithmetik*, which applied to each and every expression, is now reduced to the triviality that variables have meaning only in the context of a statement, whereas by contrast proper names and relational expressions also have meaning – both sense and referent – when they occur isolated, that is, outside of the context of statements.

3 Critical Remarks I

In the first two sections of this chapter I have assumed an uncritical stance with regard to Frege's theory of sense and referent. In fact, in section 1 I have simply expounded that theory, and in section 2 I have shown that the Context Principle of *Die Grundlagen der Arithmetik* is not easy to reconcile with Frege's semantics of sense and referent. This would explain why Frege did not explicitly propound the

---

[26]'Aber die Buchstaben sind ganz anderer Art als die Zahlzeichen >2<, >3< usw. oder als die Beziehungszeichen >=<, >><. Sie sollen gar nicht Zahlen, oder Begriffe, oder Beziehungen, oder irgendwelche Funktionen bezeichnen, sondern sie sollen nur andeuten, um dem Satze, in dem sie vorkommen, Allgemeinheit des Inhalts zu verleihen. Also nur im Zusammenhang eines Satzes haben sie eine gewisse Aufgabe zu erfüllen, haben sie zum Gedankenausdrucke beizutragen. Aber außer diesem Zusammenhange besagen sie nichts.' ['Über die Grundlagen der Geometrie' II, I, 1906, in *Kleine Schriften*, p. 293.]
[27]Ibid.

Context Principle after 1890 and would support the contention that he abandoned it, even if there are some residues of it in a pair of passages of his later work.

However, Frege's semantics is not free from difficulties, and in this and the three subsequent sections I will be considering them. The difficulties can be divided into two groups; some concern the notion of sense itself, whereas others concern, not the notion of reference itself, but Frege's particular answers to the question about the referent of some sorts of expressions.

As Gottfried Gabriel argued in his interesting paper 'Einige Einseitigkeiten des Fregeschen Logikbegriffs',[28] Frege considered as differences in the colouration or illumination of expressions such that, nonetheless, are relevant for the determination of the truth-value of statements in which they occur. For Frege, e.g., the differences between 'horse', 'thoroughbred', 'jade', 'hack', 'nag' and 'pony' do not concern the sense of the expressions but only that part of the content that belongs to the colouration, to the nuances. Thus, given any statement S, the thought expressed by S would remain the same if we replace one of such expressions by another, and the truth-value of the statement would also remain the same. However, Gottfried Gabriel has shown that this is not always the case. Let us consider the following statement: (S*) 'All winners of the Epsom Derby are great thoroughbreds'. Surely, people who know that the Epsom Derby is one of the most important horse races in the world would agree to consider the thought expressed in S* as true. However, if we replace the word 'thoroughbred' by the word 'jade' in S*, we obtain the clearly false statement (S') 'All winners of the Epsom Derby are great jades'. Moreover, S' will be considered false by the same persons considering S* true, and precisely because they consider S* true. Thus, S* and S' not only do not have the same truth value and, thus, do not express the same thought, but seem to express incompatible thoughts, that is, such that could not both be true. Thus, the difference between 'thoroughbred' and 'jade' is not irrelevant for the truth or falsehood of statements in which they occur. Hence, it is not a mere difference of colouration or illumination, as Frege had thought.

The difficulty that we have here considered, however, does not represent any serious treat to Frege's semantics, since we could very well modify a little Frege's views and consider the difference between 'thoroughbred' and 'jade' a difference of sense, not one of colouration.

4 Critical Remarks II

As we saw in Chapter 1,[29] in *Begriffsschrift* Frege makes use of three notions that are only vaguely explained, namely, 'content', 'judgeable content' and 'conceptual content', which are not parts of his technical philosophical vocabulary after 1890. The notion of 'content', which seems to be the most general and is also the most

[28]In M. Schirn (ed.), *Studies on Frege II*, pp. 67-86. On Frege's views on this issue, see 'Der Gedanke', in *Kleine Schriften*, p. 348.
[29]See especially sections 4 and 5.

vaguely delimited, is the only one used – and only exceptionally – in his mature philosophy. This occurs, e.g., in 'Der Gedanke',[30] where he distinguishes in a statement (that is, assertive sentence) between the assertion and the content, and he adds that the thought is sometimes the whole content of the statement, whereas sometimes it is only a part of the content. In the latter case, the rest of the content is precisely the colouration and illumination discussed in the preceding section.

The notion of judgeable content is probably the least enigmatic of the three notions mentioned above. The judgeable content of *Begriffsschrift* is what is recognized as true in an assertive sentence. In fact, in *Begriffsschrift*, the content sign '—' as well as the compound judgement sign '|—' can only precede a judgeable content. At the beginning of *Grundgesetze der Arithmetik*,[31] Frege states that on the basis of his general distinction between sense and referent, he has divided what he had called 'judgeable content' in *Begriffsschrift*, into thought – the sense of an assertive sentence – and truth-value – the referent of an assertive sentence. Hence the notion of judgeable content has become superfluous. It must be stressed, however, that the notion of judgeable content is much nearer to the notion of thought than to the notion of truth-value. The judgeable content is simply a content that is capable of being judged. Thus, it is basically what many have called 'the proposition' expressed by an assertive sentence. But the proposition is nothing other that what Frege called 'the thought'.

By far the most enigmatic – and probably the most interesting – of the three notions mentioned above is that of conceptual content. As mentioned in Chapter 1, in *Begriffsschrift* Frege explains the notion of conceptual content as follows:[32]

(1)   Two statements, one in the active mode and the other the corresponding statement in the passive mode, have the same conceptual content.

(2)   Two statements such that we can infer the same statements from them, while maintaining fixed the remaining premises, have the same conceptual content.

(3)   The concept-script does not need to differentiate between two statements with the same conceptual content. In fact, for the concept-script the conceptual content is the only thing that counts.

It is interesting to observe that (2) is not easy to reconcile with (3). (2) is essentially concerned with some sort of interderivability, since each statement is derivable from itself. Thus, since two statements with the same conceptual content have the same logical (here in the sense of syntactical rather than semantic) consequences, each of the statements has to be derivable from the other, while the remaining premises remain fixed. More generally, two statements S and S' have

---

[30]See 'Der Gedanke', in *Kleine Schriften*, pp. 346 and 348.
[31]*Grundgesetze der Arithmetik I*, section 5, p. 9, footnote 2.
[32]See Chapter 1, section 5 above.

the same conceptual content if they are such that for any set Γ of statements of the same language as S and S' – e.g., the language of *Begriffsschrift* – and for all statements S* of the same language, Γ∪S |—S* if and only if Γ∪S' |—S*. Hence, e.g., *Modus Ponens* and *Modus Tollens* would have the same conceptual content, since, with the help of *Reductio ad Absurdum*, they are derivable from each other in propositional logic. Also, statements of propositional logic, such as, e.g., 'p→q', '¬p∨q' and '¬(p∧¬q)' would have the same conceptual content. Moreover, on the basis of (2) more interesting equivalences could be interpreted as sameness of conceptual content. Thus, in Zermelo-Fraenkel set theory, the Axiom of Choice, the Well-ordering Principle, Zorn's Lemma, and many other very different mathematical statements would have the same conceptual content. However, contrary to what (3) says, it seems to be convenient that a logical language clearly differentiate between 'p→q', '¬p∨q' and '¬(p∧¬q)', and it is not merely convenient but indispensable that a mathematical language differentiates between the Axiom of Choice and its many and varied equivalents in set theory, algebra, topology and, if the language is of first order, in logic. In fact, if a mathematical language were not capable of differentiating between the Axiom of Choice and its equivalents, that would be a sufficient reason to consider such a language inadequate for mathematics. Hence, (2) and (3) are by no means easy to reconcile.

It is interesting to observe that in 'Der Gedanke'[33] Frege offers as examples of statements expressing the same thought pairs of statements constituted either by an arbitrary statement in the active mode and its corresponding passive counterpart, or by a statement that contains the verb 'to give' and the corresponding statement obtained from it by replacing the verb 'to give' by the verb 'to receive', interchanging the words in the nominative and dative cases, and making the indispensable syntactic adjustments. Similarly, on the basis of such an explanation, the inequalities '9>3' and '3<9' would have the same sense, that is, would express the same thought. Moreover, in 'Der Gedanke'[34] Frege asserts that a language that is adequate for science does not need to differentiate between statements expressing the same thought. Thus, in 'Der Gedanke' Frege assigns to thoughts two of the three distinctive traits assigned in *Begriffsschrift* to conceptual contents.

However, as was shown above, the notion of conceptual content was not free from confusions. Something similar occurs with the notion of sense in 'Der Gedanke'. In that paper Frege even identifies facts with true thoughts.[35] But this would seem to erase important differences. In 'Über Sinn und Bedeutung'[36] and in *Grundgesetze der Arithmetik*,[37] Frege had made it clear that statements like 'The

---

[33]'Der Gedanke', in *Kleine Schriften*, p. 348. See also Frege's posthumous paper of 1897 'Logik', in *Nachgelassene Schriften*, p. 153.

[34]Ibid., p. 347.

[35]Ibid., p. 359.

[36]'Über Sinn und Bedeutung', in *Kleine Schriften*, p. 148.

[37]*Grundgesetze der Arithmetik I*, section 2, p. 7. On this issue, see also a letter to Paul F. Linke, in *Wissenschaftlicher Briefwechsel*, p. 156, in which Frege borrows an example from

morning star is a planet' and 'The evening star is a planet' express different thoughts, as do the equations '2+2=4' and '2²=4'. The four statements express true thoughts. Moreover, on the basis of 'Über Sinn und Bedeutung' and *Grundgesetze der Arithmetik*, inequalities like '5+2<9', '4+3<9' and '8-1<9' and infinitely many other inequalities corresponding to the same fact, namely, that the number 7 is smaller than the number 9, would have to be rendered as expressing different thoughts. If facts were identical with true thoughts, it would by no means be clear how indefinitely many thoughts could be identical to the same fact. Furthermore, if two thoughts, e.g., '5+2<9' and '8-1<9' were identified with the same fact, while being different from each other, the transitivity of (absolute) identity would be violated. On the other hand, if we were to identify those two thoughts – or the thoughts expressed by the statements 'The morning star is a planet' and 'The evening star is a planet' – with different facts, that could only add more confusion, since the latter distinction would be one without a difference. In any case, the identification made by Frege in 'Der Gedanke' between facts and true thoughts is hardly compatible with his notion of sense of 'Über Sinn und Bedeutung' and *Grundgesetze der Arithmetik*.

Some light can be thrown into this discussion, if we consider Frege's two letters to Husserl of 1906.[38] In the first letter Frege takes equipollency as a criterion to establish that two statements express the same thought.[39] Thus, with the help of this letter, the analogy between the explanation of conceptual content in *Begriffsschrift* and the explanation of the notion of thought present in 'Der Gedanke' is completed, since two statements are equipollent if they have the same logical – that is, syntactical – consequences.[40] Using this criterion for the identity of sense of two or more statements, Frege could say that equipollent statements correspond to the same fact, and that if they were true, the thought expressed by them would be identical to that fact. This seems to be the most plausible explanation of the enigmatic identification of true thoughts with facts.

Now, such an explanation of sense and, especially of thought, given by Frege in 'Der Gedanke' and the letter to Husserl to which I have referred, is not only similar to the explanation of conceptual content in *Begriffsschrift*, but is also surrounded by the same difficulties, mentioned at the beginning of this section, surrounding the notion of conceptual content. Most importantly, the notion of thought – and of sense – expounded in 'Der Gedanke' and the above mentioned

---

Husserl's *Logische Untersuchungen II*, U.I, to illustrate the distinction between sense and referent; as well as *Wissenschaftlicher Briefwechsel*, p. 197, letter to Peano, and pp. 234-5, letter to Russell.

[38] *Wissenschaftlicher Briefwechsel*, pp. 101-6.

[39] Ibid., p. 102.

[40] It is interesting that in the second letter Frege uses a semantic and somewhat more imprecise criterion – see *Wissenschaftlicher Briefwechsel*, pp. 105-6. Moreover, it is a pity that all of Husserl's letters to Frege of that period have been lost, since Frege was identifying notions – those of thought and conceptual content – which Husserl clearly would have differentiated.

letter is clearly different from the official notion of thought of 'Über Sinn und Bedeutung' and *Grundgesetze der Arithmetik*. According to the latter writings, '2+2=4' and '2^2=4' express different thoughts, as do statements like 'p→q' and '¬p∨q'. However, according to the letters to Husserl of 1906, they should express the same thought, as would also do the Axiom of Choice and its many and varied equivalents. Nonetheless, though it is true that – according to the notions of sense and thought of 'Über Sinn und Bedeutung' and *Grundgesetze der Arithmetik* – two statements with the same sense, that is, that express the same thought, would be equipollent, not all equipollent statements would express the same thought.

On the other hand, it should be stressed that on the basis of Frege's notion of sense in 'Über Sinn und Bedeutung' it is not clear how in the following pairs of statements the members of each pair have the same sense: (i) {'The Greeks defeated the Persians in the battle of Platea', 'The Persians were defeated by the Greeks in the battle of Platea'}; (ii) {'John gave a book to Mary', 'Mary received a book from John'}; (iii) {'9>3', '3<9'}. Let us consider the last example, though the argumentation for the other two cases is essentially the same. If on the basis of Frege's understanding of the notions of thought and, in general, of sense in 'Über Sinn und Bedeutung' and *Grundgesetze der Arithmetik*, we were to assert that '9>3' and '3<9' express the same thought, then either (i) there is no difference in sense between '>' and '<', or (ii) the reordering of the arguments in some way exactly compensates for the difference of sense between '>' and '<'. However, (i) is absurd, since if '>' and '<' had the same sense, then '9>3' and '9<3' would express the same thought. But those inequalities do not even have the same truth-value and, thus, cannot express the same thought. Nonetheless, though '>' and '<' express different senses, those senses are clearly related (as are the senses of 'to defeat' and 'to be defeated', as well as those of 'to give' and 'to receive'). We could say that they are dual senses. Now, if '9>3' and '3<9' were still to express the same thought, then (ii) above would have to be true and, thus, the reordering of the arguments would have to compensate exactly (or nullify) the difference in sense between '>' and '<'. However, on the basis of Frege's official notion of sense, that is, that of 'Über Sinn und Bedeutung' and *Grundgesetze der Arithmetik*, there is no satisfactory explanation of such a compensatory effect of the reordering of the arguments. Hence the presumed identity of the thoughts expressed by '9>3' and '3<9' – as well as the identity of the thoughts expressed by the members of the remaining two pairs of statements mentioned above – remains a complete mystery, to say the least. The mystery disappears completely if we understand by 'thought' (and by 'sense') what Frege says about such notions in his first letter to Husserl of 1906 referred to above, since it is a very plausible assumption that '9>3' and '3<9', as well as the members of the other two pairs, are equipollent. Thus, since according to that letter, two equipollent statements express the same thought, the members of each of the three pairs of statements under consideration would express the same thought, that is, would have the same sense.

The preceding discussion allows us to conclude that – very probably without being conscious of it – Frege had two different notions of sense, namely,

(i) the official notion of sense of 'Über Sinn und Bedeutung' and *Grundgesetze der Arithmetik*, discussed in section 1 of this chapter, and (ii) an unofficial and not completely clear notion of sense, rooted in his old notion of conceptual content, and present in 'Der Gedanke', the letters to Husserl of 1906 and in 'Kurze Übersicht meiner logischen Lehren',[41] written also in 1906.

5 Critical Remarks III

As we have seen in section 1 of the present chapter, in Frege's semantics the referent of a statement is a truth-value, that is, either the True or the False. Such a referent is determined both by the sense of the statement, that is, by the thought expressed by the statement, and by the referents of its constituent parts and, thus, in the case of atomic statements, by the objects and concepts that are the referents of the proper names and, respectively, the conceptual words, which are the constituent parts of the statement. In other words, the diagram presented in section 1 of the present chapter must be commutative.

Now, the problem lies not in the commutativity of the diagram, but in the last vertex of the diagram. It seems arbitrary that, on the one hand, one should assign as referent one of two truth-values to an infinite number[42] of thoughts expressible in a language and, on the other hand, that one should assign one of two truth values to a possibly finite, but in any case very large number of n-tuples of objects and concepts. It seems that the relation between thoughts and truth-values should be a more mediate one, and that between the two there are some intermediate entities that could be considered legitimate candidates to the title of referents of statements. In fact, from the semantic investigations of Edmund Husserl in *Logische Untersuchungen*,[43] *Erfahrung und Urteil*,[44] and *Vorlesungen über Bedeutungslehre*[45] we can obtain two different sorts of entities that could very well be considered the referents of statements, namely, states of affairs and what he called 'situations of affairs' [in German: *Sachlage(n)*]. To express it briefly and without digressing, states of affairs are for Husserl the facts that are described by the statements, but are categorialized, whereas the situations of affairs would be the non-categorialized facts. Let us consider an example similar to some already discussed. According to Husserl, as well as to Frege's official notion of sense, the inequalities '5+2>4' and '6+1>4' express different thoughts, since '5+2' and '6+1' are names with the same referent but different sense. However, according to Husserl the referent of the two inequalities is not a truth-value – in this case: the True – as for Frege, but a state of affairs (a categorialized fact), namely, the state of affairs that the number 7 is greater than the number 4. On the other hand, the

---

[41] In *Nachgelassene Schriften*, pp. 213-18. See pp. 213-14.
[42] I mean here 'denumerably infinite', that is, as many as there are natural numbers.
[43] *Logische Untersuchungen II*, U. I and IV.
[44] *Erfahrung und Urteil* 1939 (Hamburg, 1985), p. 285.
[45] *Vorlesungen über Bedeutungslehre* (Dordrecht, 1987). See pp. 98-102.

inequalities '7>4' and '4<7' refer to different states of affairs, which have the same situation of affairs (non-categorialized fact) as basis. Husserl would consider in a similar way some of the examples discussed in the previous section, namely, those concerning pairs of statements, one in the active mode and the other the statement obtained from it by the transformation from the active to the passive mode, as well as those concerning pairs of statements obtained from each other by replacing the verb 'to give' with the verb 'to receive', and interchanging the substantives in nominative and dative, together with the corresponding syntactic adjustments.

On the basis of the preceding point, one can ask whether Frege ever attempted to offer a justification of his choice of truth-values as the referents of statements. In fact, he did attempt this, namely, in 'Über Sinn und Bedeutung' and in his posthumous 'Einführung in die Logik', presumably written in 1906 – interestingly, in the same year of his letters to Husserl referred to above – but published only in 1969.[46] In 'Über Sinn und Bedeutung' Frege argues as follows:[47] Let us suppose that a statement has a referent. Let us then replace in such a statement an expression with another having different sense but the same referent. Such a replacement cannot have any influence on the referent of the statement. However, under such a transformation the thought related to the statement does not remain invariant. Hence, the thought cannot be the referent of the statement. Thus, the thought is the sense expressed by the statement. We can very well exclude any consideration of the referent of a statement and consider only its sense, that is, the thought expressed by it. Only our search for the truth of statements takes us from their sense to their referent. We have to look for a referent of the statement, if we are interested in the referents of its constituent parts. But we are interested in the referents of the constituent parts of a statement only if we are interested in the truth-value of the statement. Thus, we have to consider the truth-value as the referent of the statement.

In 'Einführung in die Logik' Frege argues as follows:[48] Only when we are interested in the truth of a statement, do we require that each proper name occurring in the statement have a referent. Moreover, we know that it is indifferent to the sense of a statement, that is, to the thought expressed by it, whether the constituent parts of the statement have a sense or not. There must be something different from the thought and connected with its truth, for which it is essential that the constituent parts of a statement have a referent. But the only thing for which it is essential that each of the constituent parts of the statement have a referent is for its truth-value. Hence, the referent of a statement is a truth-value.

The argumentation in 'Über Sinn und Bedeutung' as well as that in 'Einführung in die Logik' is by no means compelling. On their basis – especially on the basis of the more detailed one in 'Über Sinn und Bedeutung' – Frege can only conclude (i) that the thought is not the referent of a statement, since it does not remain invariant under the transformations of statements in statements, in

---

[46]See *Nachgelassene Schriften*, pp. 201-12.
[47]See *Kleine Schriften*, pp. 148-50.
[48]See *Nachgelassene Schriften*, pp. 210-11.

which expressions are replaced by expressions having a different sense but the same referent, and (ii) that since the truth-value remains invariant under such transformations, it is a possible candidate for the referent of statements. Frege, however, by no means establishes that it is the only possible candidate, that is, the only thing related to statements that remains invariant under such transformations. Moreover, as can be easily shown,[49] both Husserl's states of affairs and situations of affairs remain invariant under such a transformation.

It should be mentioned here that other important authors in the analytic tradition have tried to establish that only the referent remains invariant under a transformation, in which an expression is replaced by another expression having a different sense but the same referent. In particular, in his *Introduction to Mathematical Logic*,[50] Alonzo Church has argued on behalf of Frege's thesis that the truth-value is the only possible referent of statements. Nonetheless, Church considers a much broader group of transformations of statements in statements, under which only the truth-value remains invariant. However, precisely because he does not restrict his consideration to transformations of statements in statements, in which expressions are replaced by other expressions having a different sense but the same referent, his argument is by no means conclusive.[51]

6 Critical Remarks IV

In the preceding section I asked about the reasons Frege had for considering truth-values to be the referents of statements. One can also ask about the reasons he had for considering concepts as the referents of conceptual words – not as their senses – and, thus, preferring them for that role to their extensions. It should here be mentioned that not only Husserl,[52] but also their – so far as I know – only common student, Rudolf Carnap, in *Meaning and Necessity*[53] opted for the extension as the referent and the concept as the sense of what in the terminology of such authors corresponds to conceptual words. In 'Ausführungen über Sinn und Bedeutung',

---

[49]See my 'Remarks on Sense and Reference in Frege and Husserl', 1982, reprinted in Hill and Rosado Haddock, pp. 23-40.

[50]See A. Church, *Introduction to Mathematical Logic*, pp. 24-5.

[51]For a detailed refutation of Frege's argumentation, see my 'Remarks on Sense and Reference in Frege and Husserl'. See also Barwise and Perry's paper 'Semantic Innocence and Uncompromising Situations', *Midwest Studies in Philosophy VI* (Minneapolis, 1981), pp. 387-403, as well as Hermann Weidemann's paper 'Aussagesatz und Sachverhalt: ein Versuch zur Neubestimmung ihres Verhältnisses', *Grazer Philosophische Studien* 18, (1982): 75-99. For a refutation of Church's argument, see my 'To be a Fregean or to be a Husserlian: that is the Question for Platonists', 1999, reprinted also in Hill and Rosado Haddock, pp. 199-220. For a detailed discussion and refutation of the most important versions of the so-called slingshot argument, see Chapter 4 of Oswaldo Chateaubriand's excellent book *Logical Forms I* (Sao Paulo, 2003).

[52]See *Logische Untersuchungen II*, U. I, Chapter I.

[53]*Meaning and Necessity* (Chicago, 1947), p. 19.

Frege argues on behalf of his contention that concepts are the referents of statements, but – as we will soon see – such an argumentation also is by no means compelling.

Frege argues as follows:[54] Without affecting its truth, in each statement one can replace conceptual words with one another, if the same extension of a concept corresponds to them. Thus, with respect to inferences and logical laws concepts behave in a different manner only if their extensions diverge. The fundamental logical relation is that of an object falling under a concept: all other logical relations can be reduced to it. When an object falls under a concept, it falls under all other concepts having the same extension. In the same fashion in which proper names of the same object can be replaced by each other, conceptual words can also be replaced by each other, if the extension of the concept is the same.

Now, such an argument not only does not favour Frege's thesis that the referent of a conceptual word is a concept but also clearly seems to confirm the rival thesis that takes extensions as the referents of conceptual words. In fact, Frege seems to be conscious of where his argumentation really leads, adding that one could very well think of taking the extension as the referent of conceptual words, and such a choice would contain a nucleus of truth. Nonetheless, this choice is excluded by the fact that extensions of concepts are objects.[55]

It seems that what does not allow Frege to embrace the thesis that the referents of conceptual words are the extensions of concepts is just his belief – about which more will be said in the next chapter – that an unsaturated expression, as are conceptual words, needs to have an unsaturated referent – as are concepts – not a saturated one, an object, – as are extensions. But this is more of a prejudice than a ground on which Frege's choice could be based. A more weighty ground for his preference of concepts over their extensions as the referents of statements is to secure a referent for conceptual words, even in the case in which the extension of the concept is empty.

The advocates of the thesis that the referents of conceptual words are extensions of concepts, whereas concepts are senses of conceptual words, can use diverse arguments against Frege's views. Firstly, they can use precisely Frege's argumentation, since it really advocates in favour of their views against Frege's. Secondly, they can ask Frege to explain what is the sense of a conceptual word, in case it is not the concept, and they can urge Frege to give examples of replacements of conceptual words having different senses – in which case the thought expressed by the statement changes – but in such a way that the concept that corresponds to the conceptual word remains invariant. In other words, one could require Frege to show that, as in the case of proper names, the mappings from conceptual words to their respective senses and from these to the corresponding concepts are both many-one, not bijective. Frege does not give any such example, and most surely could not have given any regardless of how hard he

[54]See 'Ausführungen über Sinn und Bedeutung', in *Nachgelassene Schriften*, pp. 128-36, especially pp. 128-9.
[55]Ibid., p. 129.

had tried. Moreover, though it is true that a variation in the extensions of concepts entails a variation in the concepts, the concepts can very well vary without necessarily entailing any variation in their extensions – under the presupposition here adopted that all contexts in which the conceptual words are present are extensional. In fact, it is not difficult to find an example of the replacement of a conceptual word with another linked to a different concept, without thereby changing neither the extension of the concept or the referent of the statement. As a matter of fact, the referent of the statement remains invariant even if, contrary to Frege's choice, we choose situations of affairs, or even states of affairs as the referents of statements. Thus, let us consider the following pair of statements; (i) '2 is an even prime number', and (ii) '2 is an even number smaller than 3'. (ii) is obtained from (i) by the replacement of a conceptual word with another linked to a different concept but having the same extension of the concept, which contains the number 2 as its only member. Since the truth-value of (i) – as well as the corresponding state of affairs and the corresponding situation of affairs – remains invariant under such a replacement, the referent of the statement is not affected by a replacement of a conceptual word by another linked to a different concept but with the same extension. Hence, contrary to what Frege believed, the extension, not the concept, is the referent of the conceptual word, whereas the concept seems to be the sense expressed by the conceptual word. This last argumentation is perfectly similar to Frege's argumentation in 'Über Sinn und Bedeutung' – and mentioned in section 5 above – which intends to show that thoughts cannot be the referents of statements, but must be their senses, and is, thus, as valid as Frege's.

With respect to the difficulty that would be represented in the possibility of the extension of a concept being empty, the defenders of the rival thesis can very well stipulate that: (i) if the concept is absurd and, thus, no object can fall in its extension, then the referent of the conceptual word will be the empty extension (or empty class), and (ii) if the concept is not absurd and, thus, even if no object falls in its extension in the actual world, then there are possible worlds in which there are objects that fall in the extension of the concept. One could, e.g., take the union of the extensions of the concept in all those possible worlds – which will not be empty – as the referent of the conceptual word. If one prefers to avoid the notion of possible worlds – as Frege probably would – then the distinction between cases (i) and (ii) loses its importance, and one may very well assign as referent to every conceptual word whose sense is a concept with empty extension, precisely the empty extension. In any case, (ii) has no importance for science, and conceptual words like 'centaur' or 'unicorn', which as a matter of fact have an empty extension, could very well be excluded from the language of science, as Frege does with proper names devoid of a referent.

7 Identity Statements

In 'Über Sinn und Bedeutung' Frege introduces the notion of sense to solve the problem of assessing identity statements. At the very beginning of the paper,[56] Frege asserts that if what is expressed in an identity statement of the form 'a=b' were – as he had believed in *Begriffsschrift* – a relation between signs, then, since the connection between a sign and what is designated contains a certain arbitrariness, the truth or falsehood of such a statement would depend on such an arbitrariness. Hence, an identity statement of the form 'a=b' would always be empirical.[57] On the other hand, if such an identity statement were rendered as merely expressing that the referent of 'a' is the same as the referent of 'b', in case the statement were true, there would be no difference in cognitive value between such a statement and the statement 'a=a'.[58] Hence, 'a=b' does not express any relation of an object with itself. What distinguishes the statements 'a=a' and 'a=b' from one another – in case 'a=b' is true – and makes the cognitive value of the latter much greater than that of the former is the fact that, connected with the diversity of signs, there is a diversity in the way the designated is given. Thus, Frege concludes[59] that one should acknowledge that the sign is connected not only with the object designated by it, that is, the referent of the sign, but also with what he calls 'the sense of the sign', which is responsible for the way in which an object is given. This would explain the fact that, in general, the statements 'a=b' and 'a=a' have different cognitive value, since for the cognitive value – not the truth-value – of a statement is its sense, not its referent, which is decisive.[60]

Nonetheless, Frege is not completely explicit and does not erase all doubts concerning the content of an identity statement of the form 'a=b', or, more specifically, does not make totally clear what such a statement expresses. Thus, even in his mature writings, Frege's rendering of identity statements is not as neat as desired. On this issue, I would like to mention that in *Grundgesetze der Arithmetik*[61] Frege says that an identity statement is concerned merely with a relation of an object with itself. In general, such an unclear and sometimes even careless treatment by Frege of identity statements has originated some unacceptable renderings of his views on this issue, even by some of the most prominent Fregean scholars, e.g., giving too much importance to Frege's assertion in *Grundgesetze der Arithmetik*, while ignoring his analysis in 'Über Sinn und Bedeutung', or claiming that for Frege all identity statements of the form 'a=b' –

---

[56]See *Kleine Schriften*, p. 143.
[57]On this issue, the reader should remember Frege's definitions of 'analytic', 'synthetic', '*a priori*' and '*a posteriori*' in *Die Grundlagen der Arithmetik*, reproduced above in Chapter 2, section 3.
[58] See *Kleine Schriften*, p. 143.
[59]Ibid., p. 144.
[60]See ibid., p. 162.
[61]*Grundgesetze der Arithmetik I*, section 7, p. 11.

including those like '7-1=4+2' are synthetic.[62] Nonetheless, in the framework of Frege's semantics of sense and referent, there is only one adequate rendering of identity statements that does justice to the difference in cognitive value between identity statements of the forms 'a=a' and 'a=b', and at the same time allows for the possibility that an identity statement of the form 'a=b' be analytic, though its cognitive value is much greater than that of identity statements of the form 'a=a'. Moreover, it is precisely such a rendering that receives more textual support from 'Über Sinn und Bedeutung'. We can express it as follows: An identity statement of the form 'a=b' expresses a congruence relation between the senses of the proper names 'a' and 'b' determined by the sameness of the referent. Thus, when the referent of 'a' is the same as that of 'b', the senses of 'a' and 'b' belong to the same equivalence class, and the statement 'a=b' is true. In the contrary case, the statement is false, and the senses of 'a' and 'b', not having the same referent, belong to different equivalence classes. In the trivial case of an identity statement of the form 'a=a', it is always true and, of course, 'a' belongs to the same equivalence class as 'a' under the congruence relation '='. I will now show that all other possible interpretations of identity statements confront insurmountable difficulties.[63]

Let us consider the following six possible renderings of identity statements: (1) They express an identity relation between the two objects that are the referents of the expressions at each side of the identity sign. (2) They express the identity relation of an object with itself, which is the common referent of the expressions at each side of the identity sign. (3) They express an identity relation between the expressions at each side of the identity sign. (4) They express a congruence relation, determined by the sameness of referent, between the expressions at each side of the identity sign. (5) They express an identity relation between the senses of the expressions at each side of the identity sign. (6) They express a congruence relation, determined by the sameness of referent, between the senses of the expressions at each side of the identity sign. We will see that renderings (1)-(5) are unsustainable.

According to (1), identity statements express an identity relation between two objects that are the referents of the expressions at each side of the identity sign. But if they are two objects, then one cannot properly talk about identity. They could not have exactly the same properties, since each one of them, e.g., the object referred to by 'a', would have the property of not being the other, namely, the object referred to by 'b', and this property of not being the object referred to by 'b'

---

[62]An example of the first kind of misunderstanding is Michael Dummett's *Frege: Philosophy of Language*, p. 544, whereas Hans Sluga offers a good example of the second kind of misunderstanding, which is by no means limited to Sluga. See, e.g., his 'Semantic Content and Cognitive Sense', in L. Haaparanta and J. Hintikka (eds), *Frege Synthesized* (Dordrecht, 1986), pp. 47-64, especially p. 60.

[63]For a more detailed discussion of this issue, see my paper 'Identity Statements in the Semantics of Sense and Reference', in *Logique et Analyse* 100, 1982, reprinted in Hill and Rosado Haddock, pp. 41-51.

could not be a property of the object referred to by 'b', since no object is different from itself. In fact, according to Leibniz's Principle of the Indiscernibility of Identicals, to which Frege adheres, if two objects have exactly the same properties, they are one and the same object. Moreover, on the basis of such a rendering, there could at most be a partial identity between two objects or, more precisely, an identity in some aspect. In such a case, one would have to explain in which aspect are the two objects identical, and to establish this, one could not rest on the corresponding statement, if one wants to avoid a vicious circle. Furthermore, it could very well be the case that the referent of 'a' is identical in some determined aspect to the referent of 'b', while being identical in a completely different aspect to the referent of 'c'. In such a case, the statements 'a=b' and 'b=c' would be true, but the statement 'a=c' would be false, thus violating the transitivity of identity. Moreover, under such a rendering, the identity sign would be ambiguous.

According to (2), identity statements express the identity relation of an object with itself. On the basis of such a rendering, there would not be a difference in cognitive value between an identity statement of the form 'a=a' and one of the form 'a=b', in case the latter were true. Moreover, on the basis of such a rendering, every true identity statement of the form 'a=b' would be necessarily true, since it is true in all possible worlds that all objects are identical with themselves. Hence 'the morning star = the evening star' would be as necessary as 'Venus = Venus'. On the other hand, one could ask the defenders of (2) whether a false statement of the form 'a=b' expresses the identity of an object with itself or not. If it were to express the identity of an object with itself, it could not be false. In such a case, all statements of the form 'a=b' would have to be necessarily true. If it were to express something different than a true statement of the form 'a=b', what is expressed by an identity statement of the form 'a=b' would be a (non-constant) function of its truth-value. But this is simply absurd.

According to (3), an identity statement expresses an identity relation between expressions. However, in such a case all identity statements of the form 'a=b' would be false, since 'a' and 'b' are different expressions. Even a triviality like 'London = Londres' would be false on the basis of such a rendering. Only identity statements of the form 'a=a' would be true (and this only under the assumption that we are considering expression-types and not expression-tokens). Thus, this rendering also leads to untenable consequences.

According to (4), an identity statement expresses a congruence relation, determined by the sameness of referent, between the expressions at each side of the identity sign. Thus, (4) is essentially Frege's view on this issue in *Begriffsschrift*. However, the relation between an expression and its referent is arbitrary. Hence, we could never establish either the truth or the falsity of an identity statement of the form 'a=b' only by means of an analysis of its constituent parts or derive it, in case it were true, only from logical laws, or even from general laws, logical or not. Therefore, on the basis of such a rendering, all identity statements of the form 'a=b' would be synthetic and, moreover, empirical, since dependent on the empirical fact that the convention under which the expression 'a' is linked with a referent and the convention under which the expression 'b' is linked with a referent have their second term, that is, the referent, in common. Hence, on the one hand, it is arbitrary and conventional that the Romans used the sign 'vii' to refer to the number 7, and it is also arbitrary and conventional that we use the sign '7' to refer to the number 7; but it is an empirical fact that 'vii' and '7' refer to the same number. Thus, even statements like 'vii=7', '$2^2 = 4$' and 'London = Londres' would be synthetic *a posteriori* under such a rendering.[64]

According to (5), identity statements express an identity relation between senses. But in such a case, if 'a' and 'b' are expressions with different senses, an identity statement of the form 'a=b' would be false. Thus, the statements 'Hesperus = Phosphorus', 'the morning star = the evening star' and '3+2 =5' would be false. Clearly, such a rendering clashes directly with Frege's analysis of identity statements. Only identity statements like 'London = London', 'London = Londres' and 'France's capital = die Hauptstadt Frankreichs', whose sides express the same sense, would be true.

On the basis of the preceding argumentation, one can conclude that none of the renderings (1)-(5) of identity statements in a semantics of sense and referent is acceptable. Only rendering (6) avoids all the difficulties mentioned above, and, moreover, does justice to Frege's analysis.[65]

---

[64]In the last example, the conventional component seems to disappear, since it was not as a result of a stipulation, but of language evolution, that English speakers began to call the city of London 'London' or that Spanish speakers began to call it 'Londres'. However, the arbitrary and the empirical components are present in that example as well as in the others, and, thus, my analysis is in no way stymied by such an inessential difference.

[65]A discussion similar to the above is presented in my paper mentioned in footnote 62, which also contains a critique, based on that analysis, of Kripke's views on identity statements. See also my paper 'Necessità a posteriori e contingenze a priori in Kripke: alcune note critiche', in *Nominazione*, 2, (1981): 205-19.

Chapter 5

The Basic Distinctions II:
Function and Object

1 The Nature of Functions

In Chapter 1 of this work, we saw that in *Begriffsschrift* Frege distinguished between variable constituents of sentences and constituents that remain invariant with regard to such changes. Frege called 'function' that part of the sentence that remains constant through change, and 'argument' the part that changes. More precisely, functions have empty places filled sometimes by an argument, sometimes by other arguments. Thus, in *Begriffsschrift* functions are conceived in a syntactic fashion. They are some kind of incomplete expression, with empty places to be filled by their arguments.

In Frege's mature writings functions experience an ontologization. They are not conceived any more as a kind of expression with empty places, but as a sort of entities, namely, as one of the two fundamental sorts of entities, objects being the other fundamental sort. Objects are complete, or saturated entities, which do not require any complementation, whereas functions are incomplete, or unsaturated entities, which require complementation. When a function is saturated, a new saturated entity, that is, an object, results.[1]

Functions are for Frege the possible referents of one of the two basic sorts of expressions, namely, functional expressions, which are conceived in a fashion similar to how functions were conceived in *Begriffsschrift*. They are essentially incomplete, or unsaturated expressions, having empty places, which need to be filled by proper names, that is, by names of objects. Proper names, on the other hand, have no empty places. They are saturated. When the empty places of a functional expression are filled with proper names, we obtain a saturated expression, a proper name of an object. This object is the value of the function for the argument whose name filled the empty places of the functional expression that refers to the function.

Thus, according to Frege, there is on the side of the expressions a perfectly similar structure and categorization as on the ontological side. Saturated expressions – proper names – correspond to saturated entities – objects – referred to by them, whereas unsaturated expressions – functional expressions – correspond to unsaturated entities – functions – referred to by them. Moreover, to the saturation

---

[1] See, for example, 'Funktion und Begriff', in *Kleine Schriften*, pp. 125-42.

of a function by saturated entities, which produces a new saturated entity – the value of the function – there corresponds the saturation of the corresponding functional expression by the corresponding proper names, which gives rise to the proper name of the value of the function.

This correspondence is even more harmonious, since to the saturated expressions correspond not only saturated referents, but also saturated senses, and to unsaturated expressions correspond not only unsaturated referents, but also unsaturated senses. Nonetheless, the distinction between saturated and unsaturated senses does not receive the same attention as the corresponding distinctions on the side of expressions and on the ontological side.[2]

Now, not all functions have a single argument. There are functions of two or more arguments. Frege calls functions having two arguments 'doubly unsaturated'. Their saturation by an object does not eliminate the unsaturation, but diminishes it by its transformation into a simple unsaturation. To eliminate such an unsaturation, an object is still required. The saturation of doubly unsaturated functions by an ordered pair of objects gives rise to a new object, which is the value of the function for such an ordered pair of objects as arguments.[3] Something similar occurs at the level of senses and at the level of expressions. The corresponding sense will be doubly unsaturated, and the corresponding expression will also be doubly unsaturated. To saturate them both the sense and the expression would require a double saturation. Such a doubly unsaturated expression will have two different empty argument places – which should be clearly distinguished from two occurrences of the same empty argument place in the expression – and would require not one but two proper names to obtain a saturated expression. The insertion of a proper name in one of the two empty argument places of the expression would merely reduce but not eliminate the unsaturation. Something similar would occur with a doubly unsaturated sense.

Frege's notion of function is considerably broad. In contrast with current set-theoretical mathematics, according to which a function of one argument is a relation of two arguments uniquely determined in its second argument and, in general, a function of n arguments is a relation of n+1 arguments uniquely determined in its last argument – hence, making functions special cases of relations – for Frege both concepts and relations are special cases of functions. For Frege, a concept is a function of one argument, whose value is always a truth-value, that is, either the True or the False. Similarly, a (dyadic) relation is a function of two arguments, whose value is always a truth-value.[4]

On the side of expressions – as well as on the side of senses – we have a corresponding situation. Both conceptual words and relational expressions are

---

[2]In fact, it is not clear what are the senses of function expressions and, especially, of conceptual words. See on this issue section 6 of the previous chapter.

[3]Subtraction and division functions among integers, as well as asymmetrical relations – see the next paragraph – make it clear that the pairs of arguments have to be ordered.

[4]Frege usually discusses only dyadic relations, but it is clear that similar considerations apply to relations of any finite number of arguments.

special cases of functional expressions, and are, thus, unsaturated, that is, they contain empty argument places. When the empty argument places of such expressions are filled with proper names – one in the case of conceptual words, two in the case of (dyadic) relational expressions – a statement is obtained, which is a saturated expression and, thus, a proper name of an object, in this case a truth-value, either the True or the False.

Since concepts and relations are functions, they are not only entities, but also entities of a completely different nature from that of objects. They are unsaturated entities requiring a complementation by saturated entities. Both the saturation of a concept and the double saturation of a (dyadic) relation give rise to an object which is a truth value, namely, the True when the object falls under the concept (or, respectively, the ordered pair of objects is in the relation), or the False when the object does not fall under the concept (respectively, the ordered pair is not in the relation). Frege frequently calls this unsaturated nature of concepts and relations their 'predicative nature'.[5]

Finally, it should be mentioned that both in 'Funktion und Begriff'[6] and in *Grundgesetze der Arithmetik*[7] Frege explicitly considers functions whose arguments are functions, thus, taking the first decisive steps for the development of a hierarchy of functions. In fact, as we have seen in Chapter 1, already in *Begriffsschrift* Frege considers functions whose arguments are functions, though he is less explicit about the possibility of developing a hierarchy of functions.[8] At the first level of the hierarchy there are functions of one or more arguments, whose arguments are objects: the first level functions. There are also functions of one or more arguments, whose arguments are first level functions, that is, functions of objects: the second level functions. There are also functions – Frege mentions only two sorts in section 24 and again in section 31 of *Grundgesetze der Arithmetik* – of one or more arguments, whose arguments are second level functions: the third level functions. In principle, there remains the possibility of extending the hierarchy of functions, by introducing functions of nth level, for any positive integer n. Moreover, Frege also considers functions of two or more arguments, whose arguments are of different levels. Thus, we can obtain a somewhat more complex hierarchy than the former, of what could be called mixed functions. There can, for example, be a function of two arguments, one of whose arguments is an object and the other a first level concept, or a function of three arguments, one of

---

[5]See, for example, 'Über Begriff und Gegenstand', in *Kleine Schriften*, pp. 167-78.
[6]'Funktion und Begriff', in *Kleine Schriften*, pp. 141-2.
[7]See *Grundgesetze der Arithmetik I*, section 31, pp. 48-9.
[8]See Chapter 1, section 9 above. In contrast to *Begriffsschrift*, in *Grundgesetze der Arithmetik* there are third level functions, that is, functions, whose arguments are functions having functions as arguments.

whose arguments is an object, another a first level function, and the remaining one a second level function.[9]

2 The Predicative Nature of Concepts

In the preceding section we have seen that both concepts and relations are special cases of functions, namely, functions whose value is always a truth-value. Thus, they have in common with the remaining functions that peculiar property of unsaturation, which – as already mentioned in the preceding section – in the special case of concepts (and relations) Frege frequently calls the predicative nature of concepts. In contrast with functions, objects are saturated entities and, thus, of a completely different nature than concepts.

On the side of expressions, there is also a fundamental difference between proper names, whose referents are objects, and conceptual words, whose referents are concepts. The predicative nature of conceptual words distinguishes them from proper names. Hence, in a statement neither a proper name can be replaced by a conceptual word nor a conceptual word can be replaced by a proper name, without affecting the sentential nature of the statement. The result of either of such substitutions does not form a statement, since its parts do not glue together.

Now, due to the fact that natural languages are not uniquely determined by logical considerations, and suffer also psychological and, in general, empirical determinations, one has sometimes the false impression that substitutions as the above are possible. The fact of the matter, according to Frege, is that such empirical influence tends to hide the underlying logical structures. As Frege repeatedly underscores,[10] the task of philosophy is the continuous battle with everything psychological in language and with grammar itself, since both tend to hide logical relations. Thus, it should be perfectly clear why Frege concedes such an importance to the construction of an artificial language, the concept-script, for conveying the logical relations unadulterated by anything empirical, an importance that he extends to all the exact sciences. Nonetheless, in general, Frege seems to coincide with the Husserl of *Logische Untersuchungen*[11] and elsewhere, and the Wittgenstein of the *Tractatus Logico-Philosophicus*[12] in believing that there is some sort of logical nucleus in natural language.

---

[9]See *Grundgesetze der Arithmetik I*, sections 21-3, pp. 36-41, where Frege introduces examples of functions of different sorts from the beginning of the hierarchy, including a concrete one of a third level function on p. 41, end of section 23.

[10]See, for example, *Begriffsschrift*, pp. XII-XIII, as well as his late 'Erkenntnisquellen der Mathematik und der mathematischen Naturwissenschaften', in *Nachgelassene Schriften*, pp. 286-94, especially pp. 288-9.

[11]See *Logische Untersuchungen II*, U. IV. See also, for example, *Formale und transzendentale Logik* (1929, Den Haag, 1974), Beilage I, and *Vorlesungen über Bedeutungslehre* (Dordrecht, 1987).

[12]See *Tractatus Logico-Philosophicus* (1922, German original, *Logisch-philosophische Abhandlung*, 1921, bilingual edition, London, 1961).

Let us consider, for example, the following two statements: 'The Morning Star is a planet' and 'The Morning Star is Venus'. Superficially, it would seem that the two statements have the same structure and that, thus, a conceptual word – a planet – and a proper name Venus – can be replaced by each other in statements without anomaly. But such a similarity is superficial, and hides a profound structural difference. In the statement 'The Morning Star is a planet' the particle 'is' is the so-called copula, which serves to express that an object falls under the concept. In fact, as already mentioned,[13] for Frege, the presence of the indefinite article in the singular – as in 'a planet' – serves to indicate that the referent is a concept, whereas the presence of the definite article – as in 'the Morning Star' – serves to indicate that the referent is an object. On the other hand, in the statement 'The Morning Star is Venus' the particle 'is' serves to express an identity – it is a sort of abbreviation for 'is identical with' – and the whole statement expresses an equation. More precisely, the statement is an identity statement and – as shown in section 7 of the preceding chapter – expresses a congruence relation between the senses of the two proper names at the sides of the identity sign. However, we could reinterpret such a statement by means of a reinterpretation of the particle 'is' as a copula. But in such a case the predicate would be 'is Venus' or, more explicitly, 'is nothing else than Venus', of which the proper name 'Venus' is only a part. But here there is no anomaly, since the fundamental difference between proper names and conceptual words does not exclude that a proper name occur as part of a conceptual word or that a conceptual word occur as part of a proper name. Thus, for example, the conceptual word 'teacher' occurs as part of the proper name 'the teacher of Alexander the Great', whereas the proper name 'Frege' occurs as part of the conceptual word 'sibling of Frege'. That which is excluded is that a proper name occur as the whole predicate of the statement, and that a conceptual word occur as the whole subject of a predication, in which usually proper names occur, since what can be asserted of an object cannot be asserted of a concept.

In natural languages there are uses that could originate serious confusions, for example, when we want to talk about a concept, let us say following Frege, the concept of being a horse, briefly, the concept 'horse'. In such a case, Frege says in 'Über Begriff und Gegenstand',[14] we properly do not predicate anything about a concept, since the referent of the expression 'the concept ''horse''' is not a concept but an object. A similar situation presents itself when we try to talk about relations. For example, the expression 'the kindred relation' does not refer to a relation but to an object. Although such examples produce some sort of tension in natural language, they do not abolish the distinction between conceptual word and proper name, or between concept and object, and simply serve to make us conscious of the fact that natural language is not the best vehicle for logical communication of thoughts.

---

[13]For example, in section 2 of Chapter 3.

[14]See *Kleine Schriften*, pp. 167-78. See also 'Ausführungen über Sinn und Bedeutung', in *Nachgelassene Schriften*, pp. 127-36.

It should be mentioned here that Frege does not explain what are the objects that substitute concepts (and relations) when we want to talk about them by means of expressions like 'the concept "horse"'. This unclearness has given rise to the postulation by some Fregean scholars of some mysterious objects.[15] As already mentioned in Chapter 3, I consider such an *ad hoc* hypothesis completely unnecessary, since due to the strict relation between a concept and its extension, it seems perfectly reasonable that the extensions of concepts are the objects referred to when we try to talk about concepts – and the value ranges of the functions, in general, when we try to talk about functions. (In the special case of relations, the referents would be double extensions, or sets of ordered pairs that are in the corresponding relations.) This contention receives a decisive support from the footnote in section 68 of *Die Grundlagen der Arithmetik*, in which Frege asserts that one could perfectly well replace the expression 'the extension' in the definition of number by the expression 'the concept'. This is so because the expression 'the concept' refers to the extension of the concept, not to the concept. If it would refer to any other object different from the extension of the concept, such a replacement would have affected the meaning – both sense and referent – of the expression, and probably the truth-value of the statement.[16] Briefly, the postulation of such mysterious objects would seem to have been introduced exclusively to defend the distinction between concept and object from criticisms like those of Kerry, whereas the much more natural interpretation here propounded has independent support in a writing that antecedes Kerry's critique.[17]

According to Frege, it is possible to predicate something about a concept. However, such a predication is of a different level than the usual predications about objects. Concepts are functions, and not all functions that are concepts are of first level. There are concepts of second level, whose arguments are concepts of first level. An example of a concept of second level is existence. Thus, existence is predicated of concepts and, hence, not of objects. When we say, 'There exists a square root of 4', to use Frege's example, we do not say anything about a definite number, neither about 2 nor about -2 (nor about any other number), but simply assert the non-emptiness of the concept 'square root of 4'. When we assert that there exists a great philosopher, we do not say anything about Plato or Aristotle, or any other philosopher, but simply assert that the concept of 'great philosopher' is non-empty. The predication of a second level concept of one of first level is similar to, but different from, that of a first level concept of an object. Hence, to underscore both the similarity and the difference, Frege says that an object falls

---

[15]See, for example, the references to some writings of M. Schirn in footnote 57 to section 5 of Chapter 3.

[16]The objection that the interpretation given above would be prone to an infinite regress is completely unfounded, since to speak about the extension of the extension of a concept is nonsense.

[17]The discussion of this issue will be completed below, after the introduction of Frege's notion of a second level concept. See also Chapter 3, section 5 above, where some relevant literature is mentioned.

under a first level concept and that a first level concept falls in a second level concept.[18]

As mentioned some paragraphs back, the interpretation given by Frege in 'Über Begriff und Gegenstand' of presumed counterexamples to his distinction between concept and object, for example, the statement 'The concept "horse" is a non-trivial concept', is not completely clear. Moreover, it is not free of serious difficulties. According to Frege, 'the concept "horse"' is a proper name and its referent is an object that replaces the concept that is the referent of the conceptual word 'horse' and is strictly related to the concept in some unspecified way. I have argued above that such an unspecified object is the extension of the concept, and that the *ad hoc* postulation of mysterious objects can only multiply the difficulties. However, Frege himself seemed not to be completely satisfied with his answer in that famous paper to Kerry's critique, and in his posthumously published 'Ausführungen über Sinn und Bedeutung'[19] suggests the replacement of the expression 'the concept "horse"' by the much less natural phrase 'what the conceptual word "horse" refers to'. Thus, the expression 'the concept "horse"' could be seen as a sort of abbreviation for the phrase 'what the conceptual word "horse" refers to'. Now, in view of the hierarchy of functions – and, thus, of concepts – the above two expressions cannot be replaced by one another in statements without making some corresponding adjustments. If the statement 'The concept "horse" is a trivial concept' is to have any sense, the expression 'is a trivial concept' has to refer to a first level concept, since the expression 'the concept "horse"' refers to an object. If, on the other hand, the statement 'What the conceptual word "horse" refers to is a trivial concept' is to have any sense, the expression 'is a trivial concept' has to refer to a second level concept, since 'what the concept "horse" refers to' refers to a first level concept. This last rendering of the phrase 'is a trivial concept' seems intuitively more adequate. In this fashion the statement 'What the conceptual word "horse" refers to is a trivial concept' would be expressing that the concept which is the referent of the conceptual word 'horse' falls in the second level concept 'trivial concept'. In such a case, one would have to render the statement 'The concept "horse" is a trivial concept' as an inadequate abbreviation – and strictly devoid of sense – of the statement 'What the conceptual word "horse" refers to is a trivial concept', or one would have to assign the expression 'the concept "horse"' a first level concept as referent, not an object. The latter would be inconsistent with Fregean logico-linguistic strictures, forcing us to abandon Frege's linguistic criterion that the presence of the definite article in the singular is an indicator that the expression following the article is a proper name. Of course, Frege does not opt for such a solution to the difficulties presented by Kerry, though it would have seemed very natural from a non-Fregean standpoint. In fact, Frege's solution is also less compelling than the solution mentioned above, which takes the statement 'The concept "horse" is a trivial concept' as a mere abbreviation, strictly devoid of sense, of the statement 'What the conceptual word

---

[18]See 'Über Begriff und Gegenstand', p. 174.
[19]'Ausführungen über Sinn und Bedeutung', p. 133.

"horse" refers to is a trivial concept'. Briefly, the difficulties besieging Frege are the following: (1) He asserts that an expression like 'the concept "horse"' does not denote a concept, but an unsatisfactorily explained related object, which has to be the extension of the concept, if one wants to avoid bigger problems. (2) But even if we avoid those problems, to make sense of the statement 'The concept "horse" is a trivial concept', Frege has to render the conceptual word 'trivial concept' as a first level conceptual word referring to a first level concept, though the concept referred to by the expression 'trivial concept' seems intuitively to be a second level concept, in whose extension first level concepts fall. (3) Contrary to what Frege asserts in 'Ausführungen über Sinn und Bedeutung', regardless of whether we render the conceptual word 'trivial concept' as a first level or as a second level conceptual word, either the statement 'The concept "horse" is a trivial concept' or the statement 'What the conceptual word "horse" refers to is a trivial concept' is devoid of sense. That is, if 'trivial concept' is a second order conceptual word, the first statement is devoid of sense – since it would be predicating a second order concept of an object – and if 'trivial concept' is a first level conceptual word, the latter statement would be devoid of sense since it would be predicating a first level concept of a first level concept. Hence, Frege does not adequately answer Kerry's objections. I will continue, however, with the exposition of Frege's views.

Both the relation of an object falling under a first level concept as the relation of a first level concept falling in a second level concept differ radically from the relation of subordination of a concept to another concept. The latter relation is one between concepts, but between concepts of the same level. For example, in the statements 'All squares are rectangles' and 'All tigers are felines' what is expressed is that the first concept is subordinated to the second one, that is, that the extension of the first concept is contained in the extension of the other concept. In such statements nothing is said about particular objects, squares, tigers, rectangles, felines or whatever, but about the relation of subordination of a concept to another concept, whose extension then contains that of the first one. The relation of subordination between concepts does not have to be proper subordination. Thus, it is possible that the extensions of the two concepts coincide. In such a case, Frege speaks of mutual subordination. Thus, when all Y are X, and all X are Y, we have the relation of mutual subordination between the concepts X and Y. In such a case, the extension of the concept X is identical with the extension of the concept Y. Extensions are objects and, thus, the identity relation can be applied to them. Mutual subordination does not apply to objects, but applies to concepts. It is the relation for entities of a predicative nature that corresponds to identity, but it is not identity.

A first level concept is a property of an object that falls under it. Similarly, a second level concept is a property of a first level concept that falls in it. On the other hand, if a first level concept X is subordinated to another first level concept Y, then Y is a note of the concept X and a property of the objects that fall under X. Thus, one should clearly distinguish between note [in German: *Merkmal*] and property. If we have the concepts $X_1,...,X_n$, $n \geq 2$, we can obtain the new concept Z such that an object w falls under Z if and only if w falls under exactly

$X_1,\ldots,X_n$. In such a case, all X_i, i=1,…n, are properties of w, and notes of Z, but are not properties of Z. Only a second level concept could be a property of Z. Thus, if Z is a first level concept, for a concept Y to be a property of Z it is a necessary, though not a sufficient condition for Y that it be a second level concept. On the other hand, for Y to be a note of the first level concept Z, it is a necessary, but not a sufficient condition for Y that it be a first level concept. Hence, Y can never be both a property and a note of Z. Of course, Y could be at the same time both note and property. It could be a note of the first level concept Z and, if Z does not have an empty extension, it would be a property of the objects that fall under Z. However, this possibility not only does not blur the distinction, but also reaffirms and clarifies it.

Finally, it should be mentioned that, as in his early (and later) writings, Frege requires of every first level concept, of every first level relation and, in general, of every first level function not only that it be defined for all objects, but that it be clearly demarcated, that is, that, for example, in the case of concepts it could be decided if any given object falls or does not fall under it. In fact, Frege does not establish any hierarchy of objects parallel to that of functions. Moreover, he equates the requirement that each and every first level function of a scientific language be defined and clearly demarcated for each and every object with the *Tertium non Datur.*[20]

This last point brings to the fore a sort of logical objects that play a decisive role both in the edification of Frege's logical system in *Grundgesetze der Arithmetik* and in its demise. As we shall later see, Frege's above mentioned requirement has to be applicable to these logical objects. Here lies the Achilles' heel of Frege's logical system, the source of the Zermelo-Russell Paradox.

3 Value Ranges

In his 1891 paper 'Funktion und Begriff' Frege introduces a notion that could be considered the greatest novelty of the logical system of *Grundgesetze der Arithmetik* with respect to that of *Begriffsschrift*, namely, the value ranges [in German: *Wertverlauf*]. Value ranges have for Frege a decisive importance, since he considers them a generalization of the notion of the extension of a concept, and this view will allow him to express with full generality the notorious Axiom V of *Grundgesetze der Arithmetik*, that is, precisely the principle that – together with other features of Frege's logico-philosophical views – will give rise to the Zermelo-Russell Paradox.

In the introductory informal discussion of the logical system of *Grundgesetze der Arithmetik*[21] Frege asserts that the words 'the function $\Phi(\xi)$ has the same value range as the function $\Psi(\xi)$' have the same referent as the words 'the functions $\Phi(\xi)$ and $\Psi(\xi)$ have for the same argument always the same value'. It

[20]See, for example, *Grundgesetze der Arithmetik II*, section 56, p. 69.
[21]*Grundgesetze der Arithmetik I*, section 3, p. 7.

should here be mentioned that in 'Funktion und Begriff'[22] Frege asserts that the two above mentioned statements express the same sense, an assertion that is much stronger than that made in *Grundgesetze der Arithmetik*. This will become important in the discussion of some difficulties, which I will consider in the next section. In any case, what Frege wants to secure is the transformation of the generality of an equation in an equation between value ranges, and vice versa. That is precisely the content of Axiom V, which in non-Fregean notation reads as follows:

$$[\hat{u}\Phi(u)=\hat{a}\Psi(a)]=(\forall x)(\Phi(x)=\Psi(x))$$

The expression '$(\forall x)(\Phi(x)=\Psi(x))$' asserts that for each argument x, the functions $\Phi(\xi)$ and $\Psi(\xi)$ have the same value. On the other hand, the expression '$[\hat{u}\Phi(u)=\hat{a}\Psi(a)]$' asserts that the value ranges of the functions $\Phi(\xi)$ and $\Psi(\xi)$ are one and the same. It should be observed that, in contrast to functions, value ranges are objects, and, thus, we can talk about the equality of value ranges. Hence, Axiom V asserts that the generality of an equation between the values of two functions for the same argument means the same as the claim that the objects that are the value ranges of the two functions are one and the same – where 'means' should be rendered as 'refers to', if we are discussing *Grundgesetze der Arithmetik*, and as 'expresses the same sense', if we are discussing 'Funktion und Begriff'. In this fashion, the introduction of a special notation for value ranges in the logical system of *Grundgesetze der Arithmetik* and Axiom V allow us to transform, with all generality, any arbitrary expression for functions in a proper name of the corresponding value range.

If the function is a concept, Frege speaks of the extension of the concept instead of the value range of the concept. Thus, extensions of concepts are value ranges of functions of one argument, whose value is a truth-value. It should be mentioned here that in the very special case of a conceptual word that refers to a concept under which exactly one object falls, besides the name for the value range, Frege introduces in *Grundgesetze der Arithmetik* an expression that has as a referent the unique object that falls under the concept. Such a name is obtained from the variable, for example, ξ, by prefixing it the symbol '\'. Thus, the resulting expression '\ξ' will play a similar role in Frege's logical system as the definite article in natural languages having such a tool.[23]

The preceding discussion has not made the notion of a value range completely clear. As we will see shortly, that notion as well as Axiom V, offer some serious difficulties. In fact, Frege himself was not totally unaware of possible difficulties, since some passages of *Grundgesetze der Arithmetik I*[24] seem to indicate that he saw that notorious principle as a sort of necessary evil that he would have preferred avoiding. Moreover, Frege's Epilogue to the second

---

[22]'Funktion und Begriff', p. 130.
[23]See *Grundgesetze der Arithmetik I*, section 11, pp. 18-20.
[24]Ibid., p. VII.

volume,[25] written after Russell had communicated to him the derivation of the Zermelo-Russell Paradox in his logical system, leaves little doubt about it.

It should be observed first that Axiom V does not completely determine value ranges. Frege is perfectly conscious of this fact, and even shows it convincingly with the help of the so-called permutation argument of section 10 of *Grundgesetze der Arithmetik*, which essentially shows that given two functions $\Phi(\xi)$ and $\Psi(\xi)$ for which Axiom V holds and, thus, their courses of values are one and the same, one can find a function $\vartheta(\xi)$ that never has the same value for different arguments, and is such that:

$$[\vartheta(\hat{u}\Phi(u))=\vartheta(\hat{a}\Psi(a))=[(\forall x)(\Phi x)=\Psi(x))]$$

Moreover, as Frege clearly expresses it,[26] such a principle allows us to recognize a value range only when it is referred to by a name of the form '$\hat{u}\Phi(u)$', but we cannot decide whether an object that is not thus given is a value range or not, or to what function it corresponds. More generally, we cannot decide whether or not a value range has a property, except if we already know that the property is linked to a property of the corresponding function.

As stressed by Christian Thiel[27] and Michael Resnik,[28] the introduction of value ranges in *Grundgesetze der Arithmetik* is very similar to the second attempt at defining number in *Die Grundlagen der Arithmetik*. Incidentally, Axiom V seems like a contextual definition of value ranges,[29] and the difficulties mentioned by Frege and reproduced in the preceding paragraph are essentially the same that affected such an attempt. In both cases, what Fregean scholars have named the 'Julius Caesar Problem' plays an important role. However, though the difficulties encountered by the second attempt at defining number were sufficient to force the abandonment of such an attempt, he does not make a similar decision in the case of Axiom V. Frege seems to consider that since Axiom V is not a definition, he does not need to eliminate with one stroke such sort of indetermination mentioned above, but can proceed stepwise, eliminating such an indetermination in the case of each single function through stipulations made when introducing the function in the system, that fix the values that the function is going to have for value ranges as arguments.[30] Since, on the other hand, Frege identifies truth-values with particular

---

[25] *Grundgesetze der Arithmetik II*, Nachwort, pp. 253-65, especially p. 253.

[26] *Grundgesetze der Arithmetik I*, section 10, p.16.

[27] See his 'Wahrheitswert und Wertverlauf', in Matthias Schirn (ed), *Studies on Frege I*, pp. 287-99, especially p. 291.

[28] See his *Frege and the Philosophy of Mathematics* (Ithaca, 1980), p. 209.

[29] Although it looks like a definition, Frege explicitly rejects this possibility in *Grundgesetze der Arithmetik II*, section 146. Moreover, if Axiom V were really a definition, it would violate both the requisite of completeness for any object – see ibid., section 56 – and the requisite of the simplicity of the term in the role of *definiendum* – see ibid., section 66. On the issue of definitions, see section 5 of the next chapter.

[30] See *Grundgesetze der Arithmetik I*, section 10, pp. 16-18.

value ranges, namely, the True with the value range û(—u) of the function —ξ, whose value is the True only when its argument is the True, and whose value is the False for all other arguments, and the False with the value range û(u= [¬(∀x)(x=x)]) of the function ξ=[¬(∀x)(x=x)], whose value is the True when its argument is not the True, and is the False when its argument is the True, Frege does not need to presuppose value ranges other than truth-values.[31] Hence, if the introduction of each and every function in the logical system were accompanied by a stipulation of the values of the function for value ranges as arguments, the indetermination mentioned above would disappear. However, as we will shortly see, this is not the only sort of indetermination besieging Axiom V.

4 Some Difficulties

In *Grundgesetze der Arithmetik* Frege states that Axiom V, namely, $\vdash[\hat{u}\Phi(u)=\hat{a}\Psi(a)]=[(\forall x)(\Phi(x)=\Psi(x))]$, expresses in symbolic language that the statements 'Function $\Phi(\xi)$ has the same vakue range as function $\Psi(\xi)$' and 'Functions $\Phi(\xi)$ and $\Psi(\xi)$ always have for the same argument the same value' have the same 'meaning' (in German: *sind gleichbedeutend*).[32] According to Frege's technical use of the word *Bedeutung*, which is usually rendered into English either as reference, denotation or – as I prefer – as referent, the two sides of Axiom V would have the same referent. More precisely, on the basis of the only acceptable rendering of identity statements in a semantics of sense and reference, expounded in the preceding chapter, Axiom V would be expressing the claim that the senses at each side of the principal identity sign have the same referent, that is, that they are congruent modulo sameness of referent. According to this rendering – as well as to the renderings (2) and (4) discussed and rejected in Chapter 4 – an identity statement is true if the proper names at the sides of the identity sign have the same object as referent, regardless of whether their senses differ. In the special case of an identity statement between statements – as is the case of Axiom V – the preceding condition reduces to the condition that the two statements have the same truth-value, since in Fregean semantics the referents of statements are truth-values. Thus, in order for Axiom V to be true – as is presupposed in the logical system of *Grundgesetze der Arithmetik* – it would suffice that the truth value of '$\hat{u}\Phi(u)=\hat{a}\Psi(a)$' be the same as that of '$(\forall x)(\Phi(x)=\Psi(x))$', that is, that both are the True or that both are the False. However, there are $\aleph_0$ different statements in *Grundgesetze der Arithmetik* having the same truth-value as '$(\forall x)(\Phi(x)=\Psi(x))$', namely, all theorems, if the referent of '$(\forall x)(\Phi(x)=\Psi(x))$' is the True, or all negations of theorems, if the referent is the False. Hence, on the basis of the only rendering of identity statements in Fregean semantics that is free of difficulties – and even on the basis of the rejected renderings (2) and (4) – Axiom V remains

---

[31] Ibid., pp. 17-18.
[32] Ibid., section 3, p. 7.

completely undetermined in a much more radical sense than that envisaged by Frege.

If to eliminate such a total indetermination, one were to try to render Axiom V as expressing an identity between the senses of the two statements at the sides of the principal identity sign – which, as I mentioned above, was Frege's rendering two years earlier in 'Funktion und Begriff' – in which case the verbal expression *sind gelichbedeutend* would be rendered in a non-Fregean fashion as 'have the same sense',[33] the following difficulties would come to the fore. (i) This rendering is not easily reconcilable with what Frege says about senses in 'Über Sinn und Bedeutung'. (ii) Under such a rendering Axiom V would transform into a triviality, since, in general, identity statements in which the proper names at the sides of the identity sign have the same sense do not express any profound truth. Moreover, it would then be very difficult to accept that such a triviality like Axiom V could have given rise to the Zermelo-Russell Paradox, or that its elimination from the logical system of *Grundgesetze der Arithmetik* would stymie the derivation of the arithmetical principles from the remaining logical axioms. (iii) It would also be difficult to understand Frege's concern with the lack of intuitiveness of Axiom V.[34] (iv) Finally, let us suppose for a moment that such a rendering were correct. In such a case, if we were to replace one of the names of value ranges in Axiom V with another name having a different sense, we would obtain a statement that would differ from Axiom V only in virtue of such a replacement, but that would be false on the basis of the presupposed rendering of the notorious principle, since in the new statement the senses of the partial statements do not coincide. Thus, under such a rendering the truth of Axiom V would depend on the mode of designation. But that would be totally unacceptable not only for Frege – remember his rejection of the first attempt to define number in *Die Grundlagen der Arithmetik* – but in general. Moreover, under such a rendering, the Principle of Substitution *salva veritate* of expressions having different sense but the same referent would be violated, a principle that Frege surely would not have liked to abandon.[35]

Thus, if we base our understanding of Frege's semantics on his exposition in 'Über Sinn und Bedeutung', Axiom V remains completely unintelligible. If we were to render Axiom V as expressing that the statements at the sides of the principal identity sign have the same referent, which for Frege means that they have the same truth-value, it would be totally undetermined. On the other hand, if

---

[33]Sluga clearly prefers to render Axiom V as expressing sameness of sense, and in his 'Semantic Content and Cognitive Sense' tries to dismiss – see p. 61 – Dummett's interpretation of Axiom V in *Grundgesetze der Arithmetik* as expressing the sameness of referent. Sluga forgets that Frege explicitly rejects such a rendering in a footnote to section 10, p. 16 of that work. That footnote leaves no doubt that the expression '*gleichbedeutend*' used in that passage of section 10 of *Grundgesetze der Arithmetik* should be rendered as 'having the same referent'.

[34]See *Grundgesetze der Arithmetik I*, p. VII.

[35]See *Die Grundlagen der Arithmetik*, section 65, as well as 'Über Sinn und Bedeutung', in *Kleine Schriften*, pp. 143-62.

we interpret Axiom V as expressing that the statements at the sides of the principal identity sign have the same sense, and understand 'sense' as in 'Über Sinn und Bedeutung' and *Grundgesetze der Arithmetik*, then such a principle would be trivialized and it would be incomprehensible how such a triviality could have given rise to the Zermelo-Russell Paradox. Furthermore, in such a case, Axiom V would violate the Principle of Substitution *salva veritate*.

There are only two possible related explanations of such a quandary in Frege's philosophy. The first one is that Frege really understands Axiom V as in 'Funktion und Begriff', that is as expressing an identity between the senses of the expressions at the sides of the principal identity sign, but he understands by 'sense of a statement' not the thought expressed, but that unofficial notion of sense – discussed in the preceding chapter – which, in the case of statements, coincides essentially with his old notion of conceptual content of *Begriffsschrift*. This rendering of the very special identity statement that is Axiom V is, however, not free of difficulties, since it clashes directly with Frege's official notion of sense in 'Über Sinn und Bedeutung' and *Grundgesetze der Arithmetik*, and with the ensuing rendering of identity statements. The second possible explanation would consist in rendering Axiom V as expressing that its two sides have the same referent, but a different sense, while maintaining the official notion of sense, but abandoning the thesis that the referents of statements are truth-values, and replacing them with conceptual contents. Thus, on this rendering, statements express thoughts but refer to conceptual contents, and identity statements between statements would be expressing a congruence relation between senses modulo sameness of conceptual content. This is a more satisfactory solution to the quandary, though not one that Frege would have accepted. Moreover, it would bring Frege nearer to Husserl, in whose semantics of sense and reference there is a notion, namely, that of a situation of affairs [in German: *Sachlage*], which can be seen as a refinement of Frege's notion of conceptual content. Nonetheless, even such a modification of Frege's views would not be Husserlian enough, since it would still lack the notion of a state of affairs [in German: *Sachverhalt*], which in Husserl's semantics occupies an intermediate role between the thought and the situation of affairs, and prevents their collapse. Statements – like the members of the pairs ['2+3=5', '6-1=5'], ['5+2>6', '8-1>6'] and ['The Morning Star is a planet', 'The Evening Star is a planet'] – express different thoughts but refer to the same state of affairs. The notion of a situation of affairs is more profound than that of a state of affairs, and would express a sort of logical or mathematical equivalence. Axiom V, which is really a sort of biconditional would, if true, be rendered as expressing that the expressions at the sides of the biconditional have the same situation of affairs, though they express different thoughts and have different states of affairs as referents. A perfectly similar interpretation would apply to Frege's second attempt at defining number in *Die Grundlagen der Arithmetik*.

5 Value Ranges and Extensions

The problems with the notion of value range are not limited to those considered in the preceding section. As already mentioned in section 3, Frege identifies the value ranges of concepts – which they should have in virtue of being a special case of functions – with the extensions of the concepts. But as we will see shortly, this is by no means clear. Now, the same Fregean notion of the extension of a concept has not been exempt of misunderstandings.[36] Thus, it is convenient to make it precise.

The extension of a concept is for Frege an object. Hence, we can talk about the identity of two extensions of concepts. We can also talk about the inclusion of an extension in another extension, though in the case of those special extensions of concepts that are numbers none is included in any other, since their intersection is always empty.[37] The identity of two extensions corresponds to the mutual subordination of their corresponding concepts.[38] The extension of a concept is always completely determined by the concept.[39] An object falls under a concept if and only if it belongs to the extension of the concept.[40] This relation of belonging an object to an extension should be clearly distinguished from the relation of being a physical part of a whole.[41]

Thus, the extension of a concept is a kind of set determined by such a concept, and to which belong exactly those objects that fall under the concept. Hence, if we put in the empty place of a conceptual word a name of an object that falls under the concept referred to by the conceptual word, the referent of the statement so obtained will be the True. The remaining entities that could be arguments of the function that is the concept but that do not fall under the concept, do not belong to the extension of the concept. Since Frege requires a complete demarcation of each and every function, in the case of first level concepts, the latter collection – which nowadays is sometimes called the 'anti-extension'[42] of the predicate (or conceptual word) – is formed by all objects of the system that do not belong to the extension of the concept. Hence, if the concept of a peaceful human being is clearly defined, not only do Adolf Hitler and Napoleon not belong to its extension, but also neither do my personal computer nor my copy of Frege's *Kleine Schriften*.

Although Frege never defined his notion of a value range, and, moreover, did not believe that such a definition was possible, since for him value ranges were

---

[36]For example, in Currie's *Frege: an Introduction to his Philosophy*, p. 68, and in Sluga's *Gottlob Frege*, p. 147.
[37]See *Die Grundlagen der Arithmetik*, section 69, p. 77.
[38]See 'Über Schoenflies: Die logischen Paradoxien der Mengenlehre', in *Nachgelassene Schriften*, pp. 191-9, especially pp. 197-8.
[39]Ibid., p. 199.
[40]Ibid., p. 198.
[41]Ibid., p. 199.
[42]See, for example, Saul Kripke's 'An Outline of a Theory of Truth', 1975, reprinted in Robert L. Martin (ed.), *Recent Essays on Truth and the Liar Paradox* (Oxford, 1984), pp. 53-81, especially p. 64.

logically simple objects and, thus, indefinable,[43] from his above mentioned elucidation it should be clear that value ranges are a sort of sets of all ordered pairs <a,b>, where 'a' belongs to the domain of the function and 'b' is the value of the function for the argument 'a'. Thus, a value range is a sort of generalization of the graph of a function, in a similar way in which Frege's notion of function is a generalization of the notion of function of mathematical analysis. Since in the logical system of *Grundgesetze der Arithmetik* all first level functions have the same domain, namely, the totality of objects of the system, one can say that two functions have the same set of values, if and only if they always assign the same value to the same argument. In such a case, the set of ordered pairs <a,b> of the two functions coincide.

Let us suppose now that the set of values of the functions contains only two members, namely, the True and the False. In other words, let us consider only first order functions of one argument, whose value is always a truth-value, that is, functions that are concepts.[44] One can ask about the value range of such a concept. A value range is the set of all ordered pairs <a,b> such that 'a' is any object and 'b' is one of the two truth-values. Thus, two concepts have the same value range when for any first member 'a' of such an ordered pair, they have as second member of the ordered pair the same truth-value, either the True or the False.

If we now compare this value range of a concept with the extension of the concept, we immediately find the following difference. The value range is a set of ordered pairs, whereas the extension of the concept is not a set of ordered pairs. One could try to shorten the gap between the two notions by redefining the extension of a concept as a set of ordered pairs, such that the second member of each pair is always, that is, for each first member, a truth-value. However, this value would always be the True, since the objects that do not belong to the extension of the concept could not be first members of such ordered pairs. Hence, even after the arbitrary stipulation of conceiving the extensions of concepts as sets of ordered pairs, the following differences with the value range of a concept still remain: (i) The second member of an ordered pair that belongs to the value range of a concept can be either the True or the False, whereas that of the extension of a concept can only be the True. (ii) The first member of an ordered pair belonging to the value range of a concept can be any object of the system, whereas the first member of an ordered pair belonging to the modified notion of the extension of a concept can only be one of those objects of the system to which corresponds the True as second member. Hence, if we insist in identifying the extension of a concept with the value range of that concept, the concept can only be a partial function, since it would not be defined for arguments that do not have the True as value. This is, however, incompatible with Frege's requirement that all functions and, in particular, all concepts be defined for all objects of the system. Thus, the

---

[43]For more on this issue, see my discussion of Frege's views on definitions in the next chapter.
[44]To simplify the discussion, I am considering only functions of one argument in this section.

extension of a concept, modified or not, is not simply a special case of the value range of a function.

Moreover, such an interpretation of extensions as ordered pairs – propounded by Sluga and Currie in their respective books on Frege – would make it impossible for an extension to be included in another extension and, thus, for a concept to be subordinated to another concept. Thus, notwithstanding the residual difference mentioned above between the modified extensions of concepts and the value ranges of concepts, if concepts are defined for all objects, as Frege believed, and extensions were ordered pairs, as conceived by Sluga and Currie, the extension of the concept of tiger would not be properly contained in the extension of the concept of feline, since for all objects that are not tigers, the Slugian extension of the concept of tiger would have as second member the False, whereas for some of those non-tigers as first argument, for example, for lions, the Slugian extension of the concept of feline would have as second member the True. Furthermore, the Slugian empty extension would not be really empty and properly included in any other extension, since it would always have the False as second member, whereas any non-empty Slugian extension would have the True as second member at least once. Thus, the Slugian empty extension would not be contained in any other Slugian extension. It would not be empty at all. Finally, since there is no really empty Slugian extension, if Frege had used such a bizarre notion of extension as the basis of the definition of numbers in logical terms, he would not have been able to define the number '0' and, of course, any other number. His reduction of arithmetic to logic would have been a blunder from the very beginning.[45]

Returning to Frege, his confusion between extensions of concepts and value ranges of functions of one argument, whose value is a truth-value, can be expressed in a more familiar way as the confusion between a set **M** and the field (domain × range) of the characteristic function of the set **M** (where the true is rendered by '1' and the false by '0'), which is composed of all ordered pairs <a,1> and <b,0> such that a∈ **M** and b∉ **M**. If we define – as is usual in the post-Kripkean literature on the semantic notion of truth for natural languages – the anti-extension of a conceptual word (predicate) as the set of all objects of the system that do not belong to the concept, we can see that, in a strict sense, the value range of the concept is the union of the extension and anti-extension of the concept. Hence, though the notion of the extension of a concept and that of the value range of a (first level) function of one argument, whose value is a truth-value, are clearly

[45]Recently, some authors have argued that Frege's logical system had more fundamental difficulties than that disclosed by Russell's famous letter of June 1902. See on this issue, the paper by Peter Aczel, 'Frege Structures and the Notion of Proposition', in J. Barwise, H.J. Keisler and K. Kunen (eds), *The Kleene Symposium* (Amsterdam, 1980), pp. 31-59, and the paper by Hartwig Frank, 'Freges Waagerechter und die Logik der Begriffsumfänge', in Ingolf Max and Werner Stelzner (eds), *Logik und Mathematik*, pp. 49-57. For another difficulty in Frege's logical system of *Grundgesetze der Arithmetik*, see Werner Stelzner's paper 'Wahrheits-und Falscheitsfunktionen in der Begriffsschrift der *Grundgesetze*', ibid., pp. 58-67.

related, they are not identical, and, thus, in a strict sense extensions of concepts are not special cases of value ranges of functions.

Chapter 6

Fundamental Philosophical Issues in
Grundgesetze der Arithmetik

1 Introduction

In the preceding chapter I discussed a fundamental issue of *Grundgesetze der Arithmetik* already, namely value ranges. They were properly introduced in 'Funktion und Begriff' and, in some sense their discussion belonged with that of the notions of 'function', 'concept' and 'object'. In the remaining two chapters, I will be concerned with other philosophical issues discussed by Frege in *Grundgesetze der Arithmetik* and in other (usually later) works. In this chapter, some fundamental themes of Frege's philosophy take central stage, while in the last chapter I will round my critical exposition with some other less central but not less interesting themes.

As we saw in Chapters 2 and 3, Frege's views can be assessed sometimes while analysing his criticism of other views. In Chapter 2, I expounded Frege's criticism both of psychologistic conceptions of mathematics and of what I called there the 'naturalistic views of mathematics'. But such criticism did not refute two less vulnerable views very popular in the academic quarters of those days. Firstly, there is the psychologistic view of logic. For a logicist like Frege, his refutation of psychologism in mathematics in *Die Grundlagen der Arithmetik* would not be conclusive if it were not completed by a refutation of psychologism in logic. In fact, if arithmetic were independent of psychology but logic were not independent of psychology, it would be unheard of to try to derive arithmetic from logic. Thus, the refutation of psychologism in logic was an extremely important and unavoidable task for Frege, and he sets out to accomplish it in the Preface to *Grundgesetze der Arithmetik*. Secondly, there is the formalist conception of mathematics, whose refutation by Frege is dispersed in different writings extending over some three decades. Already at the end of *Die Grundlagen der Arithmetik* Frege criticizes formalism in arithmetic, but he elaborates such criticism with more details both in the second volume of *Grundgesetze der Arithmetik* and in shorter writings, beginning with his 1885 paper 'Über formale Theorien der Arithmetik'.[1]

---

[1] 'Über formale Theorien der Arithmetik', in *Kleine Schriften*, pp. 103-11. See also 'Antwort auf die Ferienplauderei des Herrn Thomae', ibid., pp. 324-8, and 'Die Unmóglichkeit der Thomaeschen formalen Arithmetik aufs neue nachgewissen', ibid., pp. 329-33.

In addition to expounding Frege's criticisms of psychologism in logic and of the pre-Hilbertian formalism in mathematics, I will say a few words in this chapter on Frege's logicism and Platonism. The chapter ends with an exposition of Frege's views on definitions.

2 Frege's Criticism of Psychologism in Logic

Even a Fregean scholar like Michael Dummett has acknowledged in the preface to the second edition of Findlay's translation of Husserl's *Logische Untersuchungen*[2] that Frege's criticism of psychologism in logic did not play a decisive role in the refutation of psychologstic foundations of logic, whereas Husserl's criticism was much more decisive. Dummett does not try to explain, however, why Husserl, and not Frege, nearly annihilated psychologism. The most natural and also superficial explanation of such a situation is that Frege's refutation of psychologism occurs in a logical treatise loaded with a very strange symbolism, whereas Husserl's occurs in a book on philosophy. I think, however, that there are at least two other no less important reasons. Firstly, it should be pointed out that Frege's argumentative style is very – sometimes extremely – disrespectful not only of his adversaries' views but even of his adversaries as persons. Frege has the tendency to ridicule and even misrepresent the views of others, and is very reluctant to acknowledge their merits. One of the best examples of this way of proceeding is precisely Frege's late review of 1894 of Husserl's early writing *Philosophie der Arithmetik*, in which Husserl incurs in a form of mild Brentanian psychologism, which is distorted and exaggerated in Frege's review. Moreover, *Philosophie der Arithmetik* was an extension of Husserl's professorship writing [*Habilitationsschrift*] of 1887 *Über den Begriff der Zahl*, and represented his views at most up to the first half of 1890. At the beginning of 1891 Husserl sent Frege a copy of the book together with his review of the first volume of Schröder's *Vorlesungen über die Algebra der Logik I*, both published early that year. In that review Husserl makes the distinction between sense and reference, and – though both writings were published almost simultaneously – an attentive reader should have taken note of the evolution of Husserl's thought from the book to the review. In a letter of Frege to Husserl dated 24 May 1891, Frege acknowledges that Husserl had also made the distinction between sense and reference. However, in none of his writings published during his lifetime did he acknowledge as much, and in 1894 he distorted the young Husserl's views in order to ridicule him, without any mention of Husserl's review of Schröder's book.[3] Something similar – if not worse – occurred with Georg

---

[2] Michael Dummett, 'Preface to Edmund Husserl's *Logical Investigations*' (Routledge, second edition 2001), p. XVII.

[3] It should be mentioned, however, that in the posthumously published 'Ausführungen über Sinn und Bedeutung' there is such a recognition – see *Nachgelassene Schriften*, pp. 134-5. Scholars that still believe in the myth that Husserl obtained the distinction between sense and reference from Frege seem not to have read that paper or Frege's letter to Husserl of 24

Cantor. Frege's criticism of the mathematician who can be considered the founder of modern mathematics was vicious and personal, and the mild recognition of Cantor's contributions to mathematics at the end of *Die Grundlagen der Arithmetik* in no way does justice to their greatness.

The third example of misrepresentation of the views of an adversary is precisely Frege's criticism of the clearly radical psychologistic logician Benno Erdmann's views, with which we will be concerned below. But this brings us directly to the second decisive difference between Frege's refutation of psychologism in logic (and mathematics) and Husserl's refutation of psychologism in logic. Husserl is not only very respectful of his adversaries – which he usually quotes extensively – but also makes much finer distinctions than Frege and offers a more detailed and compelling argumentation. Thus, for example, in Chapter VII of the first volume of *Logische Untersuchungen*[4] Husserl clearly distinguishes between specific and individual relativism. Specific relativism has either as a thesis or as a consequence of its theses the relativization of logic to a species, usually the human species, whereas individual relativism would relativize logic to the individual subjects. Husserl says that in modern times nobody has dared to propound individual relativism. Moreover, he adds that psychologism, as well as Kantianism, are forms of specific relativism. Frege not only does not make such a simple distinction, but he also uses their confusion to misrepresent and ridicule his opponents. Let us illustrate this point with an exposition of Frege's criticism of psychologism in logic with special reference to Benno Erdmann's views.

According to Frege,[5] the presumed psychological foundation of logic so popular in his days is based on a series of confusions and on the ambiguous use of some terms. For Frege, logic is the science whose objects of study are the laws of truth or, to put it more precisely than Frege does, the science concerned with the derivability relations between statements expressing true thoughts. But the word 'law' is ambiguous, and this ambiguity has originated the psychological distortion of logic. As is well known, on the one hand, one speaks of moral and state laws, and understands under 'law' a sort of duty or obligation, something that ought to be, even if it in fact is not. On the other hand, one speaks of 'law' as is usual in the natural sciences, namely, as expressing the generality of some events. It is in this last sense that the term 'law' is used in mathematics and logic, though they concern

----

May 1891 in *Wissenschaftlicher Briefwechsel*, pp. 94-8, especially p. 98. That Frege did not feel comfortable with such acknowledgements of Husserl's writings seems to be attested by his borrowing in a letter to Paul F. Linke of 1919 – see *Wissenschaftlicher Briefwechsel*, p. 156 – of an example of Husserl – see *Logische Untersuchungen II*, U. I, section 12 – to explain the distinction between sense and reference, but without mentioning Husserl. Of course, Linke, who was acquainted with Husserl's views, knew where the example came from. I thank Claire O. Hill for reminding me in a private communication some years ago of this passage in Frege's letter to Linke.
[4]*Logische Untersuchungen I*, (1900, Den Haag, 1975), Chapter VII, section 34.
[5]This exposition is mostly based on the Preface of *Grundgesetze der Arithmetik I*, pp. XIV-XXVI. On this point, see p. XV, as well as similar remarks at the beginning of 'Der Gedanke', pp. 342-3.

not the generality of certain events occurring in nature but the generality of what is, and thus in the case of logic, of what is true.[6] Now, both logical laws, as well as geometrical, arithmetical or physical laws, can very well be conceived as prescribing what ought to be or, more explicitly, as prescribing that we should think according to them, if we want to think correctly.[7] The latter, combined with the generality of logical laws, made it possible for logical laws to be frequently called laws of thought. This, however, creates the confusion of considering logical laws as natural laws of correct thinking. But to think is a sort of psychological activity. Thus, the distortion of logical laws is completed by considering them psychological laws, and taking logic to be founded on psychology.

In this way, psychologism blurs, according to Frege, the distinction between the objective and the subjective. It confounds the laws of truth with the laws of considering something to be true. The latter are clearly psychological. If logical laws were laws for considering something to be true, they would in the best of cases only express the empirically determined average of how people think, and such a content could very well change with time in the way fashion changes. However, logic is not concerned with such laws but with the laws of truth, and being true is fundamentally different from being considered true, regardless of whether it is so considered by one, many or all human beings. In fact, a thought can very well be true even if nobody considers it true. But if logical laws are independent of being considered true, logical laws are not psychological.

The psychological misrepresentation of logic inevitably leads to a sort of relativism. If we were to find other beings whose laws for considering something true were different from ours, psychologistic logicians could only accept that as a fact, but could not appeal to any objective logical laws that could serve as judge for deciding whether human beings or those beings, or neither of the two thinks according to the logical laws. On the contrary, those who believe that logical laws are laws of truth or, even, normatively understood, laws that prescribe how to think correctly, would ask themselves whether our or those beings' laws for considering something true, or neither of them, coincide with the laws of truth. The psychologistic logician cannot ask the same question, since if he does, he would be acknowledging laws of truth that are not of psychological nature. Moreover, psychologism tends to confuse what is clearly fundamentally different. Logical laws, as laws of what is true, prescribe how one should judge regardless of where or when and of who judges, since truth is completely independent of the one who judges. On the contrary, what Erdmann calls 'objective certainty' is not

---

[6]See 'Der Gedanke', p. 342.
[7]See *Grundgesetze der Arithmetik I*, p. XV. There have been some clear misunderstandings on this issue. As Dummett recently put it in his Preface to the new edition of Findlay's translation of Husserl's *Logische Untersuchungen*, for Frege logic was as theoretical as for Husserl, and both also agreed that not only logic, but also other theoretical disciplines admit normative applications. Once more, Husserl's discussion was more detailed and clear, leaving no doubt about his position, whereas some isolated remarks by Frege seem to have generated the confusion about his views.

independent of the judging subjects and could change with a change in our nature.[8] Frege acknowledges the existence of an objective non-real region of entities, whereas psychologism does not. But it is in no way clear why what is independent of judging subjects has to affect our senses, has to belong to the region of physical reality.[9]

Up to this point Frege's argumentation is both sober and compelling, and the arguments are similar to some of Husserl's later arguments. However, instead of adding still more compelling arguments – as Husserl does –[10] Frege turns to the use by some psychologistic logicians of the word 'representation', imbuing it with his particular subjective rendering,[11] to unjustly accuse psychologistic logicians like Erdmann of the most ridiculous subjectivism, essentially, an individual relativism that – according to Husserl – none of them, and certainly not Erdmann, propounded.

Frege adds that psychologism is prone to confound concepts with representations. But, as Frege acknowledges, the word 'representation' is ambiguous, since sometimes it seems to refer to something belonging to the individual consciousness and is related to other representations by psychological laws, whereas sometimes it refers to something in front of all of us in the same way and, thus, does not presuppose any individual consciousness. Frege opts to attribute to psychologistic logicians the first of the two meanings of the word 'representation', though they seemed, sometimes in an unclear, sometimes in a more clear way, to be using the word 'representation' in the second rendering. Although psychologistic logicians did not acknowledge the validity of logical, mathematical or any scientific laws, independently of any knowing subject, they were eager to accept their intersubjective validity for all ('normally constituted') human beings. Thus, psychologistic logicians were what Husserl called specific relativists, not subjectivists in the sense of individual relativists. They thought – whether clearly or unclearly – that truth was dependent on the general structure of our consciousness as human beings, not on the peculiar individual traits of the consciousness of the judging subject. Precisely that is the reason why they tried to found logic and mathematics on psychology, that is, on the study of general laws of consciousness, and not on the peculiarities of any individual consciousness – what would be almost insane.

Thus, Frege asserts,[12] on the basis of his preferred rendering of the word 'representation', that neither logic nor any other science, nor anything objective

---

[8]See *Grundgesetze der Arithmetik I*, pp. XV-XVI.
[9]Ibid., p. XVIII.
[10]*Logische Untersuchungen I*, Chapter VII, section 36. Husserl's fourth to sixth arguments against specific relativism, which are totally foreign to Frege, are still more compelling, and applicable not only to psychologism, but also to biologism, for example, Darwinism, and even to Kantianism. For a general exposition of Husserl's argumentation see my paper 'The Structure of the Prolegomena', in *Manuscrito* XXIII/2 (2000): 61-99.
[11]*Grundgesetze der Arithmetik I*, pp. XVIIIff.
[12]Ibid., p. XIX.

would be possible. Representations are subjective, belonging to an individual consciousness and being indissolubly linked to that consciousness. My representation of a determinate number is as such different from your representation of the same number, and if they do not have the same properties, psychologism could not decide between them, since it cannot appeal to any objective number. My representation of a determinate number would be as linked to my consciousness as my state of sorrow, and as incomparable with your representation of the same number as my sorrow is incomparable with yours. Frege correctly asserts that the view he is criticizing – which is not that of psychologism – converges to solipsism. Frege tries to ridicule Erdmann's assertion that everything that is an object can be represented and that everything that can be represented is an object by rendering representation as linked to the individual consciousness. Thus, he argues that if both the subject and the predicate were representations, then one could never say that an object is green, since there are no green representations.

Frege concludes triumphantly that psychologism is untenable and that psychological analyses are as irrelevant for logic as they are for astronomy.[13]

3 Logicism in *Grundgesetze der Arithmetik*

In *Begriffsschrift* the logicist thesis of the reduction of arithmetic to logic is presented as a possibility deserving to be investigated. In *Die Grundlagen der Arithmetik* that thesis appears in the form of a programme that has to be and will be executed in a future writing. Frege does not pretend to establish such a thesis in his philosophical masterpiece, but only to make it plausible, or very probable. On the other hand, in *Grundgesetze der Arithmetik* Frege tries to establish the programme sketched in *Die Grundlagen der Arithmetik*. Hence, he presents the logicist thesis in a more categorical fashion. Thus, in section 1 of that work[14] Frege states that he is going to confirm his thesis that arithmetic is a part of logic by deriving by logical means only the most simple and basic arithmetical laws. Of course, due to the prior seminal work of Weierstraß, Dedekind and Cantor, such a derivation would serve to reduce all analysis to logic. Frege is perfectly conscious of this situation and, in the second volume of *Grundgesetze der Arithmetik*, extends his presumed reduction to the theory of real numbers.

Frege is also perfectly conscious that Richard Dedekind had also propounded the logicist thesis in his monograph *Was Sind und was Sollen die*

---

[13]Similar arguments are to be found in many of Frege's writings, for example, in 'Über Sinn und Bedeutung' and, especially, in 'Der Gedanke', in which the subjective rendering of 'representation' is presupposed without further notice.
[14]Ibid., section 1. For comparison, see on this issue Chapter 2, section 1, and Chapter 3, section 7 above.

Zahlen?,[15] and in the Preface of *Grundgesetze der Arithmetik* he acknowledges that fact, but, on the other hand, criticizes Dedekind for the lack of rigor of his 'proofs'. Thus, it is not enough to propound the logicist thesis and to sketch how we could obtain some theorems, but one has to establish the thesis with complete rigor, which is the objective of *Grundgesetze der Arithmetik*.[16] To eliminate any sort of doubt, Frege will make all proofs explicit, dividing them in their most simple logical steps. In particular, that will also include making explicit all axioms, rules of inference and also all definitions on which the derivations are based. The axioms are listed in section 47, the rules of inference in section 48, and the definitions at the end of the first volume. Thus, by avoiding any holes in the inference chain, Frege will be able to bring to the fore the presuppositions on which the proofs are based, since only by making explicit all such presuppositions on which the members of the different inference chains are founded, will the logicist thesis be established.

4 Frege's Platonism

As we have seen both in the exposition of Frege's views in *Die Grundlagen der Arithmetik*, especially in Chapter 2 above, and in the first section of this chapter, Frege clearly distinguished between what is physically real – that is, has spatial coordinates, or, in more recent terminology, spatio-temporal coordinates – and what is objective. For Frege, not everything that is not physically real is subjective, since the physically real is just a proper part of the objective. The equatorial line that divides the earth in two hemispheres is objective, but does not belong to the realm of physically real objects perceived by our senses. In the same way, numbers are objective, without belonging to the realm of the physically real.[17]

In Chapters 4 and 5 we saw how in Frege's mature philosophy there is a tendency towards ontologization. Functions and concepts are now objective unsaturated entities – not unsaturated signs – though not objects, which are saturated entities. Numbers, truth-values and, in general, value ranges are objects, that is, saturated entities. Moreover, senses and, in particular, thoughts are conceived as a sort of entities. Senses are saturated or unsaturated, depending on whether they refer to saturated or unsaturated entities or, what is the same in view of Frege's pre-established harmony between grammar and ontology, if they are expressed by saturated or unsaturated expressions. They are neither subjective nor physically real, and belong – together with numbers, truth-values and, in general, value ranges, and with concepts, relations and, in general, functions – to a third realm of entities, that is, to the realm of the neither physically real nor subjective realm of entities. None of those entities is perceived by us and, thus, does not

---

[15] *Was Sind und was Sollen die Zahlen?* (Braunschweig: Vieweg, 1888, English translation 1901, reprint, Dover 1963).
[16] See *Grundgesetze der Arithmetik I*, p. VII.
[17] See Chapter 2, section 7 above.

belong to the physically real. But they are in no way dependent on our consciousness, and are the same for all of us. Moreover, they would not disappear if mankind or any rational beings in the universe were to disappear. Thus, they are not subjective, not even merely intersubjective, but objective.[18]

In his 1918 paper 'Der Gedanke',[19] Frege expounds his views about the realm of the objective non-physically real with great detail, using thoughts as an example of an entity belonging to such a third realm and contrasting them both with entities belonging to the realm of the physically real and with representations – in Frege's subjectivist rendering – that, as well as decisions, belong to the subjective realm of our individual consciousness. In contrast with the entities of the physically real world – the first realm – the entities of the non-physically real but objective third realm are not perceived by us, have no spatio-temporal coordinates, and cannot suffer the effects of the causal chains of events permeating the physically real world. Hence, a thought is non-temporal and its truth or falsity is also non-temporal. Thus, thoughts exist even if no one has ever thought them, and they are either non-temporally true or non-temporally false. Thoughts and, in general, entities of the third realm are, on the other hand, as objective as the entities of the first realm, and as capable of being the object of intersubjective knowledge. Frege is perfectly conscious[20] of the fact that in our natural languages there exist expressions – Husserl called them 'occasional expressions –[21] which seem to express different thoughts in different situations. Such imperfections of natural languages do not affect the objective nature of thoughts. What varies with every use of words like 'I', 'yesterday' or 'here' is the referent. In any case, such expressions would not occur in a perfect language adequate to thought.[22]

Entities of the second realm, that is, decisions and representations – in Frege's rendering – which include among others sensations, sentiments, volitions, etc.,[23] have in common with the objects of the third realm that they are not perceived by us. But they differ clearly from the entities of the third realm by being subjective, or more exactly, by being dependent on a consciousness that is the bearer of such a representation (or decision), and that is its only bearer, since there is no way to compare representations occurring in two different consciousnesses.

Although Frege did not discuss the issue sufficiently in any of his writings, he seems to sustain[24] that there is in us a sort of faculty that allows us to get acquainted with the entities of the realm of the objective non-physically real, in a similar fashion to that in which sense perception makes it possible for us to get

---

[18]For an excellent treatment of Frege's views on the third realm, its coincidences with and differences from Popper's World 3, see the recent MA thesis of my former student Pedro Rosario Barbosa, *El Platonismo de Gottlob Frege y el Mundo 3 de Karl Popper*, 2004.
[19]*Kleine Schriften*, pp. 342-62.
[20]See ibid., pp. 348-50.
[21]See *Logische Untersuchungen II*, U. I, section 26.
[22]I prefer not to digress with a discussion of Frege's views on this issue, which do not attain complete clarity, probably because the issue is not relevant for Frege's concept-script.
[23]'Der Gedanke', p. 351.
[24]Ibid., p. 360.

acquainted with the objects of the physical world. In fact, Frege distinguishes – though without sufficiently developing the distinction – three sources of human knowledge, namely: the logical source of knowledge, the geometrical (and temporal) source of knowledge and the sensible source of knowledge.[25] The first one would be the source that would allow us access to the entities of the realm of the objective non-physically real, without intervention of any of the other two sources. It seems that the logical source of knowledge would also be present in our geometrical knowledge, in which the second source of knowledge is present in a decisive way, and even in sensible knowledge, in which the presence of the third source of knowledge is decisive.

5 Frege's Critique of Formalism in Mathematics

At the end of Chapter 3 I briefly expounded Frege's criticism in *Die Grundlagen der Arithmetik* of Hankel's formalist views on mathematics. In later writings Frege returns to his critique of the so-called 'formalist arithmetic' propounded by some mathematicians in the late nineteenth century and at the beginning of the twentieth century. Of course, he is not considering the more sophisticated formalism of Hilbert's school, which developed in the first decades of the twentieth century, though, as we will see in the last chapter, he criticized Hilbert's formal new axiomatics as applied to geometry. Frege's criticism is directed especially to the writings of his colleague Thomae, whose formalist views he examines in papers of 1885, 1906 and 1908,[26] and in *Grundgesetze der Arithmetik*,[27] and to those of Heine, criticized also in the latter book. It should be mentioned, however, that such arguments probably could had been directed to a late blossoming formalism of Hilbert's student, Haskell B. Curry, whose views in his monograph *An Outline of a Formalist Philosophy of Mathematics*[28] seem to be a return to pre-Hilbertian formalism.

For formalists of the Thomae sort, numerical signs and numbers coincide, and it is completely irrelevant whether or not numerical signs serve to express a content – or better: have a referent – whether because, as Heine seemed to have thought, they lacked a referent, or, as Thomae seemed to have thought more confusedly, because in this way we avoid metaphysical considerations. The sign

---

[25]For more details, see Frege's last papers in *Nachgelassene Schriften*, especially 'Erkenntnisquellen der Mathematik und der mathematischen Naturwissenschaften', pp. 286-94, and my discussion below in Chapter 7, section 3.
[26]See his 'Über formale Theorien der Arithmetik', 1885, 'Antwort auf die Ferienplauderei des Herrn Thomae', 1906, and 'Die Unmöglichkeit der Thomaeschen formaler Arithmetik aufs neue nachgewiesen', 1908, in *Kleine Schriften*, pp. 103-11, 324-8 and 329-33 respectively.
[27]*Grundgesetze der Arithmetik II*, sections 86-137.
[28]*An Outline of a Formalist Philosophy of Mathematics* (North Holland, Amsterdam, 1951).

itself, the numerical figure, is what should be considered as being the number by formalist arithmetic.[29]

On this issue Frege observes that since in formalist arithmetic signs do not refer, when we speak about the properties of, for example, the numerical sign '2', we should have to consider the physical, chemical and geometrical properties of such a geometrical sign, some of which – for example, the chemical ones – would vary, depending on whether we write the sign with a pencil, a pen or a chalk. However, properties like that of being the smallest even positive number, or the smallest prime, could not be obtained in such a fashion, since the sign '2' does not have such properties. Moreover, if 5/6 and 25/30 were mere combinations of signs, one could not prove the equation 5/6=25/30. Moreover, adds Frege,[30] the use of definitions would be excluded, since they do not concern mere signs.[31] On the other hand, a formalist arithmetic, by being completely devoid of any content, would be incapable of any applications. But it is precisely the applicability of mathematics, sustains Frege,[32] what distinguishes it from a mere game like chess. Thus, the possibility of being applied belongs necessarily to mathematics.

Furthermore, from a formalist perspective it is in no way clear on what grounds are we to exclude some pairs of numerical signs from the domain of application of arithmetical operations like subtraction or division. For example, it is in no way clear why we cannot stipulate that in the same fashion as the numerical signs '5-3' can be substituted by the numerical sign '2', the numerical signs '3-5' can also be substituted by the numerical sign '2', nor is it intelligible why we have to extend the set of numerical signs in order to consider numerical signs like '3-5'.[33] Moreover, it is in no way clear why the set of numerical signs '1/0' is not as legitimate as the set of numerical signs'1/2'. Evidently, a formalist cannot argue that '1/0' is senseless, whereas '1/2' is not, since for formalist arithmetic the second set of signs is as devoid of meaning (that is, sense and referent) as the first.[34]

Moreover, phrases like 'is greater than' or 'is smaller than' are completely unintelligible from a formalist point of view. Let us consider the inequality '3 is smaller than 7'. Evidently, a formalist cannot render the phrase 'is smaller than' in that context as is usual in mathematics, namely, as expressing that the number being the referent of the numerical sign '3' is smaller than the number which is the referent of the numerical sign '7'. However, it would be totally unwarranted to render the above inequality as somehow trying to say that the numerical sign '3' is

---

[29]See *Grundgesetze der Arithmetik II*, section 88, p. 98.

[30]Ibid., section 107, p. 114.

[31]For Frege's views on definitions, see the next section.

[32]*Grundgesetze der Arithmetik II*, section 91, p. 100.

[33]Ibid., section 105, pp. 112-13, in which Frege refers to Heine's formalist views, but immediately adds in section 106, p. 113, that the same difficulties are present in Thomae's views.

[34]Ibid., section 113, pp. 119-20.

in the geometrical or physical sense of that word smaller than the numerical sign '7'.[35]

The position of the formalists is even more difficult to sustain if we consider mathematical analysis. Thus, Frege asserts[36] that formalism makes mathematical analysis impossible, since if numbers were mere geometrical figures on a piece of paper or on the blackboard, they would be physical entities subjected to the rigours of material existence, and as such there could only be a finite number of them. But since we can only write finitely many numerical figures and since for formalists the existence of a number that has never been written would be absurd, we could not have representations of infinite series and, thus, could not obtain irrational numbers.[37]

According to Frege, the presumed plausibility of formalist arithmetic originates in the fact that it surreptitiously presupposes the usual arithmetic with content. If we were to deprive formalist arithmetic of the support in content arithmetic, it would be reduced to a few absurd theses. As a confirmation of the preceding assertions, in 'Die Unmöglichkeit der Thomaeschen Arithmetik aufs neue nachgewissen'[38] Frege observes that it is interesting that Thomae and the other formalists always make use of the same signs 0,1,2, etc. used in content arithmetic. In the game of chess, for example, none of its rules would be affected if we were to replace the figures of the king, queen, etc. with figures of a general, a colonel, etc. The game would remain the same, since the figures have no other meaning than the one conferred by the rules of the game. However, if we were to replace the well-known numerical signs 0,1,2,3 etc. with symbols like @,#,&,* etc., arithmetic would become completely unintelligible. But if arithmetic were a mere formal game with rules and figures, without any content, it should not be affected by a mere replacement of the symbolism. Such a replacement is not possible simply because it would destroy the surreptitious support of formalist mathematics in content mathematics.

6 On the Nature of Definitions

Frege's mature philosophy contains interesting but nonetheless questionable philosophical reflections on the nature of definitions and on axiom systems – which he simply calls 'systems'.[39] In this section I will discuss Frege's views on definitions on the basis of his most detailed treatments in *Grundgesetze der*

---

[35]Ibid., section 121, p. 126.
[36]See ibid., section 131, p. 134, and section 137, p. 139.
[37]Ibid.
[38]See *Kleine Schriften*, pp. 329-33, especially p. 332. Similar remarks are also present in *Grundgesetze der Arithmetik II*, section 83, p. 93 and in Frege's critique of Cantor's views see section 88, p. 98 – , though Cantor was no formalist, as Frege clearly acknowledges.
[39]See his long paper – or short monograph – 'Logik in der Mathematik', in *Nachgelassene Schriften*, pp. 219-70.

Arithmetik and 'Logik in der Mathematik'. I will make some references to his views on axiom systems, though I will give that issue a more thorough treatment in the last chapter while exposing Frege's views on the foundations of geometry.

It is clear that in an axiom system, if we want to avoid both a vicious circle in the proofs and in the definitions, not every statement can be proved and not every concept can be defined. The axioms of the system are not provable and do not require any proof. In fact, for Frege – as for traditional axiomatics – axioms should posses no less evidence than any other statement of the system, even a sort of self-evidence that makes superfluous not only any attempt at proving them, but also at proving their consistency with each other.[40]

In the same fashion, some concepts belonging to the system are not definable in the system. They are primitive concepts of the system or, in Fregean terminology, simple concepts.[41] In the case of a system of logic – like that of *Grundgesetze der Arithmetik* – which does not presuppose any more fundamental system, there are notions that are simple in an absolute sense, and are called by Frege 'logically simple concepts'.

However, the fact that a concept is indefinable does not preclude trying to clarify it, so as to avoid any misunderstandings. Such clarifications are especially important, due to the fact that in natural languages many words are equivocal, and when we want to incorporate them to the vocabulary of an axiom system, we have to clearly demarcate our chosen meaning from any other meanings the words have in everyday language. This task of clarifying primitive expressions cannot be done by definitions. For this task we have to make use, according to Frege, of what he called 'elucidations'.[42] Elucidations serve to fix the sense and referent of the primitive expressions, without having the intent of being definitions properly speaking. In fact, contrary to definitions, elucidations take the sense of the expression as a whole, and attempt merely to convey it to us by some sort of indication. Elucidations do not belong to the statements of the system, but are previous to the system. Thus, it would seem that elucidations belong to a sort of propedeutic of the axiom system, in the particular case of a logical system like that of *Grundgesetze der Arithmetik*, to a propedeutic of logic. Other authors, like Husserl in *Logische Untersuchungen*, who had no qualms with entering the realm of the foundations of logic itself, tried to clarify the linguistic and epistemological foundations of logic, for example, in the second volume of his masterpiece. Frege, however, thought that logic did not require any sort of foundation. As Wittgenstein later put it, logic should take care of itself.[43]

Although I cannot enter here in such a discussion, it should be mentioned that herein can be located the most important divergence between the soundest

---

[40]See 'Logik in der Mathematik', pp. 267-8.
[41]It is interesting that in his critique of Frege's *Die Grundlagen der Arithmetik* in *Philosophie der Arithmetik*, pp. 119-20, Husserl used precisely such terminology of simple concepts to argue that the notion of number is indefinable.
[42]See, for example, 'Logik in der Mathematik', p. 224.
[43]*Tractatus Logico-Philosophicus*, 5.473, p. 94 (German), p. 95 (English).

analytical philosophy originating in Frege and the equally soundest phenomenology originating in Husserl.[44] For Frege, there is no proper propedeutic of logic besides the informal elucidations. For Husserl, logic – as well as mathematics – needs a clarification of its foundations, which in the case of the former is both linguistic (semantic – First Investigation – and syntactical – Fourth Investigation) and epistemological (Fifth and Sixth Investigations). The linguistic foundation is itself founded on more general ontological issues (Second and Third Investigations). Of course, as we have seen, *malgré lui* Frege had to address both semantic and ontological issues, and had to try to clarify them in order to have a better understanding of logic and mathematics. Thus, after all, the two great philosophers were nearer to each other than what they thought and much nearer than what their so-called followers – with a few exceptions, like Michael Dummett – have ever believed. But let us now continue with our exposition of Frege's views on definitions.

The definitions of expressions are very different from the elucidations. They introduce a simple sign and stipulate that such a simple sign is going to have the same sense and the same referent as a group of already known signs. In this fashion, the new sign acquires a sense and a referent, and the definition itself is transformed into a new statement of the system and, thus, can be used in deriving theorems. The most simple form of definition introduces an expression for a new concept formed from other already known concepts, which would then be notes of the new concept and properties of the objects – if any – that fall under the new concept.

Frege stresses[45] that definitions cannot be creative, that is, they cannot surreptitiously have the role of an existential axiom. If such anomaly were to occur, the presumed definition would not be a mere definition, and behind it there would be hidden a statement requiring either to be proved or to be acknowledged as an axiom. Besides so-called creative definitions, Frege disallows many other sorts of 'definitions' used by his mathematical contemporaries. Nonetheless, some of those sorts survived Frege's attempt at ostracizing them and presently are in good mathematical health. Frege's rejection of such sorts of definition is based in one way or another on two general requirements he made, namely, the requisite of completeness and the requisite of simplicity. The requisite of completeness is nothing other than his already mentioned conviction that a definition of a concept should be such that for any object it has to be determinable whether it falls or does

---

[44]I underscore in both cases the word 'soundest' to distinguish Frege's and others' analyses from the very questionable linguistic dilletantism of some so-called analytic philosophers of ordinary language, as well as from naturalism of the Quinean variety, with whose writings Frege would not have liked to be associated; and, on the other hand, to distinguish Husserl's views from the so-called phenomenology of Scheler, Heidegger and many others, with whom Husserl did not want to be associated. Of course, I am not ignoring the fact that after the publication of *Logische Untersuchungen* the bulk of Husserl's research distanced itself considerably from Frege's relatively limited philosophical interests.

[45]See, for example, *Grundgesetze der Arithmetik I*, Vorwort, p. VI.

not fall under the concept defined.[46] In the contrary case, one could not properly assert that the concept has been defined. Moreover, the expression introduced by a definition has to be simple, that is, the expression cannot have meaningful constituent parts, it cannot have any part with an independent sense and, thus, with a possible referent.[47] In the contrary case, there would exist the possibility that the constituent part, taken in isolation, has a sense incompatible with the definition of the compound expression.

On the basis of such requirements, and especially that of completeness, Frege stipulates the following conditions on definitions:[48] (i) It is not allowed to give two (or more) definitions of the same concept, since in such a case one would have to establish the concordance of the two (or more) definitions, thereby excluding not only the possibility of the non-concordance between the two definitions, but also their incompatibility. (ii) One has to reject stepwise definitions, which consist in defining the expression first for a particular case, using that definition to derive some theorems, and afterwards introduce a definition for another case, and by means of this new definition sometimes one tries to make determinations concerning the first particular case already defined. Such a presumed definition would violate the requirement of completeness – except in the limiting case in which the expression had been completely determined by the first part of the definition. In such a case, however, the second part of the definition either could have been derived as a theorem on the basis of the first part, or is incompatible with it. On the other hand, in the most important case, in which the defined expression is not completely determined by the first part of the definition, it is possible that the subsequent explanations of the concept are not compatible with the first one. (iii) One has to reject any sort of conditional definition, and especially those whose correction is dependent on a proof of a result that one has first to establish. It is clear that also in this case the completeness requirement is violated. (iv) One has to reject also contextual definitions. It is not allowed to explain a sign or word by means of an explanation of the complex expression in which it occurs, since from the referent of the whole expression together with the referent of a part of a complex expression, one cannot obtain the referent of the remaining part.[49] (v) One should not explain two different concepts with the same definition. Each definition should define exactly one concept. (vi) One should reject also any system of definitions, each of whose members contains various expressions in need of explanation, and such that each of these expressions occur in various of these 'definitions' and the system as a whole is intended to be a sort of 'definition' of each of those expressions. Essentially, this last sort of system of definitions is present in Hilbert's axiomatization of geometry. Thus, it is perfectly

---

[46]See, for example, *Grundgesetze der Arithmetik II*, section 56, p. 69.
[47]Ibid., section 66.
[48]See, ibid., sections 56-63 and section 66, as well as 'Logik in der Mathematik', pp. 221ff.
[49]As already mentioned in Chapter 3, this direct rejection of contextual definitions in general is not easy to reconcile with the thesis of many Fregean scholars that Frege consciously retained the Context Principle after 1890.

understandable why Frege reacted to it in the way I will expound in the next chapter.[50]

It should be underscored here that, on the basis of his requirements on definitions, Frege explicitly rejects in *Grundgesetze der Arithmetik* the rendering of Axiom V as a definition.[51] The expression 'ûΦ(u)=âΨ(a)' is not a simple expression, but a complex one containing the sign '=', which is taken as already known. Thus, if we were to render Axiom V as a definition, that 'definition' would violate the requirement of simplicity of the expression to be explained, and – as every contextual definition – would violate the requirement of completeness. Incidentally, this rejection of contextual definitions grounded on their violation of the requirements of simplicity and completeness offers a more general and articulate basis for the rejection of Frege's second attempt at defining number in *Die Grundlagen der Arithmetik* than the one given in his philosophical masterpiece.

7 Some Critical Remarks

Frege's views on definitions are not as free from possible objections as could be gathered from my exposition. The first and most evident questioning of Frege's views is based on pure facts. Logicians and mathematicians have continued to use many of the sorts of definitions rejected by Frege without having had any logical difficulties. Recursive definitions, definitions by abstraction and contextual definitions are part of the common arsenal of contemporary mathematicians and logicians. Recursive definitions, in particular, are at the heart of logic, for example, in the rules of formation for determining the well-formed formulas of a logical system, as well as in the definitions of proof and derivation. Different sorts of definition by abstraction are used both in areas like set theory and model theory. Notions like that of ultraproduct would have been unthinkable, if logicians had taken seriously Frege's strictures on definitions. Such strictures could only have stymied the development of logic and mathematics.

Moreover, as mentioned by Tarski in his epoch-making monograph 'The Concept of Truth in Formalized Languages', recursive definitions can be transformed into essentially equivalent explicit definitions, as those advocated by Frege.[52] As a matter of fact, the recursive definition is simpler than its equivalent

---

[50]For a thorough treatment of Frege's theory of definitions, see the MA thesis of my former student José Ernesto Mieres, *La Noción de Definición en la Filosofía de la Matemática de Gottlob Frege*, 1997.

[51]See *Grundgesetze der Arithmetik II*, section 146, pp. 147-8.

[52]'The Concept of Truth in Formalized Languages', 1935, reprinted in Alfred Tarski, *Logic, Semantics, Metamathematics* 1956, second edition 1983, pp. 152-278. In the footnotes to pp. 175-6 Tarski refers to Dedekind and precisely to Frege, as well as to Russell and Whitehead's *Principia Mathematica* on this issue, whereas in the footnote to p. 177, with his exemplary usual clarity, he offers an example of such a transformation.

but more traditional explicit counterpart. Thus, simplicity is obtained, whereas nothing essential is lost by the use of recursive definitions instead of explicit ones.

Finally, it should be mentioned that Frege's expositions of his views on definitions are not free of difficulties. It is not clear whether it is the referent of the new expression that is determined by the definition, or whether it is both the sense and the referent that are being determined. Even in the same work Frege goes from one characterization of definitions to the other. Such incongruence is present, for example, in *Grundgesetze der Arithhmetik* and in 'Logik in der Mathematik'. It is pertinent to finish this chapter with some quotations from those works.

> We introduce a new name by means of a definition, by determining that it is going to have the same sense and the same referent as one [name] composed from familiar signs. By these means the new sign will now have the same referent as the explanatory [one]....[*Grundgesetze der Arithmetik I*, section 27, pp. 44-5][53]

Thus, in the first sentence of the above quotation it is said that the *definiens* and the *definiendum* of a definition must have the same sense and the same referent, whereas in the second sentence it says merely that they should be *gleichbedeutend*, that is, they should have the same *Bedeutung*, that is, the same referent. Although one could think that Frege's use of the word *gleichbedeutend* is more of a slip, the fact of the matter is that in German there exists a word *gleichsinnig* that means 'having the same sense',[54] and even if the word had not existed in the time of Frege, in German – as, for example, in Russian – it is extremely easy to form new words by composition. Moreover, six pages later (p. 51) Frege uses once more the expression *gleichbedeutend* to mean what the two sides of a definition must have in common. Other Fregean texts are worth quoting in this context.

> ...each definition must contain a unique sign, whose referent is fixed by means of it [*Grundgesetze der Arithmetik II*, section 66, p. 79.][55]

> If now, as was said, a simple sign is introduced for the group of signs, then such a stipulation is a definition. The simple sign obtains by these means a sense, namely, the same sense that the group of signs has. ['Logik in der Mathematik', p. 224][56]

---

[53]'Wir führen durch eine Definition einen neuen Namen ein, indem wir bestimmen, dass er denselben Sinn und dieselbe Bedeutung haben solle wie ein aus bekannten Zeichen zusammengesetzer. Dadurch wird nun das neue Zeichen gleichbedeutend mit dem erklärenden...' [*Grundgesetze der Arithmetik I*, section 27, pp. 44-5]
[54]See Gerhard Wahrig et al., *Deutsches Wörterbuch* (Gütersloh, revised edition 1994), p. 690.
[55]'...jede Definition muss ein einziges Zeichen enthalten, dessen Bedeutung durch sie festgesetzt wird'. [*Grundgesetze der Arithmetik II*, section 66, p. 79]
[56]'Wenn nun für eine solche Zeichengruppe ein einfaches Zeichen, wie eben gesagt, eingeführt wird, so ist eine solche Festsetzung eine Definition. Das einfache Zeichen erhält dadurch einen Sinn, nämlich denselben, den die Zeichengruppe hat.' ['Logik in der Mathematik', p. 224]

We form a sense from its constituent parts and introduce a completely new simple sign to express this sense. One can call this "structuring definition"; we prefer to call it simply "definition". ['Logik in der Mathematik', p. 227][57]

On these grounds we remain with our original conception, according to which a definition is an arbitrary stipulation by means of which a new sign is introduced for a compound expression, whose sense follows from its composition. The sign, which until then did not have any sense, receives through the definition the sense of that composite expression. ['Logik in der Mathematik', pp. 228-9][58]

...and we want to stipulate with it [the definition] that both sides of the equation should always have the same sense. ['Logik in der Mathematik', p. 246][59]

The last three quotations seem to make it clear that *definiens* and *definiendum* must have the same sense, they should be *gleichsinnig*. However, later in the same paper Frege asserts that they need only to have the same referent.

A definition is always a stipulation that a new sign or word is going to have the same referent as an already known compound sign. ['Logik in der Mathematik', p. 259][60]

The definitions are very different [from the axioms]. By their means a referent should be given to a sign or word that until then did not have one. ['Logik in der Mathematik', pp. 263-4][61]

Moreover, in a letter to Hilbert, Frege states:

Each definition contains a sign (an expression, a word) that had no referent before [and] to which by means of the definition a referent is given for the first time. [*Wissenschaftlicher Briefwechsel*, p. 62 (letter to Hilbert from 1899)][62]

---

[57]'Wir bauen einen Sinn aus seinen Bestandteilen auf und führen ein ganz neues einfaches Zeichen ein, um diesen Sinn auszudrücken. Man kann dies "aufbauende Definition" nennen; wir wollen es aber lieber "Definition" schlechtweg nennen.' ['Logik in der Mathematik', p. 227]

[58]'Wir bleiben demnach bei unserer anfänglichen Auffassung nach der eine Definition eine willkürliche Festsetzung ist, durch die ein neues Zeichen für einen zusammengesetzten Ausdruck eingeführt wird, dessen Sinn aus seiner Zusammensetzung bekannt ist. Das Zeichen, das bis dahin keinen Sinn hatte, bekommt durch die Definition den Sinn jenes zusammengesetzten Ausdrucks.' ['Logik in der Mathematik', p. 229]

[59]'...und wir wollen damit festsetzen, dass beide Seiten der Gleichung immer denselben Sinn haben sollen...' ['Logik in der Manthematik', p. 246]

[60]'Eine Definition ist immer eine Festsetzung, dass ein neues Zeichen oder Wort dasselbe bedeuten solle, wie ein schon bekanntes zusammengesetztes Zeichen.' ['Logik in der Mathematik', p. 259]

[61]'Ganz anderer Art [als die Axiome] sind die Definitionen. Durch sie soll einem Zeichen oder Worte, das bis dahin keine Bedeutung hatte, eine solche gegeben werden.' ['Logik in der Mathematik', pp. 263-4]

The preceding quotations are more than enough to show that Frege was in no way clear about what the two sides of a definition should have in common, though in his review of Husserl's *Philosophie der Arithmetik*[63] he stresses that when defining a conceptual word, what is defined is the extension of the concept and not the concept, and argues that it is so in all mathematical definitions. However, that by no means unquestionable assertion does not help much since for Frege the concept is the referent of the conceptual word, whereas the extension is neither its sense nor its referent. Thus, on the basis of Frege's semantic views, such an assertion would make Frege's confusion even more remarkable. Only if he is presupposing Husserl's theory of sense and referent, for which the sense of a conceptual word is a concept and the referent is the extension,[64] can one use Frege's assertion as supporting the view that the equality is one of referent and not of sense.

Once more, such almost schizophrenic assertions of Frege, sometimes in the same work and – as in our first quotation – even in the same passage, are explainable – if at all – only if one takes into account that he had two notions of sense. As argued in Chapter 4, his official notions of sense and thought of 'Über Sinn und Bedeutung' and of most of his mature writings are sometimes replaced by the more referential-like notions of sense and thought of his letters to Husserl of 1906. It is possible that when he asserted that the two sides of a definition ought to have the same sense, he had in mind a notion of sense corresponding to his notion of thought in the letters to Husserl of 1906, according to which sameness of thought is essentially identified with equipollency or interderivability. In the remaining more extensive quotations, Frege had in mind his official notion of sense, and believed that identity of official sense was too strong a requirement for definitions. This explanation is perfectly compatible with the rendering of Frege's words quoted above from his review of Husserl's early work as based on Husserl's semantics, but is not compatible, as already mentioned, with a rendering based on his official semantics.

---

[62]'Jede Definition enthält ein Zeichen (einen Ausdruck, ein Wort), das vorher keine Bedeutung hatte, dem erst durch die Definition eine Bedeutung gegeben wird.' [*Wissenschaftlicher Briefwechsel*, p. 62]

[63]See *Kleine Schrifen*, pp. 182 and 183. Frege says: 'Es ist der Begriffsumfang statt des Inhalts definiert.' [p. 182] That is: 'It is the extension of the concept instead of the content [what] is defined.' Moreover, he says: 'Der Vorwurf, daß nicht der Begriff, sondern dessen Umfang definiert werde, trifft eigentlich alle Definitionen der Mathematik.' [p. 183] That is: 'The objection that it is not the concept, but its extension [what] is defined, properly applies to all definitions in mathematics.'

[64]See *Wissenschaftlicher Briefwechsel*, pp. 96 and 98 (letter to Husserl of 24 May 1891), where Frege says that so far as he can see the only difference in their semantics of sense and reference concerns the sense and referent of conceptual words (p. 96), since for Husserl the concept is the sense of the conceptual word and the extension is its referent (p. 98). Of course, that was not the only difference, since Husserl never considered truth-values as the referents of statements.

My explanation of Frege's hesitations in his different discussions of definitions may not be well received by Fregean orthodox scholars. But I do not know of a better explanation. As a matter of fact, Fregean scholars usually ignore the incongruence between Frege's different assertions on definitions.

Chapter 7

Some Remaining Philosophical Issues

In this last chapter, I will try to round up my exposition of Frege's philosophy by considering some issues that probably do not belong to the nucleus of his mature philosophy, but have their immediate or mediate origin in that nucleus. In section 1, the unavoidable issue of the so-called Russell Paradox – or better: Zermelo-Russell Paradox – will come to the fore. I will be especially concerned with Frege's reaction to Russell's letter announcing the paradox in the Epilogue to the second volume of *Grundgesetze der Arithmetik*. In section 2, I shall briefly expound some fundamental aspects of Frege's reaction to the publication in 1899 of Hilbert's *Grundlagen der Geometrie* and the ensuing discussion with Hilbert and Korselt. Finally, in section 3, I will consider Frege's late abandonment of logicism and his attempt at providing a new geometrical foundation of arithmetic.

1 The Zermelo-Russell Paradox and Frege's Reaction to Russell's Letter

As is well known, on June 1902, a few months before the publication of the second volume of *Grundgesetze der Arithmetik* Frege received a letter from Bertrand Russell, in which he communicated to Frege that a paradox could be derived in the system of *Grundgesetze der Arithmetik* and in other systems of the foundations of mathematics.[1] As a matter of fact, the paradox had been also independently discovered by Zermelo and communicated to Hilbert and Husserl.[2] In a hurriedly written Epilogue to the second volume of the work, Frege formulates the paradox and discusses some possible ways out of such a logical swamp. Unfortunately, the far from intuitive presumed solution to the paradox adopted by Frege also allows the derivation of a contradiction, if one presupposes that there exist at least two objects. The great Polish logician Stanislaw Lesniewski discovered the contradiction in Frege's amended system of logic,[3] but it seems that Frege never

---

[1] See Frege's *Wissenschaftlicher Briefwechsel*, pp. 211-12.
[2] On Zermelo's discovery of the paradox, see Gregory H. Moore's book *Zermelo's Axiom of Choice* 1982, p. 89, as well as Bernhard Rang and Wolfgang Thomas' paper 'Zermelo's Discovery of the "Russell Paradox"', *Historia Mathematica* 8 (1981): 15-22, referred to by Moore, and also Edmund Husserl's brief comment in *Aufsätze und Rezensionen (1890-1910)*, (Dordrecht, 1979), p. 399.
[3] See Lesniewski's *Collected Works I* (Dordrecht, 1992), pp. 115-28, as well as his detailed discussion of the Zermelo-Russell Paradox in Chapter Two of his 'On the Foundations of

learnt about its existence. Nonetheless, Frege himself did not seem to have been completely satisfied with the patch to his system introduced in the Epilogue. Moreover, since no other presumed solution satisfied Frege more, the slow process of his abandonment of logicism began some years later, though it is difficult – if not impossible – to determine a specific year. In section 3, I will be saying more about Frege's abandonment of logicism, though mostly about the culmination of the process. Now I will be concerned firstly with Frege's formulation of the paradox in the Epilogue, as well as with the possible solutions considered by Frege. I will be following Frege's exposition closely, not only to avoid too much interpretation on my part, but also to dispel any doubts about Frege's notion of the extension of a concept as the class determined by the concept.

Frege formulates the Zermelo-Russell Paradox as follows:[4] We say that something belongs to a class, if it falls under the concept whose extension is precisely that class. Let us consider now the concept 'class that does not belong to itself'. The extension of such a concept, if we are allowed to talk about it, is the class of all classes that do not belong to themselves. Let us call this class K. Let us ask ourselves if this class belongs or does not belong to itself. Let us suppose first that it does. If something belongs to class K, then it falls under the concept whose extension is that class. Hence, if our class belongs to itself, then it is a class that does not belong to itself. Thus, our first presupposition allows us to infer a contradiction with itself. Let us suppose now that our class K does not belong to itself. Hence, it falls under the concept whose extension is that same class and, thus, it belongs to itself. Thus, our second presupposition also leads to a contradiction with itself.

Since Frege believed that the complete demarcation of functions – and, thus, of concepts and relations – was equivalent to the *Tertium non Datur*,[5] he first considered the possibility of denying classes – and value ranges, in general – the status of objects in the strict sense, and of simply considering them improper objects, in which case one could restrict the application of the *Tertium non Datur* to proper objects. In this way, value ranges could not be possible arguments for all first level functions. There would be, however, some first level functions – for example, the identity relation – that could have both proper objects and improper objects as arguments. In fact, with respect to its arguments, one would have a threefold classification of first level functions: (i) functions whose arguments could only be proper objects, (ii) functions whose arguments could be either proper or improper objects, and (iii) functions whose arguments could only be improper objects. With respect to the possible values of first level functions, one would obtain a similar threefold classification: (i') functions whose values could only be proper objects, (ii') functions whose values could be either proper or improper objects, and (iii') functions whose values could only be improper objects.

Mathematics', ibid., pp. 197-206. See also Eugene C. Luschei's book *The Logical Systems of Lesniewski* (Amsterdam, 1962), Chapter 3, section 3.

[4] *Grundgesetze der Arithmetik II*, Nachwort, pp. 253-4.

[5] See, for example, ibid., sections 56-61, 63 and 64.

Combining the two classifications, we would obtain nine sorts of first level functions. To those nine sorts of first level functions there would correspond nine different sorts of value ranges, all of which would be improper objects. We would then have to distinguish between classes of proper objects, classes of improper objects, relations between proper objects, relations between improper objects, relations – like identity – either between proper objects or between improper objects, relations between a proper object and an improper object – like the relation of an object belonging to the extension of a concept – etc. In this way, we would obtain an infinite multiplicity of species. Frege asserts[6] that objects belonging to different species could not occur as arguments of the same functions. Frege's assertion should be understood as meaning that given a function, one could not replace one of its arguments with an argument of a different species. However, if it were to mean that functions could not apply to objects of different species, it would clearly contradict his assertion that the identity relation would apply indistinctly to proper and improper objects and, more generally, would contradict the inclusion of functions that can apply either to proper objects or to improper ones as arguments.

This presumed solution considered and rejected by Frege would be a sort of type theory, in a similar fashion as the simple and ramified theories developed later by Russell and Ramsey[7] with the same goal of blocking the paradoxes. From the standpoint of Frege's *Grundgesetze der Arithmetik*, such a solution would be a natural extension of the hierarchy of functions present in that work to a hierarchy of objects and functions, together with the corresponding complications originated in such an extension. However, Frege rejects such a way out, seemingly because he believes that it is too complicated to offer a complete legislation by means of which one could decide which objects are going to be allowed as arguments of which functions.

The second possible solution considered and also rejected by Frege takes names for classes as pseudo-names devoid of referent. They would have to be considered as parts of signs that only as a whole would have a referent. In such a case, we could not explain the sign '2' by itself, but would have to consider different expressions containing the sign '2' as a dependent constituent, but that could not be logically conceived as composed of '2' and another part.

Although Frege is not especially explicit on this issue, he rejects this second attempt to avoid the paradox because he considers that such a solution would convey the abandonment of the generality of arithmetical statements, and it would in no way be clear how one could then talk about a natural number of classes or about a natural number of natural numbers.[8]

Frege opts to continue considering value ranges – and, thus, extensions of concepts, that is, classes – as proper objects, and replace Principle V with a weaker

---

[6]*Grundgesetze der Arithmetik II*, pp. 254-5.
[7]See his papers 'The Foundations of Mathematics' of 1925 and 'Mathematical Logic' of 1926, reprinted in Frank P. Ramsey, *Foundations: Essays in Philosophy, Logic, Mathematics and Economics* (London, 1978), pp. 152-212 and 213-32, respectively.
[8]*Grundgesetze der Arithmetik II*, p. 255.

version, with the hope that such weaker version could still serve the cause of logicism. According to Frege,[9] there is no difficulty in transforming the generality of an equation in the equality between its value ranges. The source of the paradox lies in the inverse transformation that would allow us to go from the equality between value ranges to the generality for all possible objects as arguments of the values of the respective functions. Furthermore, Frege adds[10] that one cannot exclude the possibility that there are functions that do not have any extension – at least, as Frege uses the expression.

The replacement of Axiom V – which Frege called 'Axiom V'' – says that the value ranges of the functions $\Phi(\xi)$ and $\Psi(\zeta)$ are identical is the same as that for every argument 'x' different both from the value ranges of $\Phi(\xi)$ and of $\Psi(\zeta)$, $\Phi(x)=\Psi(x)$. In our preferred symbolism, Axiom V' would read:

$$[\hat{u}\Phi(u)=\hat{a}\Psi(a)]\leftrightarrow[(\forall x)[\neg(x\neq\hat{u}\Phi(u)\rightarrow x=\hat{a}\Psi(a))\rightarrow(\Phi(x)=\Psi(x))]]$$

Frege's solution has the counterintuitive consequence that two first level concepts can have the same extension without having all the objects that fall under one of the concepts also fall under the other concept. In fact, Frege takes as a criterion of the identity of two extensions the following patchwork: The extension of a concept coincides with that of another concept, if every object, with the exception of the extension of the first concept, that falls under the first concept, also falls under the second, and, inversely, if every object, with the exception of the extension of the second concept, that falls under the second concept, also falls under the first one.[11]

More than any of the solutions of the Zermelo-Russell Paradox presented by Russell, Zermelo, or others, Frege's attempt at a solution seems to be an *ad hoc* solution, a sort of patch to cover a hole in Frege's logical trousers, which would hardly have generated enthusiasm among researchers in the foundations of mathematics. Moreover, as mentioned at the beginning of this section, the system of *Grundgesetze der Arithmetik* amended by the replacement of Axiom V with Axiom V' also allows the derivation of a contradiction. In fact, Frege does not seem to have seen the nucleus of the difficulty, namely, the non-exclusion of value ranges being possible arguments of the functions for which they are value ranges. The problem could not be resolved – as Frege believed –[12] simply by precluding that, given two functions having always the same value for the same argument, both have their common value range as possible argument, but by precluding that any of the two functions have their common value range as a possible argument. This last possibility is not precluded by Axiom V'. Clearly, (*) $(\forall x)[(x\neq\hat{u}\Phi(u)\wedge x\neq\hat{a}\Psi(a))\rightarrow(\Phi(x)=\Psi(x))]$ follows from Axiom V' – in fact, it is equivalent to its right hand side. The last formula is equivalent to

---

[9]Ibid.
[10]Ibid., p. 257.
[11]Ibid., p. 262.
[12]Ibid.

$(\forall x)[(\Phi(x)\neq\Psi(x))\rightarrow\neg(x\neq\hat{u}\Phi(u)\wedge x\neq\hat{a}\Psi(a))]$ – which, on the other hand, is equivalent to the strange formula $(\forall x)[(\Phi(x)\neq\Psi(x))\rightarrow(x=\hat{u}\Phi(u)\vee x=\hat{a}\Psi(a))]$. (Incidentally, this last formula, united by a biconditional with the left hand side of Axiom V', would form an extremely bizarre equivalent of that axiom.) However, the formula whose propositional matrix is the converse of the propositional matrix of (*), namely, $(\forall x)[(\Phi(x)=\Psi(x))\rightarrow(x\neq\hat{u}\Phi(u)\wedge x\neq\hat{a}\Psi(a))]$ does not follow from Axiom V', leaving the possibility that the common value range of the functions be an argument of one of the two equivalent functions. It should surprise nobody that the amended logical system also allowed the derivation of a contradiction.

The ground for the contradiction lies in Frege's requirement that functions – and, thus, concepts and relations – be defined for all objects and, hence, that there is only one sort of object. In essence, the so-called Julius Caesar Problem is also at the roots of the paradox. As mentioned above, Frege even identified this requirement with the *Tertium non Datur*. He lacked a theory of semantic categories in the tradition of Husserl-Lesniewski-Ajdukiewicz, and rejected his sketch of a theory of types, though Russell's simple theory of types would have been sufficient to block the paradox. He did not even have the now familiar notion of a universe of discourse, a notion incompatible with his Julius Caesar Dogma. Unfortunately, Frege's brilliant logical system and his duly famous philosophical analyses were built upon some dogmatically accepted theses, like the requirement of the definability of all functions for every single object, and the pre-established harmony between the grammatical domain, the realm of senses and that of ontology – the last of which, as mentioned in Chapters 4 and 5, was at the origin of important difficulties of his philosophical views – which corroded his logical endeavours from within.

2 The Controversy on the Foundations of Geometry

Someone familiar with Frege's views on geometry, expounded in Chapters 2 and 3, and especially with Frege's theory of definitions, expounded in the previous chapter, will consider Frege's reaction to the publication in 1899 of David Hilbert's duly famous *Grundlagen der Geometrie*[13] not only perfectly understandable, but a consequence of such views. In that book a conception of the role of axioms in an axiom system that is fundamentally different from that of traditional Euclidean axiomatics enters the scene – though apparently not for the first time.[14] The fundamental terms of geometry, like 'point', 'straight line' and

---

[13]*Grundlagen der Geometrie* (1899, 10th edition, Stuttgart, 1968).

[14]Only in *Grundgesetze der Arithmetik II*, section 66, published four years after Hilbert's epoch-making book, is there in that work an explicit rejection of Hilbert's implicit definitions, though it was clear already from his strictures on definitions in the first volume – see section 33 – that Frege would not allow such kind of definition. In any case, such a conception of implicit definitions seems to have been anticipated by Bernard Bolzano. On this point, see the excellent book by Jan Sebestik *Logique et Mathématique chez Bernard*

'plane', are not explicitly defined or elucidated, but occur in various axioms, which together constitute an implicit definition of the corresponding notions. Thus, the objects of study of geometry, being determined exclusively by the axioms, are devoid of any link to an intuitive basis. On this issue, Frege, who was the most important force in the revolution in logic in the second half of the nineteenth century and the founding father of a new way of doing philosophy, was especially conservative, adhering to the traditional view of axiom systems and to the clear separation of axioms from definitions. Of course, we have already seen that his related views on geometry and on definitions were correspondingly conservative, which highlights the interpretation of Frege as a man of great contrasts. He revolutionized logic and philosophy, but was extremely conservative with respect to geometry, axiomatics and the theory of definitions; he was exemplary in his logico-philosophical analyses, but built his logical and philosophical views on the basis of some unquestioned dogmas that were in the end responsible for the collapse of his logical system and for many of the difficulties encountered by his philosophical views. Furthermore, Frege was exemplarily rational and meticulous when dealing with logic and the foundations of mathematics, but had emotional affinities with extremely irrational political views.[15]

Nonetheless, though conservative with respect to axiomatic systems, as occurs with his views on geometry, some of Frege's remarks on Hilbert's views are especially interesting and cannot be ignored. Such remarks are present both in various letters of Frege to Hilbert, and in two series of articles on the foundations of geometry published in 1903 and 1906. The first series consists of two papers, whereas the second, motivated by a defence made by A. Korselt of Hilbert's views, consists of three papers.[16]

For Frege, an axiom is a thought whose truth is determined by means other than presenting a proof based on logical inference. On the other hand, a definition is – as we already saw in the preceding chapter – a stipulation by means of which the referent (or sense and referent) of a sign or word is fixed. Contrary to the remaining mathematical statements, a definition contains a word or a sign that up to then did not have any referent, and that obtains a referent exclusively by means of the definition. The remaining mathematical statements cannot contain any word or sign whose referent was not previously fixed. Moreover, definitions are arbitrary stipulations and, thus, cannot extend our knowledge. Axioms and theorems, which clearly purport to enrich our knowledge, ought never to stipulate the referent of a word or sign. Furthermore, for Frege genuine axioms are true and, thus, cannot contradict each other. Hence, in such a case, any consistency proof of the axioms with each other would be superfluous.

Bolzano (Paris, 1992), p. 142; as well as the paper by Anita von Duhn, 'Bolzano's Account of Justification', in Friedrich Stadler (ed.), *The Vienna Circle and Logical Positivism* (Dordrecht, 2003), pp. 21-33, especially p. 28.
[15]On this issue, see Frege's *Tagebuch, Deutsche Zeitscrift für Philosophie* 6, (1994): 1067-98.
[16]See *Kleine Schriften*, pp. 262-72 and 281-323.

For Hilbert, axioms play a dual role, since they purport to be constituent parts of definitions and, on the other hand, express fundamental facts, convey knowledge. Now, Frege argues[17] that if axioms assert something, then every expression occurring in them has to be completely known. If, on the other hand, axioms were definitions, they would contain expressions whose referents are not known and have to be fixed by stipulations. In such a case, they would neither assert anything nor convey any knowledge.

With respect to the dependence or independence of axioms in Hilbert's usage, Frege observes[18] that the axioms that are constituent parts of the same 'definition' must be dependent upon each other, since if some were true and others false in an interpretation, then those which are true would be acquiring a different sense, since the same notion would now be differently determined. In fact, adds Frege,[19] when we talk about the consistency or the independence of the axioms in Hilbert's usage, what is under scrutiny are not the complete axioms but those of their parts that express notes of the concept to be defined. If those notes contradict each other, there is no object possessing such properties. That is the reason why a consistency proof of the axioms consists in exhibiting an object possessing all those properties, and that an independence proof consists in exhibiting an object possessing one property but not the others.

Frege compares Hilbert's axiomatization of geometry to a system of equations with various unknowns, since in a single axiom more than one of the unknown expressions is present, in which case, the totality of the axioms is needed for their determination.[20] Frege asks whether such a system of equations has a solution and requires that if such a solution exists, it be uniquely determined. In fact, he considers that no solution is possible, and argues that by means of Hilbert's axiom system one cannot even decide whether his watch is a point or not.[21] Once more the omnipresent Julius Caesar Problem is invoked.

The fundamental error of Hilbert's 'definitions', according to Frege,[22] is the confusion between concepts of first and second level, a confusion that makes impossible a profound insight in mathematics and logic. Every point is an object and, thus, both the concept of point and all its notes are first level concepts. Now, in Hilbert's axioms the notes are not first level concepts, that is, they are not properties that an object should have in order to be a point. They are really second

---

[17]'Über die Grundlagen der Geometrie I, I', *Kleine Schriften*, p. 265. It is noteworthy that neither in *Kleine Schriften* – where the five papers of Frege on the foundations of geometry have been collected – nor in *Nachgelassene Schriften* or in *Wissenschaftlicher Briefwechsel* is the first name of Korselt given. His name was Reinhold Alwin Korselt – see Lothar Kreiser's *Frege: Leben-Werk-Zeit*, p. 638. I hope that the omission is casual, and does not illustrate any attitude of some Fregean scholars towards the authors who dared criticize their master.
[18]Ibid., pp. 265-6.
[19]Ibid., p. 266.
[20]'Über die Grundlagen der Geometrie I, II', *Kleine Schriften*, p. 268.
[21]Ibid.
[22]Ibid., p. 269.

level concepts. Thus, the relation of the Euclidean concept of point – which is a first level concept – with Hilbert's second level concept consists in the fact that the former falls within the latter. But there can also be other first level concepts of point that fall within Hilbert's second level concept of (concepts of) point. Hence, Euclidean geometry would be only a particular case of a general doctrine that would possibly contain an unlimited number of other geometries as particular cases. Thus, Frege concludes that to avoid confusions, we ought to talk about 'point in geometry A', 'point in geometry B', 'straight line in geometry C', 'axiom of parallels in geometry D', etc., and not simply of 'point', 'straight line', 'axiom of parallels', since such expressions would be equivocal.[23]

Before continuing my exposition, a digression seems pertinent. Firstly, I should mention that Frege's certainly deep and probably correct rendering of Hilbertian axiomatics cannot help to mask a limitation in Frege's views on geometry. Although Frege came to logic and philosophy from geometry and even studied some semesters and obtained his Doctor's degree at the same university in which Riemann had taught a few years before Frege's arrival, the great logician and philosopher never grasped completely the importance of Riemann's revolutionary contribution to mathematics.[24] Hilbert's views clearly take into account the general Riemannian conception of manifolds, according to which Euclidean geometry is just a particular case of a continuous threefold-extended manifold, with no special privileges. On the other hand, the nature of physical space, whether it is Euclidean or not, would have to be decided empirically. Moreover, if something could be said about intuitive, that is, non-formal and non-empirical space, then, as argued by Carnap in his dissertation, it would not validate any Euclidean or Kantian insights. Thus, Carnap turned to Husserl, who propounded a synthetic *a priori*, but was, nonetheless, strongly influenced by Riemann's views on formal manifolds, in his attempt to find a realm for intuitive space between the realm of formal manifolds and that of empirical space.[25] On the other hand, it should also be mentioned that Frege's deep interpretation of Hilbertian axiomatics put him on the verge of discovering model theory various decades earlier than Tarski. Once more, his unfounded beliefs – this time in the truth of Euclidean geometry – prevented him from making such a gigantic step forward.

Korselt's defence[26] of Hilbert's views against Frege motivated the latter to publish in 1906 a second series of papers under the same title 'Über die Grundlagen der Geometrie'. In these three papers Frege tries to answer Korselt's

[23] Ibid., p. 272.
[24] See Riemann's epoch-making monograph *Über die Hypothesen, welche der Geometrie zugrunde liegen* (1867, third edition, edited by Hermann Weyl, 1923, reprint, New York, 1960, 1973).
[25] See Rudolf Carnap's dissertation, *Der Raum*, 1922, reprint (Vaduz, 1991), especially Chapters Three and Five, as well as the notes at the end.
[26] In 'Über die Grundlagen der Geometrie', *Jahresbericht der Deutschen Akademiker Vereinigung* 12 (1903): 402-7.

criticism by expounding his views more clearly. Mostly, Frege's arguments are similar to those of the prior series of two papers. There are, however, some important aspects that did not receive due attention in the 1903 series.

Probably the most interesting and novel component of Frege's 1906 analysis of Hilbert's views on the foundations of geometry is his interpretation of 'definitions' in Hilbert's usage. Such 'definitions' are for the most part, according to Frege, dependent parts of a general theorem, which in view of the occurrence of expressions in them that play the role of what we now call 'free variables' – like 'point' or 'straight line' in Hilbert's usage – are not properly statements, and are called by Frege 'improper statements'. An authentic statement does not admit interpretations, nor is it true in some circumstances but false in other circumstances. When such a possibility is present – as happens with Hilbert's axioms – we are not dealing with proper statements, but with schemes of statements. Hilbert's axioms, for example, are not statements, they do not express a thought about whose truth or falsity it makes sense to ask, but are schemes of statements in which expressions like 'point' or 'straight line' play the role of variables in a similar fashion to that of the letter 'x' in inequalities like 'x>1' or in the equation '2x-1=9'. One could, however, obtain proper axioms from Hilbert's schemes of axioms, if they were preceded by a formulation of the circumstances of their validity. Hence, one would obtain a conditional statement whose consequent is the Hilbertian 'axiom'. Thus, in the conditional 'If x>1, then x>0' neither 'x>1' nor 'x>0' are proper statements, but the conditional is a proper statement.[27]

Another interesting issue treated by Frege in the 1906 series is that of the limits of formalization in logic. For Frege, logic is not unrestrictedly formal, since if that were the case, it would be lacking any content. In the same way in which geometry has its proper concepts and relations, logic also has its proper concepts and relations, for example, negation, identity and the subordination of a concept under another concept. In fact, for Frege no science is completely formal.

3 Frege's Abandonment of Logicism

The most radical change in Frege's views on logic, mathematics and philosophy occurred in the last years of his life. The abandonment of his views on logic, mathematics and their relation seems to have been a long process, which probably began shortly after learning about the Zermelo-Russell Paradox and by not being able to solve it satisfactorily. His 'solution' in the Epilogue of the second volume of *Grundgesetze der Arithmetik* was half-hearted, and probably he was very soon convinced that it was no solution at all. Thus, he directed his attention to geometry for the next few years, and when he returned to the discussion of logical and mathematical issues – for example, in his 1914 'Logik in der Mathematik' – he carefully avoided any reference to the logicist thesis. The logicist thesis is also not

---

[27]See *Kleine Schriften*, pp. 295-96.

explicitly mentioned in the series of papers of 1918-1920, which were supposed to be the first steps at a textbook on logic. Nonetheless, the explicit abandonment of logicism occurs in his posthumously published writings of 1924-1925. In those writings, Frege not only abandons the logicist project, but also replaces it with a new project of a geometrical foundation of mathematics. Moreover, in such writings of 1924-1925 Frege for the first time freely discusses the most general epistemological problems, and sketches a new epistemology with some general affinities to Kant's. Certainly, since his *Begriffsschrift* Frege was concerned with epistemological problems. Such concern, however, was repressed by his fear of committing the mortal sin of falling into the hands of psychologism. Thus, Frege's epistemological endeavours were limited to specific problems. Already in his 1918 paper 'Der Gedanke' the door to general epistemological concerns is half open, but it is only in his writings of 1924-1925 that the door opens completely and he dares to sketch a general epistemology.

Frege retained, however, two important theses until the end of his life, namely, that arithmetic does not require any empirical foundation and that number attributions contain a statement about a concept.[28] But he does not consider anymore that arithmetic is a branch of logic and, thus, that everything arithmetical has to be proved by purely logical means. Frege now believes that spatial and temporal intuition serve also as a foundation of arithmetic.

Frege calls a 'source of knowledge' that by means of which it is justified to judge. For the last Frege there exist three sources of knowledge, namely:

(1)   sense perception,
(2)   the logical source of knowledge, and
(3)   the geometrical source of knowledge and the temporal source of knowledge.

Thus, as in Kant, the spatial and temporal sources of knowledge are not separated, but form a sort of two-headed source of pure intuitive knowledge, which is, on the one side, not empirical and, on the other side, not logical. According to Frege, sense perception is present in our physical knowledge, but is particularly vulnerable with regard to possible distortions and deceits. In fact, in our knowledge of physics the other two sources of knowledge are also present.

In mathematical knowledge sense perception does not play any role. By contrast, both the logical and the geometrical sources of knowledge play a decisive role in mathematical knowledge. Contrary to what Frege had believed for four and a half decades, the logical source of knowledge cannot by itself give us any object. There are no logical objects. Mathematical objects are given to us by the geometrical source of knowledge. In this way, arithmetical objects are given to us by the geometrical source of knowledge, and all mathematical objects have the same geometrical origin. According to Frege, the geometrical source of knowledge

[28]See 'Neuer Versuch der Grundlegung der Mathematik', *Nachgelassene Schriften*, pp. 298-302, especially p. 298.

and the temporal one are responsible for the origin of the mathematical notions of infinitude. As a consequence of the geometrical origin of arithmetic, Frege devised a new foundational project, which in some sense turned things upside down. The geometrical foundation of arithmetic made the notion of a complex number the most fundamental arithmetical sort of number, whereas the notion of natural number would be a derivative one, probably so derivative that it would occur at the end of the foundational chain of number sorts.

None of the sources of knowledge is immune to the possibility of error, but spatial and temporal intuitions are the less vulnerable to error. In a clear reference to Hilbert's views on axiom systems, Frege asserts[29] that the possibility of error in geometrical intuition arises when one distorts the sense of the old Euclidean notion of axiom and, in this way, one assigns a different sense to the statements in which the geometrical axioms are expressed.

The logical source of knowledge is more liable to error than the geometrical or simply mathematical source, since, as mentioned above, all mathematical objects have their origin in this source. The reason for this liability to error of the logical source of knowledge lies in the fact that in virtue of our natural limitations we enter in contact with thoughts and their relations only by means of language. But language is never perfectly logical, and even the most exact language cannot free us of the possibility of distortions. The tendency of language to produce proper names to which no object corresponds as referent is particularly dangerous for the adequate grasping of thoughts. That is precisely what happens when we form a proper name according to the scheme 'the extension of concept G', and also when we try to talk about a function or a concept and say 'the function f', respectively, 'the concept G'. The paradoxes of set theory, which – according to Frege[30] – destroyed that discipline, have their origin in such muddiness of the logical caused by language. In fact, Frege considers that most contaminations of the logical source of knowledge have their origin in trying to transform into an object what is a function by means of the definite article. Thus, until his last moment Frege remained fettered to his prejudice that an expression preceded by the definite article in singular refers to an object – as if there did not exist languages – for example, Russian – without definite (or indefinite) articles.

A few words should be said on Frege's last philosophy. First of all, those Fregean scholars who have tried to make of Frege a Kantian or at least a neo-Kantian can finally find some substantial affinities between Frege's views and those of Kant. Unfortunately for them, those are the views of the old Frege, who distanced himself from some of the most basic of his previous views on logic and mathematics. Thus, in some sense, the existence of those general affinities between the old Frege and Kant can rather serve those interpreters who do not conceive Frege as a Kantian or neo-Kantian. Between the young or the mature Frege and Kant there exists only a similarity of views with respect to the nature of geometry.

---

[29]'Erkenntnisquellen der Mathematik und der mathematischen Naturwissenschaften', *Nachgelassene Schriften*, pp. 286-94, especially, pp. 292-3.
[30]Ibid., pp. 288-9.

But as was made clear in Chapters 2 and 3, Frege's arguments for the synthetic *a priori* nature of geometrical statements are very different from Kant's. Furthermore, though there exist more general affinities between the old Frege and Kant, I very sincerely doubt that Kant or the neo-Kantians would have followed the old Frege in his project of providing a geometrical foundation for arithmetic, in which the foundational order between number sorts is completely reversed. The old Frege's project looks too bizarre to produce enthusiasm in any philosophical circle. It seems more the expression of an extreme intellectual and personal frustration. His comments on the destruction of set theory by the paradoxes are not only false, but show that he either had not followed or had not understood the development of set theory in the first two decades of the twentieth century, particularly at the hands of Zermelo. Finally, his attribution of possible failures of geometrical intuitive knowledge to the abandonment of Euclidean axiomatics in favour of Hilbert's seems preposterous.

A final point that I want to make is that Frege's project and his belief that all mathematical objects have a geometrical foundation also show how disconnected he was from the development of mathematics. Already in the first two decades of the twentieth century abstract algebra had made its appearance in the mathematical scene, as had also general topology. Mathematics was much more than geometry and analysis. To be taken seriously, the old Frege – or an old-Fregean – would have had to show how algebraic notions known in his day originate in geometry. And for any new possible old-Fregean there would remain the by no means easy task of showing that the objects of study of universal algebra have a geometrical origin. The old Frege was probably right when he denied the existence of logical objects. On this point, he finally agreed with Husserl and others. He was also most surely right when he abandoned the logicist project, since not only was his logical foundation of arithmetic muddled by the Zermelo-Russell Paradox, but the most serious attempt to follow his steps, the system developed by Russell and Whitehead in *Principia Mathematica*[31] was also a failure. Their Multiplicative Axiom, which is equivalent to the Axiom of Choice seems to be set-theoretical, not logical. Their Infinity Axiom seems to be neither logical nor mathematical, but empirical. Finally, the Reducibility Axiom required by their ramified theory of types looks much more like an *ad hoc* hypothesis of doubtful validity rather than a purely logical axiom. More recent attempts by some hard-core Fregean scholars have been stymied by the illogicality of the so-called Hume's Principle. But the most important argument against logicism and even set-theoreticism is the fact that the most basic mathematical notions, like those of set, function and relation are interdefinable.[32] For Frege, relations and concepts were particular cases of functions, whereas classes (or extensions) were dependent on concepts. In set theory, sets (or classes) constitute the most basic notion. Relations are defined in terms of sets, and functions are particular cases of relations – an n-

---

[31]*Principia Mathematica*, 3 Vols. (Cambridge 1910-1913, second edition, 1925-27).
[32]On this issue, see Saunders Mac Lane's book *Mathematics: Form and Function* (New York et al., 1986), Chapter Eleven, especially pp. 359 and 407.

ary function being an n+1-ary relation uniquely determined in its last argument. But sets could also be defined in terms of relations, and in category theory both sets and relations can be defined in terms of a very abstract notion of function usually called 'morphisms' or 'arrows'.[33]

Nonetheless, the demise of logicism and the inexistence of logical objects do not imply the inexistence of non-geometrical mathematical objects. If one understands geometry as linked to our spatial intuition, as Frege and Kant did, then all objects of study of pure mathematics are non-geometrical objects. And there exists an infinity of these.

---

[33]On category theory, see, for example, Saunders Mac Lane's *Category Theory for the Working Mathematician*, Springer 1971.

Bibliography

I Writings of Gottlob Frege

(A) *In German*

Begriffsschrift (1879, reprint Hildesheim: Georg Olms, 1964a).
Die Grundlagen der Arithmetik (1884, reprint Hildesheim: Georg Olms, 1961, Centenary edition, edited and with an Introduction by Christian Thiel, Hamburg: Felix Meiner, 1986).
Grundgesetze der Arithmetik (2 vols.1893 and 1903, reprint in a single volume Hildesheim: Georg Olms, 1962).
Kleine Schriften, (Ignacio Angelelli (ed.), Hildesheim: Georg Olms, 1967, second edition 1990).
Nachgelassene Schriften (Hans Hermes, Friedrich Kambartel and Friedrich Kaulbach (eds), Hamburg: Felix Meiner, 1969, second (revised) edition 1983).
Wissenschaftlicher Briefwechsel (Gottfried Gabriel, Hans Hermes, Friedrich Kambartel, Christian Thiel and Albert Veraart (eds), Hamburg: Felix Meiner, 1976).
Tagebuch, Deutsche Zeitschrift für Philosophie 6 (1994): 1063-98.

(B) *English Translations*

Conceptual Notation and Related Articles (Terrell Ward Bynum (ed.), Oxford: Oxford University Press, 1972).
The Foundations of Arithmetic (1950, second (revised) edition Oxford: B.H. Blackwell, 1959).
The Basic Laws of Arithmetic (up to § 52 of vol. 1) (Montgomery Furth (ed.), Berkeley: University of California Press, 1964b).
Translations from the Philosophical Writings of Gottlob Frege (Peter Geach and Max Black (eds), third edition Oxford: B.H. Blackwell, 1980a).
Logical Investigations (Peter Geach and R.H. Stoothoff (eds), Oxford: B.H. Blackwell, 1977).
On the Foundations of Geometry and Formal Theories of Arithmetic (E.H.W. Kluge (ed.), New Haven: Yale University Press, 1971).
Posthumous Writings (translation of the first edition of *Nachgelassene Schriften*) (Oxford: B.H. Blackwell, 1979).
Philosophical and Mathematical Correspondence (Brian McGuinness (ed.), Oxford: B.H. Blackwell, 1980b).
Collected Papers (Max Black et al. (eds), Oxford: B.H. Blackwell, 1984).
The Frege Reader (M. Beaney (ed.), Oxford: B.H. Blackwell, 1997).

II Books on Gottlob Frege's Philosophy

Angelelli, I., *Studies on Gottlob Frege and Traditional Philosophy* (Dordrecht: Reidel, 1967).

Baker, G.P. and Hacker, P.M.S., *Frege: Logical Excavations* (Oxford: Oxford University Press, 1984).

Bar-Elli, Gilead, *The Sense of Reference* (Berlin: Walter de Gruyter, 1996).

Beaney, Michael, *Frege: Making Sense* (London: Duckworth, 1996).

Bell, David, *Frege's Theory of Judgement* (Oxford: Oxford University Press, 1979).

Belna, J.P., *La Notion de Nombre chez Cantor, Dedekind, Frege* (Paris: J. Vrin, 1996).

Birjukov, B.V., *Two Soviet Studies on Frege* (Dordrecht: Reidel, 1964).

Brisart, R. (ed.), *Husserl et Frege* (Paris: J. Vrin, 2002).

Burge, Tyler, *Truth, Thought and Reason: Essays on Frege* (Oxford: Oxford University Press, 2005).

Carl, Wolfgang, *Sinn und Bedeutung: Studien zu Frege und Wittgenstein* (Meisenheim: Anton Heim, 1982).

———, *Frege's Theory of Sense and Reference* (Cambridge: Cambridge University Press, 1994).

Currie, Gregory, *Frege: an Introduction to his Philosophy* (Sussex: Harvester Press, and Totowa, NJ: Barnes and Noble, 1982).

Demopoulos, William (ed.), *Frege's Philosophy of Mathematics* (Cambridge, MA: Harvard University Press, 1995).

Dummett, Michael A., *Frege: Philosophy of Language* (London: Duckworth, and Cambridge, MA: Harvard University Press, 1973, second edition 1981a).

———, *The Interpretation of Frege's Philosophy* (London: Duckworth, and Cambridge, MA: Harvard University Press, 1981b).

———, *Frege: Philosophy of Mathematics* (London: Duckworth, and Cambridge, MA: Harvard University Press, 1991a).

———, *Frege and Other Philosophers* (Oxford: Oxford University Press, 1991b).

———, *Origins of Analytic Philosophy* (London: Duckworth, 1993).

Gillies, Donald A., *Frege, Dedekind and Peano on the Foundations of Arithmetic* (Assen: Van Gorcum, 1982).

Greimann, Dirk, *Freges Konzeption der Wahrheit* (Hildesheim: Georg Olms, 2003).

Grossmann, Reinhardt, *Reflections on Frege's Philosophy* (Evanston: Northwestern University Press, 1969).

Haaparanta, Leila (ed.), *Mind, Meaning and Mathematics*, (Dordrecht: Kluwer, 1994).

Haaparanta, Leila and Hintikka, Jaakko (eds), *Frege Synthesized* (Dordrecht: Reidel, 1986).

Hill, Claire O. and Rosado Haddock, Guillermo E., *Husserl or Frege?: Meaning, Objectivity and Mathematics*, (Chicago and La Salle: Open Court, 2000, paperback edition 2003).

Kenny, Anthony J., *Frege: An Introduction to his Philosophy* (1995, Oxford: B.H. Blackwell, 2000).

Klemke, E.D. (ed.), *Essays on Frege* (Urbana: University of Illinois Press, 1968).

Kluge, E.H.W., *The Metaphysics of Gottlob Frege* (Den Haag: M. Nijhoff, 1980).

Kreiser, Lothar, *Gottlob Frege: Leben-Werk-Zeit* (Hamburg: Felix Meiner, 2001).

Kutschera, Franz von, *Gottlob Frege* (Berlin: Walter de Gruyter, 1989).

Largeault, Jean, *Logique et Philosophie chez Frege* (Paris and Louvain: Éditions Nauwelaerts, 1970).

Max, Ingolf and Stelzner, Werner (eds), *Logik und Mathematik* (Berlin: Walter de Gruyter, 1995).

Mayer, Verena E., *Der Wert der Gedanken* (Frankfurt: Peter Lang, 1989).

————, *Gottlob Frege* (München: C.H. Beck, 1996).

Mendelsohn, Richard L., *The Philosophy of Gottlob Frege* (Cambridge: Cambridge University Press, 2005).

Mohanty, J.N., *Husserl and Frege* (Bloomington: Indiana University Press, 1982).

Newen, Albert, Nortmann, Ulrich and Stuhlmann-Laiesz, Rainer, *Building on Frege: New Essays about Sense, Content and Concepts* (Stanford: CSLI Publications, 2001).

Notturno, Mark A., *Objectivity, Rationality and the Third Realm* (Den Haag: M. Nijhoff, 1985).

Resnik, Michael D., *Frege and the Philosophy of Mathematics* (Ithaca: Cornell University Press, 1980).

Rosado Haddock, Guillermo E., *Exposición Crítica de la Filosofía de Gottlob Frege* (publication by the author: Santo Domingo, 1985).

Rouilhan, Philippe de, *Les Paradoxes de la Représentation* (Paris: Éditions de Minuit, 1988).

Salerno, J., *On Frege* (Wadsworth: Belmont, CA., 2001).

Salmon, Nathan, *Frege's Puzzle* (Cambridge, MA: MIT Press, 1986).

Schirn, Matthias (ed.), *Studies on Frege* (3 vols, Stuttgart-Bad Cannstatt: Fromann-Holzboog, 1976).

————(ed.), *Frege: Importance and Legacy* (Berlin: Walter de Gruyter, 1996).

Sluga, Hans, *Gottlob Frege* (London: Routledge, 1980).

————(ed.), *The Philosophy of Gottlob Frege* (4 vols, New York and London: Garland, 1993).

Stelzner, Werner (ed.), *Philosophie und Logik* (Berlin: Walter de Gruyter, 1993).

Sternfeld, Robert, *Frege's Logical Theory* (Carbondale and Edwardsville: Southern Illinois University Press, 1966).

Thiel, Christian, *Sinn und Bedeutung in der Logik Gottlob Freges* (Meisenheim: Anton Heim, 1965).

————(ed.), *Frege und die Grundlagenforschung* (Meisenheim: Anton Heim, 1975).

Tichy, Pavel, *The Foundations of Frege's Logic* (Berlin: Walter de Gruyter, 1988).

Vasallo, Nicola, *La Depsicologizzazione della Logica* (Milano: Franco Angelli, 1995).

Wechsung, Gerd (ed.), *Frege Conference 1984* (Berlin: Akademie Verlag, 1984).

Weiner, Joan, *Frege in Perspective* (Ithaca: Cornell University Press, 1980)
———, *Frege* (Oxford: Oxford University Press, 1999).
———, *Frege Explained* (Chicago and Lasalle: Open Court, 2005).
Wright, Crispin, *Frege's Conception of Numbers as Objects* (Abeerden: Abeerden University Press, 1983).

III Other Works Consulted or Referred to in this Book (includes papers and monographs on Frege either especially referred to in the book or not contained in collections of papers in II)

Alemán, Anastasio, *Lógica, Matemáticas y Realidad* (Madrid: Tecnos, 2001).
Barwise, Jon, Keisler, H.J. and Kunen, K. (eds), *The Kleene Symposium* (Amsterdam: North Holland, 1980).
Barwise, Jon and Perry, John, 'Semantic Innocence and Uncompromising Situations', in *Midwest Studies in Philosophy VI* (Minneapolis: University of Minnesota Press, 1981), pp. 387-403.
Beaney, Michael, 'Russell and Frege', in Nicholas Griffin (ed.), *The Cambridge Companion to Russell* (Cambridge: Cambridge University Press, 2003), pp. 128-70.
Benacerraf, Paul, 'What Numbers Could Not Be?', (1965, reprinted in Paul Benacerraf and Hilary Putnam (eds), *Philosophy of Mathematics*, second (revised) edition, Cambridge: Cambridge University Press, 1983), pp. 272-94.
———, 'Mathematical Truth', (1973, reprinted in Paul Benacerraf and Hilary Putnam (eds), *Philosophy of Mathematics*, second (revised) edition, Cambridge: Cambridge University Press, 1983), pp. 403-20.
———, 'Frege: The Last Logicist', in *Midwest Studies in Philosophy VI* (Minneapolis: University of Minnesota Press,1981), pp. 17-35.
Bolzano, Bernard, *Grundlegung der Logik: Ausgewählte Paragraphen aus der Wissenschaftslehre, Band I und II*, second (revised) edition, edited and with an Introduction by Friedrich Kambartel (Hamburg: Felix Meiner, 1978).
———, *Theory of Science*, partial translation of *Wissenschaftslehre* (Dordrecht: Reidel, 1973).
Cantor, Georg, *Gesammelte Abhandlungen* Ernst Zermelo (ed.), (1932, reprint Hildesheim: Georg Olms, 1966).
Carnap, Rudolf, *Der Raum* (1922, reprint Vaduz, Liechtenstein: Topos Verlag, 1991).
———, *Der logische Aufbau der Welt* 1928 (fourth edition, Hamburg: Felix Meiner, 1974, English translation, Berkeley, CA: University of California Press, 1969).
———, *Die logische Syntax der Sprache* 1934 (expanded English translation, Routledge, London 1937, reprint Chicago and La Salle: Open Court, 2002).
———, *Meaning and Necessity* (Chicago: University of Chicago Press, 1947).
Chateaubriand, Oswaldo, *Logical Forms* (2 vols, Campinas: CLE, (I) 2003, (II) 2005).

Church, Alonzo, *Introduction to Mathematical Logic*, Princeton University Press, Princeton 1956.

Curry, Haskell B., *An Outline of a Formalist Philosophy of Mathematics*, (Amsterdam: North Holland, 1951).

Dedekind, Richard, *Was Sind und was Sollen die Zahlen?* (Braunschweig, 1888, English translation 1901, reprint in Essays on the Theory of Numbers, New York: Dover, 1963).

Duhn, Anita von, 'Bolzano's Account of Justification', in Friedrich Stadler (ed.), *The Vienna Circle and Logical Empiricism* (Dordrecht: Kluwer, 2003), pp. 24-33.

Dummett, Michael A., 'The Context Principle: Centre of Frege's Philosophy', in I. Max and W. Stelzner (eds), *Logik und Mathematik*, pp. 3-19.

———, Preface to the Paperback Edition of E. Husserl's Logical Investigations (London: Routledge, 2001).

Fred, Ivette, *Concepto y Objeto en la Filosofía de Gottlob Frege* (MA Thesis, UPR-RP, 1989).

Gabriel, Gottfried, 'Einige Einseitigkeiten des Fregeschen Logikbegriffs', in M. Schirn (ed.), *Studies on Frege II*, pp. 67-86.

Grattan-Guinness, Ivor, *The Search for Mathematical Roots, 1870-1940*, (Princeton: Princeton University Press, 2000).

Hilbert, David, *Grundlagen der Geometrie* 1899 (tenth edition, Stuttgart: Teubner, 1968).

Hill, Claire O., *Word and Object in Husserl, Frege and Russell: the Roots of Twentieth Century Philosophy* (Athens, Ohio: Ohio University Press, 1991).

———, *Rethinking Identity and Metaphysics* (New Haven: Yale University Press, 1997).

Hintikka, Jaakko (ed.), *From Dedekind to Gödel* (Dordrecht: Kluwer, 1995).

Hume, David, *An Enquiry Concerning Human Understanding* (1777, reprinted in David Hume, Essays and Treatises on Several Subjects II, with an Introduction by L.A. Selby-Bigge, Oxford: Oxford University Press, 1975).

Husserl, Edmund, *Philosophie der Arithmetik* (1891, Den Haag: M. Nijhoff, 1970).

———, *Logische Untersuchungen* (2 vols 1900 and 1901, Den Haag: M. Nijhoff (I) 1975, (II) 1984, English translation, London: Routledge 1970, paperback edition with a Preface by Michael Dummett and an Introduction by Dermot Moran 2001a).

———, *Formale und Transzendentale Logik* (1929, Den Haag: M.Nijhoff, 1974).

———, *Erfahrung und Urteil* 1939 (sixth edition, with Preface by Lothar Eley, Hamburg: Felix Meiner, 1985).

———, *Aufsätze und Rezensionen (1890-1910)*, (Den Haag: M. Nijhoff, 1979).

———, *Vorlesungen über Bedeutungslehre* (Dordrecht: Kluwer, 1987).

———, *Briefwechsel* (10 vols, K. Schuhmann and E. Schuhmann (eds), Dordrecht: Kluwer, 1994).

———, 'Doppelvortrag', revised edition, K. Schuhmann and E. Schuhmann (eds), *Husserl Studies*, 17 (2001b): 87-123.

Kant, Immanuel, *Kritik der Reinen Vernunft* (1781 (A), second (revised) edition 1787 (B), reprint of (A) and (B), Hamburg: Felix Meiner, 1868, 1993).

Katz, Jerrold J., 'What Mathematical Knowledge could be', *Mind*, 104 (1996): 491-522.

————, *Realistic Rationalism* (Cambridge, MA: MIT Press, 1998).

————, *Sense, Reference, and Philosophy* (Oxford: Oxford University Press, 2004).

Kripke, Saul, 'An Outline of a Theory of Truth', 1975, reprinted in Robert L. Martin (ed.) *Recent Essays on Truth and the Liar Paradox* (Oxford: Oxford University Press, 1984), pp. 53-81.

Kuhn, Thomas, *The Structure of Scientific Revolutions* (1962, second (revised) edition, Chicago: University of Chicago Press, 1970).

Leibniz, Gottfried W., *Hauptschriften zur Grundlegung der Philosophie* (edited by Ernst Cassirer, 1908, third edition Hamburg: Felix Meiner, 1966).

Lesniewski, Stanislaw, *Collected Works I* (Dordrecht: Kluwer, 1992).

Luschei, Eugene C., *The Logical Systems of Lesniewski* (Amsterdam: North Holland, 1962).

Mac Lane, Saunders, *Category Theory for the Working Mathematician* (New York et al: Springer, 1971).

————, *Mathematics: Form and Function* (New York et al.: Springer, 1986).

Mangione, Corrado and Bozzi, Silvio, *Storia della Logica* (Milano: Garzanti, 1993).

Mendelsohn, Richard L., 'Frege on Predication', in *Midwest Studies in Philosophy VI* (Minneapolis: University of Minnesota Press, 1981), pp. 59-82.

Mieres, José Ernesto, *La Noción de Definición en la Filosofía de la Matemática de Gottlob Frege* (MA Thesis, UPR-RP, 1997).

Moore, Gregory H., *Zermelo's Axiom of Choice* (New York et al.: Springer, 1982).

Ramsey, Frank P., *Foundations: Essays in Philosophy, Logic, Mathematics and Economics* (London:et al., 1978).

Rang, Bernhard and Thomas, Wolfgang, 'Zermelo's Discovery of the "Russell Paradox"', *Historia Mathematica* 8 (1981): 15-22.

Resnik, Michael D., 'Frege's Context Principle Revisited', *Philosophy and Phenomenological Research* XXVII (1967, reprinted in M. Schirn (ed.), *Studies on Frege III*), pp. 35-49.

Riemann, Bernhard, *Über die Hypothesen, welche der Geometrie zugrunde liegen* 1867, third edition, edited by Hermann Weyl, 1923, reprint, Chelsea, New York 1960, 1973.

Rosado Haddock, Guillermo E., *Edmund Husserls Philosophie der Logik und Mathematik im Lichte der gegenwärtigen Logik und Grundlagenforschung*, Doctoral Dissertation, Germany: University of Bonn, 1973).

————, 'Review of M. Schirn (ed.) *Studies on Frege*', *Diálogos* 38 (1981a): 157-83.

————, 'Necessità a posteriori e Contingenze a priori in Kripke: Alcune Note Critiche', *Nominazione* 2 (1981b): 205-19.

————, 'Husserl y Frege: Acerca de un Mito Historiográfico', Critical Study of Claire O. Hill, *Word and Object in Husserl, Frege and Russell, Diálogos* 64 (1994): 187-99.

————, 'On the Semantics of Mathematical Statements', *Manuscrito* XIX/1 (1996): 149-75.

————, 'Husserl's Relevance for the Philosophy and Foundations of Mathematics', *Axiomathes* VIII/1-3 (1997): 125-42.

————, 'Review Article of M. Schirn (ed.) *Frege: Importance and Legacy*" *History and Philosophy of Logic* 17/4 (1998a): 249-66.

————, 'The Other Philosophers of Mathematics', Critical Notice of Jaakko Hintikka (ed.) *From Dedekind to Gödel, Axiomathes* IX/3 (1998b): 361-81.

————, 'The Structure of the Prolegomena', *Manuscrito* XXIII/2 (2000): 61-99.

————, 'Review of Claire O. Hill, *Rethinking Identity and Metaphysics*', *Diálogos* 78 (2001): 205-19.

————, 'Review of Anastasio Alemán, *Lógica, Matemáticas y Realidad*', *Philosophia Mathematica* 11/1 (2003): 109-20.

Rosario Barbosa, Pedro, *El Platonismo de Gottlob Frege y el Mundo 3 de Karl Popper* (MA Thesis, UPR-RP, 2004).

Russell, Bertrand, *The Principles of Mathematics* (1903, second edition 1937, reprint London: George Allen & Unwin, 1942).

————, *Introduction to Mathematical Philosophy* (London: George Allen & Unwin, 1919).

Russell, Bertrand and Whitehead, A.N., *Principia Mathematica* (3 vols, 1910-13, second revised edition, Cambridge: Cambridge University Press, 1925-27).

Schirn, Matthias, 'Frege's Objects of a Quite Special Kind', *Erkenntnis* 32 (1990): 27-60.

————, 'Fregean Abstraction, Referential Indeterminacy and the Logical Foundations of Arithmetic', *Erkenntnis* 59 (2003): 203-32.

————(ed.), *The Philosophy of Mathematics Today* (Oxford: Oxford University Press, 1998).

Schuhmann, Karl (ed.), *Husserl-Chronik* (Den Haag: M. Nijhoff, 1977).

Sebestik, Jan, *Logique et Mathématiques chez Bernard Bolzano* (Paris: J. Vrin, 1992).

Shwayder, David S., 'On the Determination of Reference by Sense', in M. Schirn (ed.), *Studies on Frege III*, pp. 85-95.

Tait, William, 'Frege versus Cantor and Dedekind', in Matthias Schirn (ed.), *Frege: Importance and Legacy*, pp. 70-113.

Tarski, Alfred, 'The Concept of Truth in Formalized Languages', (translation of the German expanded version 'Der Wahrheitsbegriff in den formalisierten Sprachen', 1935, of the original Polish 1933 paper, in *Logic, Semantics, Metamathematics* 1956, second edition, Indianapolis: Hackett, 1983), pp. 152-278.

Tugendhat, Ernst, 'Die Bedeutung des Ausdrucks 'Bedeutung' bei Frege', in M. Schirn (ed.), *Studies on Frege III*, pp. 51-69.

Wahrig, Gerhard et al., *Deutsches Wörterbuch* (Gütersloh: Bertelsmann Lexicon Verlag, 1994).

Weidemann, Hermann, 'Aussagesatz und Sachverhalt: ein Versuch zur Neubestimmung ihres Verhältnisses', *Grazer Philosophische Studien* 18 (1982): 75-99.

Wittgenstein, Ludwig, *Tractatus Logico-Philosophicus* (1922, German original, *Logisch-philosophische Abhandlung* 1921, bilingual edition, London: Routledge, 1961).

Name Index

Subject Index

formalism   109, 117, 119
formalism, pre-Hilbertian   *See* pre-
      Hilbertian formalism
formalist   66, 109, 117-19
functional expression   75, 91-3
functional relation   59
function   4-5, 11-14, 21, 47-8, 51,
      59-60, 67, 69, 71, 75, 88,
      91-4, 96-7, 99-102, 105-8,
      130-133, 139-41
function symbol   12
function word   51, 69, 70n12

geometry   ix, 3, 23, 25, 28, 32, 64,
      117, 120, 123, 133-7, 139-
      41
geometry, Euclidean   *See* Euclidean
geometry, non-Euclidean   *See* non-
      Euclidean

Hilbertian   136-7
Hume's Principle   43, 140
Husserlian   83n51, 104
hypothetical   8

identity   vii, 10, 40, 44-5, 57, 63,
      79-80, 86-8, 95, 98, 103-5,
      126, 131-2, 137
identity relation   87-9, 98, 130-131
identity sign   10, 87-8, 95, 102-4
identity statement   ii, 9-11, 86-89,
      95, 102-4
inequality   118-119

judgeable content   viii, 4-8, 10-12,
      48, 53-4, 76-7
Julius Caesar Dogma   47-8, 133
Julius Caesar Problem   40, 46-7,
      101, 133, 135

Kantian   vii, 17, 64, 66n124, 136,
      139
Kantianism   29n47, 32, 111, 113n10

Leibniz's Principle   45, 88
logic   vii, 1-3, 7-8, 15, 17-20,
      21n18, 23, 28, 30-33, 47,

51n59, 54-5, 59, 61-2, 68,
      70, 73n20, 74, 78, 83, 109-
      114, 120-121, 123-4, 129,
      131n7, 134-9
logical   vii, ix, 1-2, 4, 6, 9, 12-13,
      16, 18-20, 23, 28-9, 41,
      43-5, 48, 51, 53-4, 57, 60,
      61-5, 67, 69-70, 77-9, 84,
      88, 94-6, 99-100, 107n45,
      110, 112-115, 117, 120,
      123, 129, 130n3, 132-4,
      138-40
Logical Empiricism   ix
logical object   41, 51-2, 99, 138,
      140-41
logicism   17, 110, 114, 129-30, 132,
      137-8, 140-41
logicist   51, 62, 65, 109, 114-115,
      137-8, 140

mathematics   vii, ix-x, 4, 6, 17-20,
      23-5, 30, 33, 62, 64-5, 78,
      92, 101n28, 109-13, 117-
      19, 121, 123, 129, 132, 134-
      141
meaning   vii, 4, 9, 12, 15, 19-20, 22,
      24, 39-42, 44, 50, 54, 56,
      58, 60, 72, 75, 83, 131
Millian   24, 64

naturalism   23, 121n44
neo-Kantian   vii, 2, 64, 139-40
non-Euclidean   28, 32
non-representability   41

object   viii-ix, 11-13, 15, 17, 19-20,
      23-4, 26, 28-34, 35-42, 45-
      51, 53-60, 63-6, 68-70, 72,
      81, 84-88, 91-102, 105-8,
      111, 114-117, 121-2, 129-
      35, 138-41
objectivity   vii, 18, 28, 33, 42
objectuality   42
ontological   9, 12, 38, 50-51, 61, 67,
      70, 91-2, 121
order type   26